The College History Series

West Liberty State College

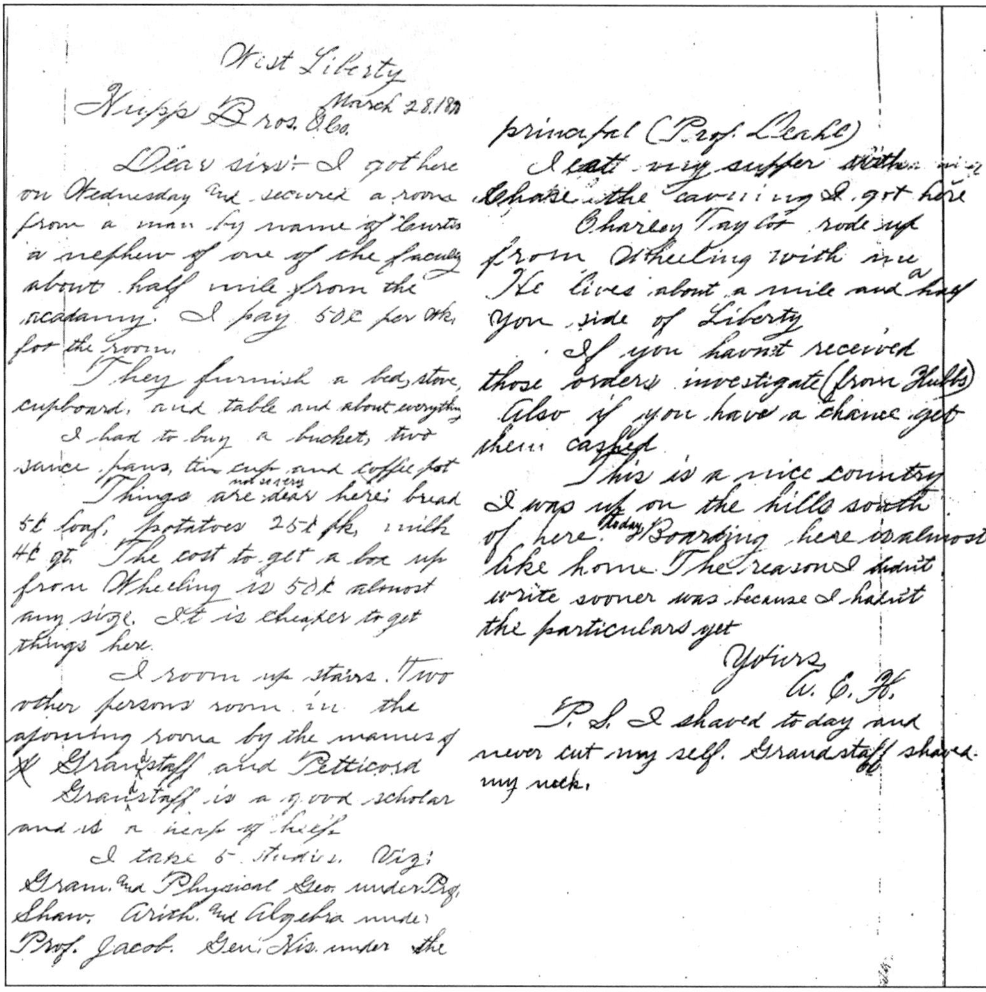

West Liberty
Kupps Bros. & Co. March 28.189

Dear sirs:- I got here on Wednesday and secured a room from a man by name of Curtis a nephew of one of the faculty about half mile from the acadamy. I pay 50¢ per wk. for the room.
They furnish a bed, stove, cupboard, and table and about everything
I had to buy a bucket, two sauce pans, tin cup and coffee pot
Things are not so very dear here: bread 5¢ loaf, potatoes 25¢ pk, milk 4¢ qt. The cost to get a box up from Wheeling is 50¢ almost any size. It is cheaper to get things here.
I room up stairs. Two other persons room in the ajoining rooms by the names of Grandstaff and Petticord
Grandstaff is a good scholar and is a heap of help
I take 5 studies. Viz: Gram. and Physical Geo. under Prof. Shaw. Arith. and Algebra under Prof. Jacob. Gen. His. under the principal (Prof. Deahl)
I eat my supper with Chase the eavning I got here
Charley Taylor rode up from Wheeling with me
He lives about a mile and a half your side of Liberty
If you havnt received those orders investigate (from Hubbs)
Also if you have a chance get them cashed.
This is a nice country
I was up on the hills south of here today. Boarding here is almost like home. The reason I didnt write sooner was because I hadnt the particulars yet
Yours
A. E. H.
P.S. I shaved to day and never cut my self. Grandstaff shaved my neck.

A Letter, Dated March 28, 1898, Sent Home from a West Liberty Student. It reads as follows:

Dear Sirs: I got here on Wednesday and secured a room from a man by name of Curtis a nephew of one of the faculty about half mile from the Academy. I pay 50¢ per week for the room. They furnish a bed, stove, cupboard, and table and about everything. I had to buy a bucket, two sauce pans, tin cup and coffee pot. Things are not so very dear here: bread 5¢ loaf, potatoes 25¢ a pk. milk 4¢ qt. The cost to get a box up from Wheeling is 50¢ almost any size. It is cheaper to get things here. I room upstairs. Two other persons room in the ajoining [sic] *rooms by the names of Grandstaff and Petticord. Grandstaff is a good scholar and is a heap of help. I take 5 studies. Viz: Gram. and Physical Geo. under Prof. Shaw. Arith. and Algebra under Prof. Jacob. Gen. His. under the Principal (Prof. Deahl). I eat my supper with Chase* [sic] *the eavning* [sic] *I got here. Charley Taylor rode up from Wheeling with me. He lives about a mile and a half your side of Liberty. If you havn't* [sic] *received those orders investigate (from Hubbs). Also if you have a chance get them cashed. This is nice country. I was up on the hills south of here today. Boarding here is almost like home. The reason I didn't write sooner was because I hadn't the particulars yet. Yours, A.E.H. P.S. I shaved today and never cut my self. Grandstaff shaved my neck.*

The College History Series

West Liberty State College

Robert W. Schramm

ARCADIA
PUBLISHING

ISBN 978-0-7385-0697-5

Published by Arcadia Publishing
Charleston, South Carolina

Printed in the United States of America

Library of Congress Catalog Card Number: 2001088389

For all general information contact Arcadia Publishing at:
Telephone 843-853-2070
Fax 843-853-0044
E-Mail sales@arcadiapublishing.com
For customer service and orders:
Toll-Free 1-888-313-2665

Visit us on the Internet at www.arcadiapublishing.com

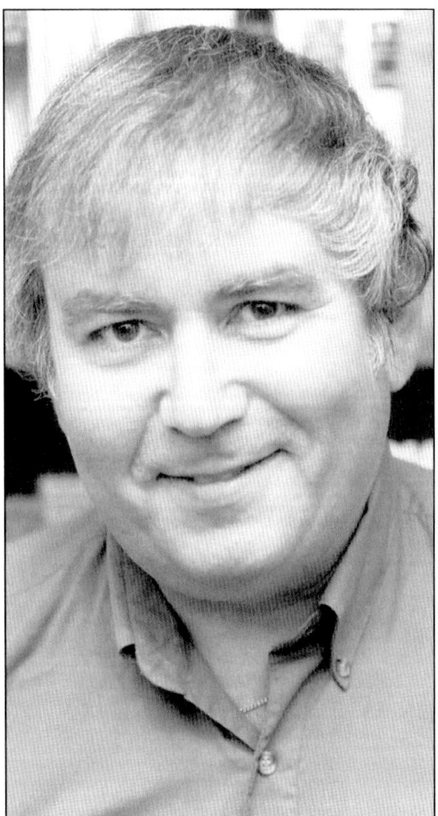

AUTHOR'S NOTES

Time travel is a recurring theme in science fiction, but science has not yet given us the capability of traveling into the past or future. A kind of time machine does exist, however—it is called a camera. Through the magic of photography we can see a 60th of a second of 1889 or a 500th of a second of 1999, and even as we look at the strange clothes on the people and the vanished backgrounds, we know that what we see was once really there. Photographs show us a single moment, and we cannot help but wonder what happened in the next moment. It is my hope that by way of the documents and photographs herein the reader will experience a glimpse of life in the past of West Liberty State College. In looking through the material contained in this history, I am reminded of a quote by Harry S. Truman, "Men make history and not the other way round. In periods when there is no leadership society stands still. Progress occurs when courageous, skillful leaders seize the opportunity to change things for the better."

—Robert W. Schramm, B.S., M.S.

CONTENTS

Acknowledgments

This pictorial history of West Liberty State College could not have been created without the help of the following people to whom I wish to express my sincere gratitude: My beloved wife, Jeanne, research librarian extraordinaire and talented actress, who provided support in every way including checking the text for grammar and spelling errors and whose opinion in the selection of photographs was invaluable; Mr. Butch Maxwell, director of public information and publicity at West Liberty State College, talented author and actor, for reading the manuscript and making suggestions as to style and structure; Professor Karen Rychlewski, talented artist and longtime friend, for teaching an "old dog" the new tricks and intricacies of Adobe Photoshop®; Dr. Paul N. Elbin, president of West Liberty State College for 35 years, mentor and friend, who thought I might have promise on the faculty and enlisted me as a member of the West Liberty family; Professor Norman Moyes and a legion of unknown *Trumpet* and *Winding Road* photographers who created most of the original photographs; my mother and father, Gladys Palmer Schramm and George W. Schramm, who gave me, at age nine, a Kodak Brownie camera, a home darkroom kit, and encouragement, which led to a lifelong interest in the medium of photography; and finally, M. Louis Jacques Mandé Daguerre and all the rest of those wonderful Frenchmen who invented what we call photography and made it all possible. I thank you one and all.

INTRODUCTION

The modern campus of West Liberty State College sits on land that was, at one time, claimed by both the British and French governments, as well as by local Native Americans. The Treaty of Paris of 1763, which ended the French and Indian War, and Pontiac's War, 1763–1764, left the British in control of the region. By 1774, settlers had come to the area from Pennsylvania, Maryland, and Virginia. In 1769, a Virginia planter by the name of Abraham Van Meter sent his apprentice, a Mr. Black, to the western part of the Virginia colony to locate and claim a suitable piece of farmland. Black found a good section of land near a spring in a valley adjacent to the Ohio River, staked a claim, built a small cabin, and began to clear the land. Around 1772, he was joined by another man, James Curtis, who staked out another claim. Other settlers, attracted by the fertility of the soil, moved into the region, which became a community known as Black's Cabin. But in 1776, inspired perhaps by the American Revolution, the name of this western outpost was changed to West Liberty.

After the formal Declaration of Independence from Great Britain, frontiersmen began to move west in ever increasing numbers, and soon a sizable community was established at West Liberty. The Virginia General Assembly, being concerned with the organization of its western frontiers, passed an act that required landowners of the region to meet for the purpose of locating and organizing a county court. In December 1776, a committee of landowners decided upon Black's Cabin in West Liberty as a suitable location for the court, which then held its first session on January 6, 1777. West Liberty grew and developed around the court, and lots and streets were laid out around the courthouse. On November 20, 1787, the Virginia General Assembly passed an act that stated that a 60-acre plot of land around the courthouse was to be established as the town of West Liberty.

As the town grew in population, it also grew in area. It is reported that on court days as many as 1,500 to 2,000 people would come to West Liberty for business and pleasure. Taverns and stores were built and a new courthouse and jail were constructed in 1778. West Liberty was the county seat and the approximate geographical center of the County of Ohio, one of three counties comprising the territory of West Augusta, which was created by the State of Virginia in 1776. This county of 1,432 square miles included parts of the present counties of Brooke, Doddridge, and Pleasants, all of the present Ohio, Wetzel, and Tyler Counties, and parts of southwestern Pennsylvania. According to local lore, Wheeling was described as a small settlement south of West Liberty.

In spite of all of this, West Liberty needed both churches and schools to become an important town. The Reverend Wilson Lee organized a Methodist congregation in the town in 1785, and while people came from miles around to attend open-air meetings, a church was not built until 1815. Rev. John MacMillan preached the first Presbyterian sermon in 1782, but it was not until 1788 that a Presbyterian Church was organized. The Episcopal Church was first established in 1792 by Dr. Joseph Doddridge.

One thing that these early preachers had in common was their interest in education. After all, a man who was educated could read his Bible in the absence of a preacher. In one way or another, these ministers imparted the idea of establishing schools. West Liberty established its first school in 1800. It was most likely the first in western Virginia. Classes were taught by Thomas Ewing and met in the log-cabin home of one of the school's patrons. It was a subscription school; the parents of the children enrolled paid in proportion to the number of their children attending. The first schoolhouse was built between 1816 and 1830 and was a crude log structure 20 feet square. By this time, West Liberty had grown considerably, and the town boasted two tanneries, a brick yard, and several hotels.

With the establishment of the University of Virginia, local residents realized the need for better education facilities than the elementary-level education provided by the subscription schools. In 1836, the General Assembly of the State of Virginia made funds available that could be used for colleges, academies, and intermediate schools. West Liberty Academy was the direct result of this.

One

The Academy

West Liberty Academy was primarily the result of the efforts of the Reverend Nathan Shotwell, a Presbyterian minister and educator who came to West Liberty in 1837 as pastor of the West Liberty Presbyterian Church. Reverend Shotwell was described by one of his contemporaries as "a man of decided intellectual force, of earnest piety and deep convictions of truth and duty." This being the case, one can easily see why he would be led to organize an academy of higher education. West Liberty Academy was chartered by the Legislature of Virginia on March 30, 1837. This is the same year that Victoria became Queen of England thus inaugurating the "Victorian Era" with its strict moral code, and two important inventions that would significantly change society were perfected. In America, Samuel F.B. Morse exhibited his electric telegraph and the special code of dots and dashes to be used with it, while in France, Louis J.M. Daguerre developed the first practical photographic process. The charter named a group of local citizens as trustees and empowered them to collect subscriptions and carry out the academy's business.

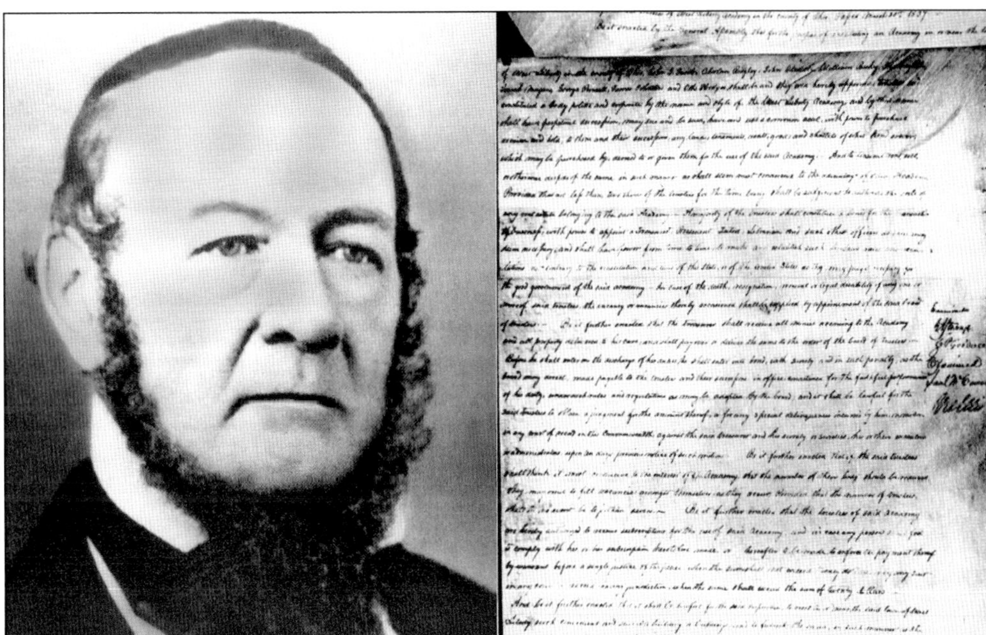

The Reverend Dr. Nathan Shotwell and The Charter. The original charter was destroyed in a fire. A photocopy is all that remains.

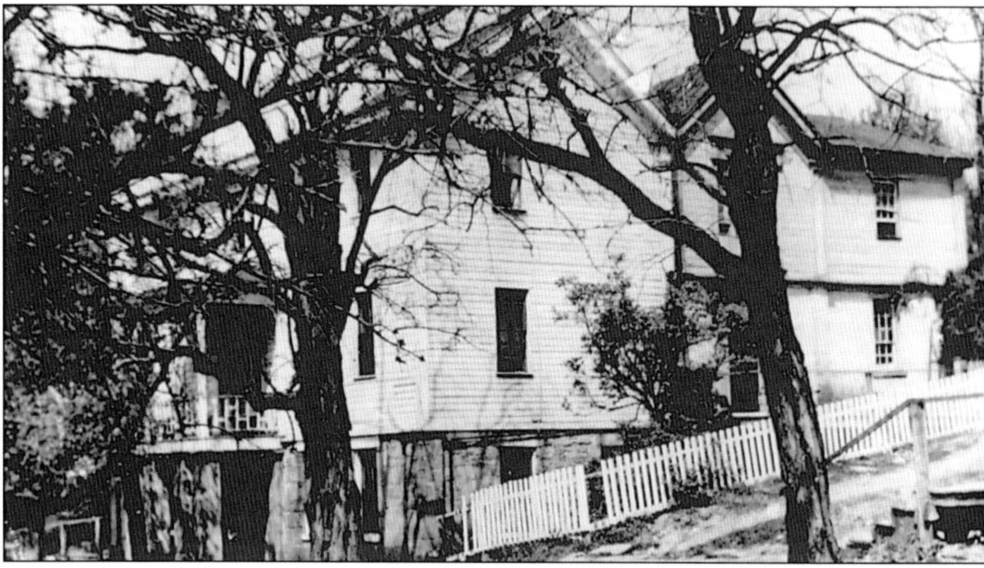

The Shotwell Residence, 1912. The academy opened the following year in the Shotwell residence, and Reverend Shotwell was named principal. In fact, Shotwell and his wife were the only faculty members. The initial enrollment was 65 male and female students, and the average first-year student was 15 years old, although some were as young as 13. The academy insisted on the strict separation of male and female students, and so the room used for classes in the Shotwell house was divided by a curtain hanging down the middle. Reverend Shotwell taught the men on one side of the curtain and his wife taught the women on the other.

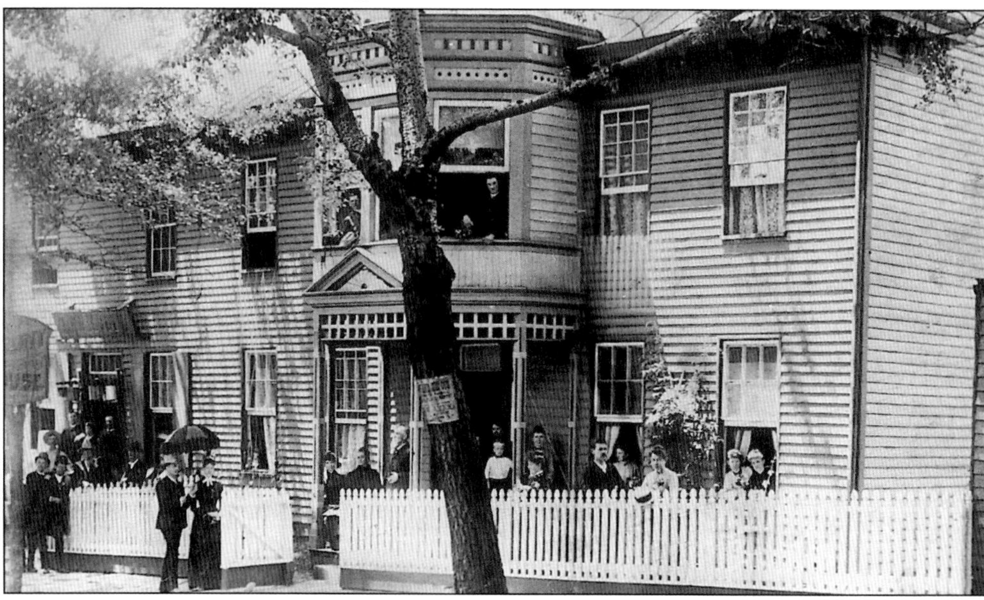

Liberty House, 1890. Most of the students stayed in boarding houses in the town. Liberty House was built by W.B. Curtis in 1860 and housed men and women students from the academy and, later, the normal school. In keeping with the strict standards of the Victorian Age, the owners of these establishments considered it their duty to look into the moral and educational well-being of their boarders. Students had to conform to a rigid set of rules of conduct enforced by the academy itself.

Regulations from the First Catalog of the Academy. The academy required students to attend daily chapel exercises and Sunday services at a church designated by the student's guardian. Male and female students were not allowed to speak to each other except in the presence of, and with the permission of a teacher. All forms of coed recreation, such as dancing or moonlight buggy rides, were forbidden. Finally, all forms of card playing or any type of gambling, frequenting of taverns, and the consumption of intoxicating beverages were likewise banned. The penalties for violating any of these rules were severe; public admonishment and immediate dismissal from the academy for second offenders were the standard.

Regulations.

1st.—All Students are required to attend church on the Sabbath at such place as his or her guardian may direct.

2nd.—Students are required to be punctual in their attendance at worship and morning exercises, and at the recitations of their Classes, and it is made the duty of the teachers every morning to report all delinquencies of the preceding day to the Principal whose duty it is to inquire into the causes of such delinquencies.

3rd.—Students are strictly forbidden frequenting Taverns or Ale Shops or any place where intoxicating liquors are kept or sold, and any Student transgressing this rule, for the first offence is to be publicly admonished before the class, and for a second to be dismissed from the Institution.

4th.—Students are forbidden card playing or gambling of any kind, and any Student so transgressing shall for a first offence be admonished before the school and for a second dismissed from the Institution.

5th.—The Students of the male and female departments are requested to confine themselves strictly to their respective sides of the building, and no intercourse is permitted between the Students of these two departments except in the presence of a teacher.

COURSE OF STUDY.

MALE DEPARTMENT.

PRIMARY CLASS.

Reading and Elocution,	(Osgood's Readers.)
Penmanship,	(Dunton's.)
Intellectual Arithmetic,	(Stoddard's.)
Written "	(Greenleaf's C. School.)
Modern Geography,	(Colton & Fitch's.)
" "	(Outline Maps.)
English Grammar,	(Primary Course, Smith)
Composition and Declamation.	

JUNIOR CLASS.

Higher Arithmetic,	(Greenleaf's.)
Physical Geography,	(Fitch's.)
Natural Philosophy,	(Primary Course.)
English Grammar,	(Advanced Course.)
Composition and Rhetoric	(Quackenbos.)
Algebra,	(Elementary.)
Latin Grammar,	(Andrews First Lessons)
Latin Reader,	(Andrews.)
Ancient Geography,	(Schmitz.)
Roman History and Antiquities.	
Physiology,	(Cutter's)
History of United States,	(Wilson's.)

SENIOR COURSE.

Algebra continued,	(Advanced course.)
Physical Geography do.	(Guyot's Earth and Man.)
Cæsars' Commentaries,	(Spencer's.)
Latin Prose composition,	(Arnold's.)
Latin Grammar contin'd.	(Andrew's & Stoddard's)
Greek Grammar,	(Fisk's.)
" Reader,	(Bullion's.)
Sallust,	"
Geometry & Trigonometry	(Davies.)
Virgil,	(Cooper's.)
Cicero's Select Orations,	(Bullion's.)
Natural Philosophy,	(Advanced course.)
Chemistry,	(Draper's.)
Botany,	(Wood's.)
Zoology,	(Agassiz.)
Xenophon,	(Cyropædia.)
Geology,	
Astronomy,	
English Language and Literature, (Latham's Hand Book,) (Trench's Study of Words,) (Trench's Past and Present of the English Language,) (Lectures,) (Shaw's English Literature.)	
Horace,	(Lincoln's.)
Herodotus,	(Johnson's.)
Surveying,	(Davies.)
Tacitus,	(Gemania & Agricola.)
Conic Sections,	(Coffin's.)
Cicero's Tusculan Questions.	
Homer's Iliad,	(Owen's.)
Demosthenes,	
Campbell's Philosophy of Rhetoric.	
Kame's Elements of Criticism.	
Logic.	
Intellectual Philosophy.—Moral Philosophy.	
Plato's Gorgias,	(Woolsey's.)
Evidences of Christianity.	
General History,	(Wilson's.)

Course of Studies from the First Catalog of the Academy. The original curriculum included arithmetic, Latin, logic, oil painting, and music. Algebra and plane geometry were added later. The first catalog, published in 1859, had a much more complex curriculum, no doubt possible only because the faculty then consisted of the principal and four teachers. Such courses as astronomy, chemistry, natural philosophy (physics), botany, zoology, geology, Greek, history, and physiology made appearances in the catalog. The total number of students attending numbered over 100, including some students from Ohio, Pennsylvania, and Louisiana.

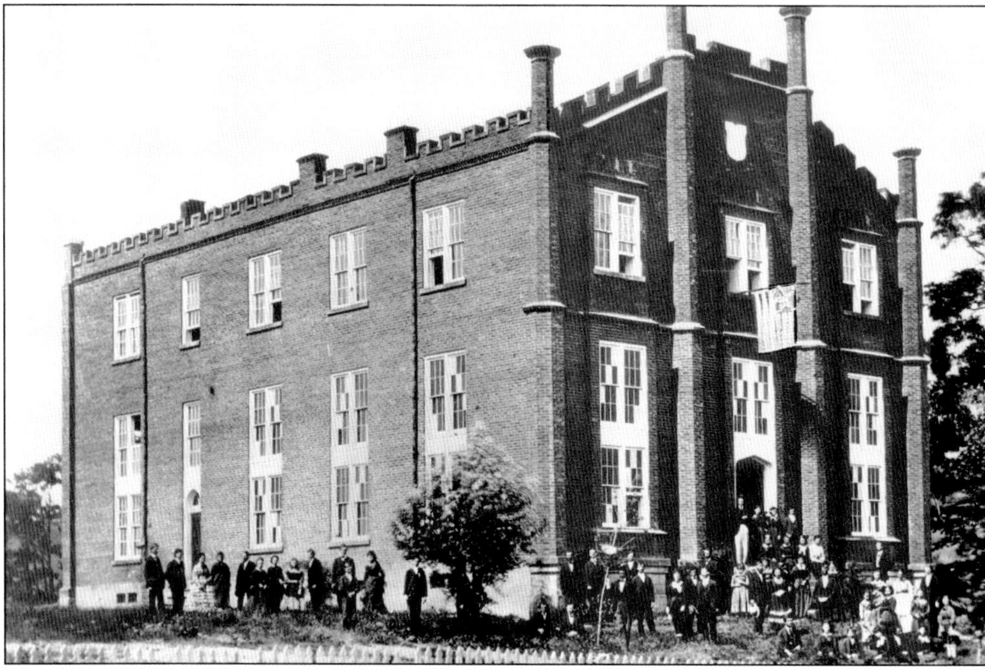

ACADEMY HALL, 1870. Around 1839, a new building was completed as a result of funds obtained by the citizens of West Liberty. Unfortunately, the new building burned to the ground in 1841, taking with it valuable records and leaving the trustees in debt. Since the academy had inadequate insurance and no financial backing, the trustees were unable to rebuild and the academy had to move back to the Shotwell residence. Friends of the academy made an appeal to the Virginia General Assembly that enabled the school to borrow funds in 1844 to continue. A public-spirited group of West Liberty residents collected sufficient funds in the amount of $30,000 to construct a new brick building, which was completed in 1857.

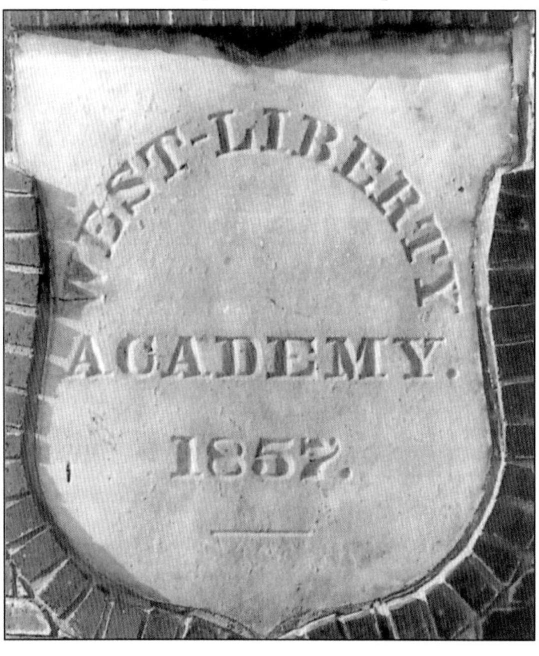

THE KEYSTONE FROM ACADEMY HALL. Academy Hall was used by the college until the early 1940s, when it was sold to the Ohio County Board of Education in 1943 and used as a high school. The building was eventually razed and replaced by a modern elementary school in 1975. This keystone, which is all that remains, is housed in the college museum.

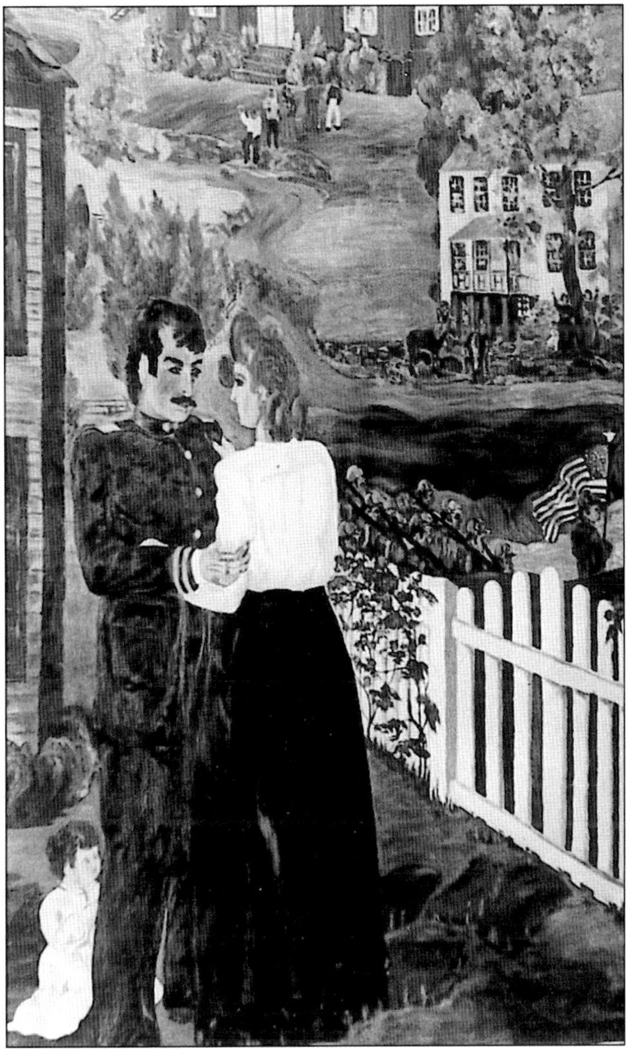

A Mural from McColloch Library Depicting Capt. W.B. Curtis Bidding Farewell to His Family. In this image, the Shotwell House is on the right and Academy Hall is in the background. The academy began attracting students from as far away as Mississippi and Louisiana but the onset of the Civil War was a detriment. West Liberty was mostly sympathetic to the Union cause and many academy students joined the Union Army. One of West Liberty's most prominent citizens, William Baker Curtis, recruited a home guard from the academy students. The following year this company became part of the Union Army as Company D, Twelfth West Virginia Volunteers. Under the leadership of Captain Curtis, this unit distinguished itself during the war and Curtis was promoted to brigadier general. While the academy was able to remain open during the war, mounting debt and low enrollment were slowly destroying the school. The board of trustees decided to sell the academy to the new state of West Virginia, which had been formed in 1863. With the help of a local committee headed by General Curtis, the West Virginia State Legislature met in Wheeling and agreed to buy the building. In February 1867, a bill was passed to purchase the academy. For three more years the academy operated as a private school. In 1869, the State Normal School Regents recommended that West Liberty Academy become a state normal school. Finally, the state legislature created West Liberty State Normal School by an act dated March 1, 1870.

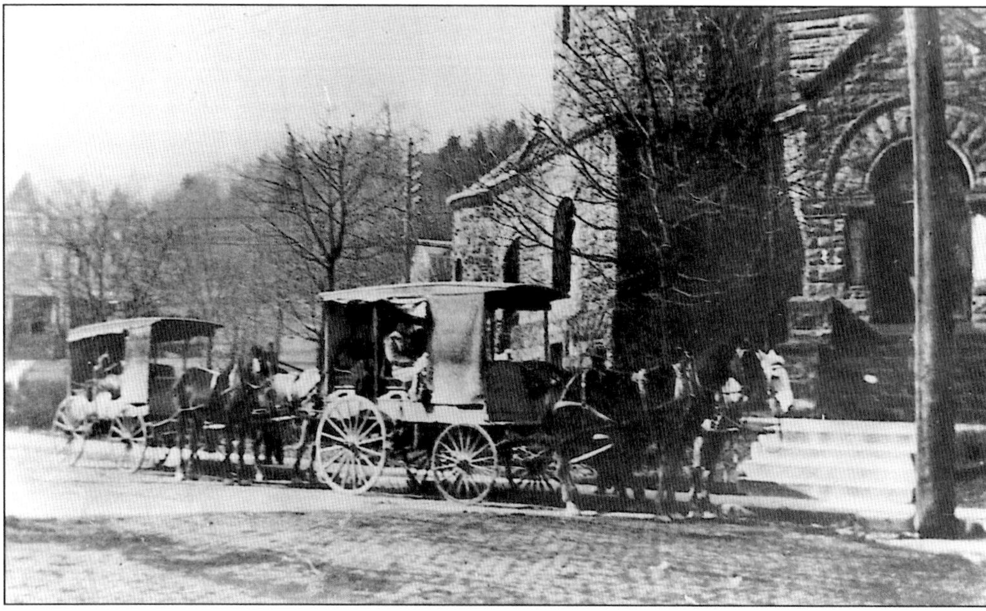

The Carriage to West Liberty at Vance Church on National Road, Wheeling. These two horse-drawn carriages traveled the 12 miles from Wheeling to West Liberty several times a day. The West Liberty "hack" took over two hours to travel the distance to the academy. A trolley car also ran from Wheeling to Short Creek and a hack traveled from there to West Liberty at regular intervals.

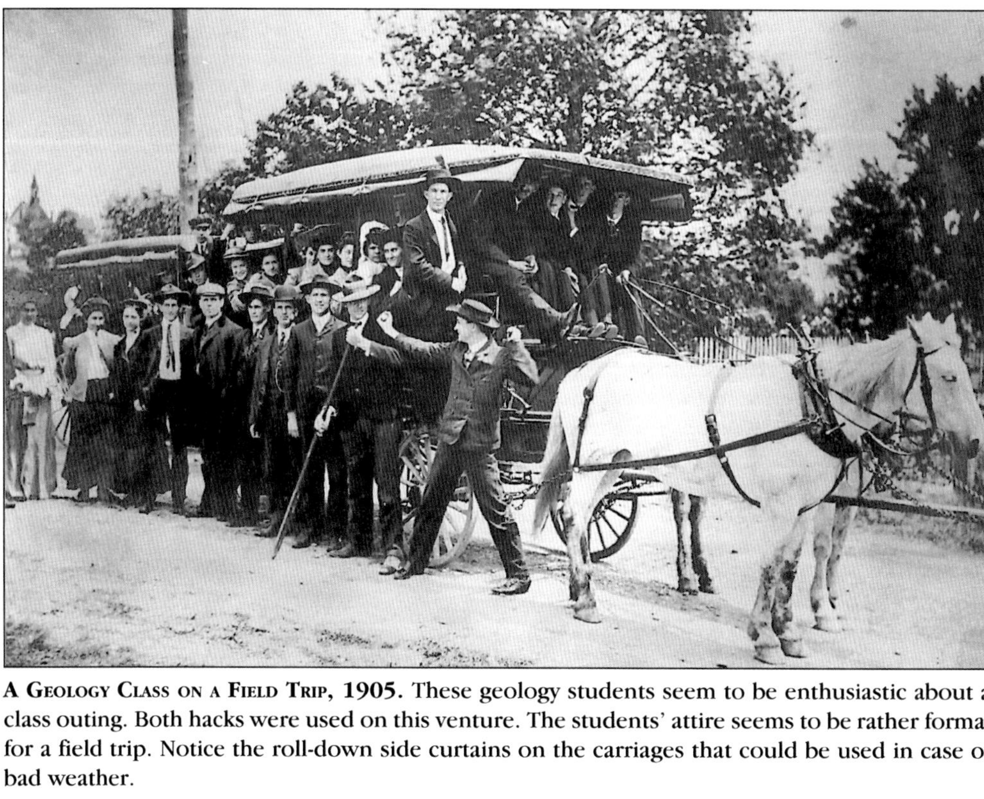

A Geology Class on a Field Trip, 1905. These geology students seem to be enthusiastic about a class outing. Both hacks were used on this venture. The students' attire seems to be rather formal for a field trip. Notice the roll-down side curtains on the carriages that could be used in case of bad weather.

Two

THE NORMAL SCHOOL

The normal school name is based on a French concept for educating teachers through the creation of a model school (école normale). *Its purpose was "to train students in the arts of the teacher, and to make them efficient and effective teachers." In addition, the school operated a secondary education program equivalent to high school until 1923. The strict rules for student conduct from the academy years were not relaxed until 1904, when male and female students were finally permitted to speak to each other in normal conversation. However, students who wished to go to games, parties, or parades had to petition the faculty for permission and young ladies were not allowed to "promenade" after dark. Incoming male students had to be at least 14 years of age and females 13. According to the catalog and other advertisements, students were attracted by "the healthful location (free of malaria and typhoid fever), small classes and moderate expenses."*

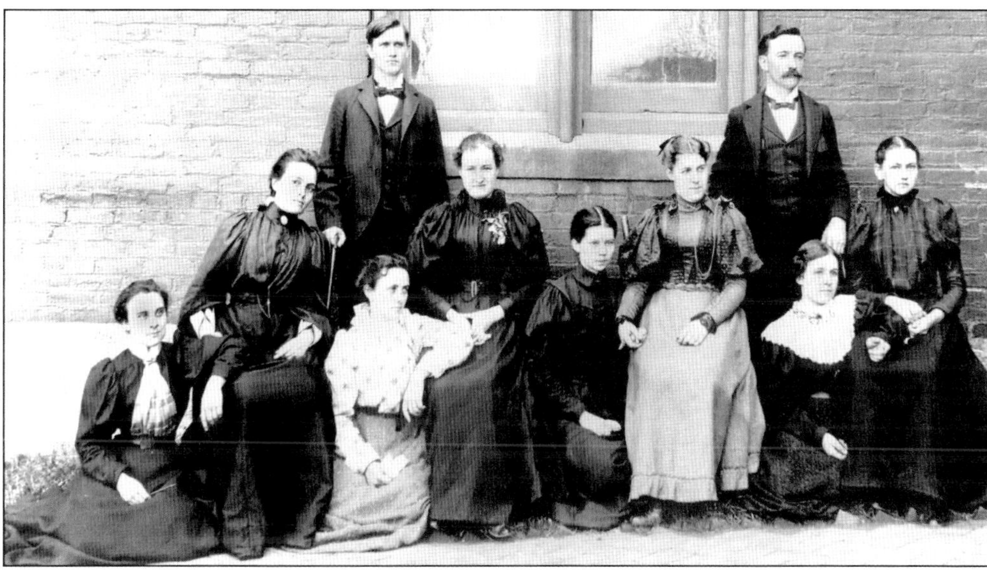

THE SENIOR CLASS OF 1898. The first commencement held in the West Liberty Normal School took place in June 1870 and exercises lasted for days. Oral examinations of candidates were conducted in the auditorium, and the public, as well as the faculty, cross-examined the students. Orations, essays, poems, readings, and music were part of the program, as were pantomimes and dialogues. An important part of the program were the literary society debates. Class histories and prophesies were read. The president, the salutatorian, and the valedictorian all addressed those present. Flowers, books, cards, and other gifts were presented to the graduates.

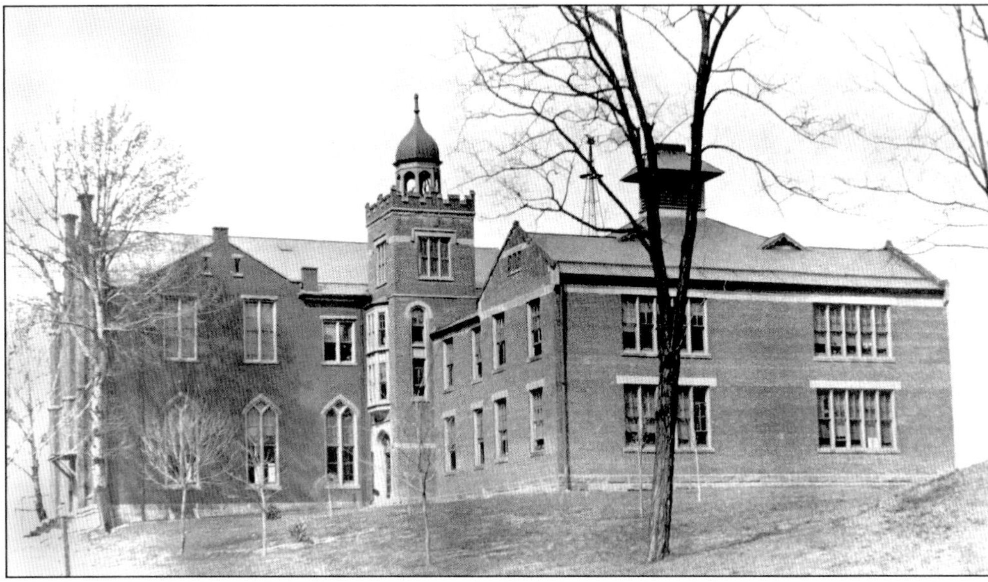

Academy Hall Annex, 1905. West Liberty Normal had developed a reputation as a school where a young man or woman could receive an inexpensive but good academic education. This and the continued increase in enrollment inspired the state legislature of 1893 to appropriate funds for an addition to Academy Hall. The building was completed in 1894 but was destroyed by fire two years later. The legislature came to the rescue and the annex was rebuilt in 1897.

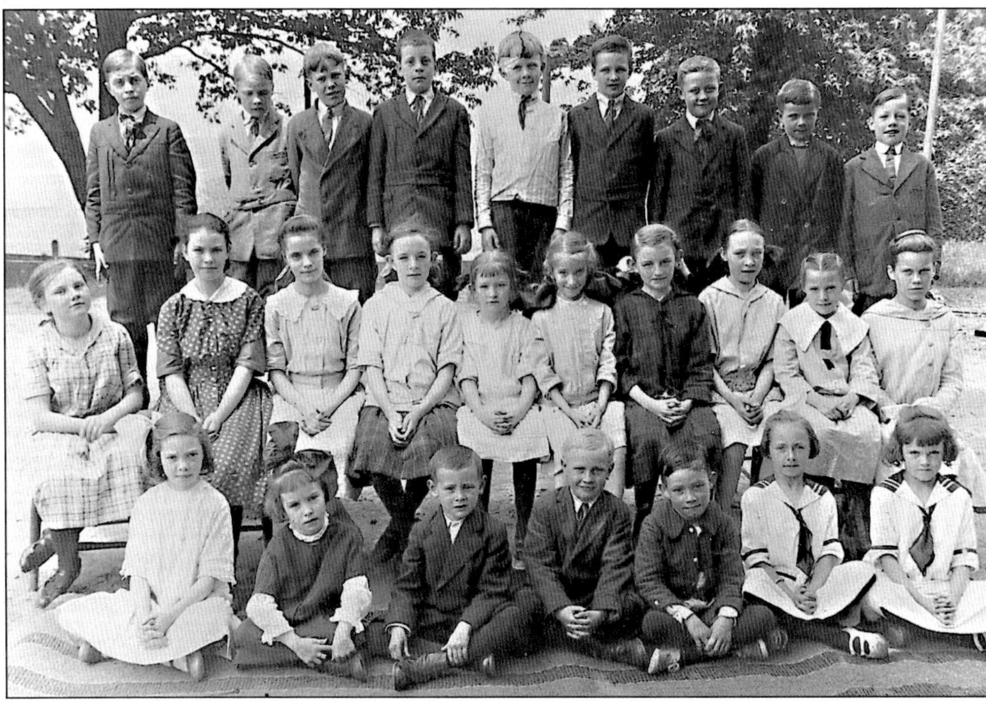

Training School Students, 1915. The new annex housed the training school, known as "Liberty Hill School." The big bell in the tower called many generations of town children to classes taught by normal school students. The training school was supervised by the members of the education faculty.

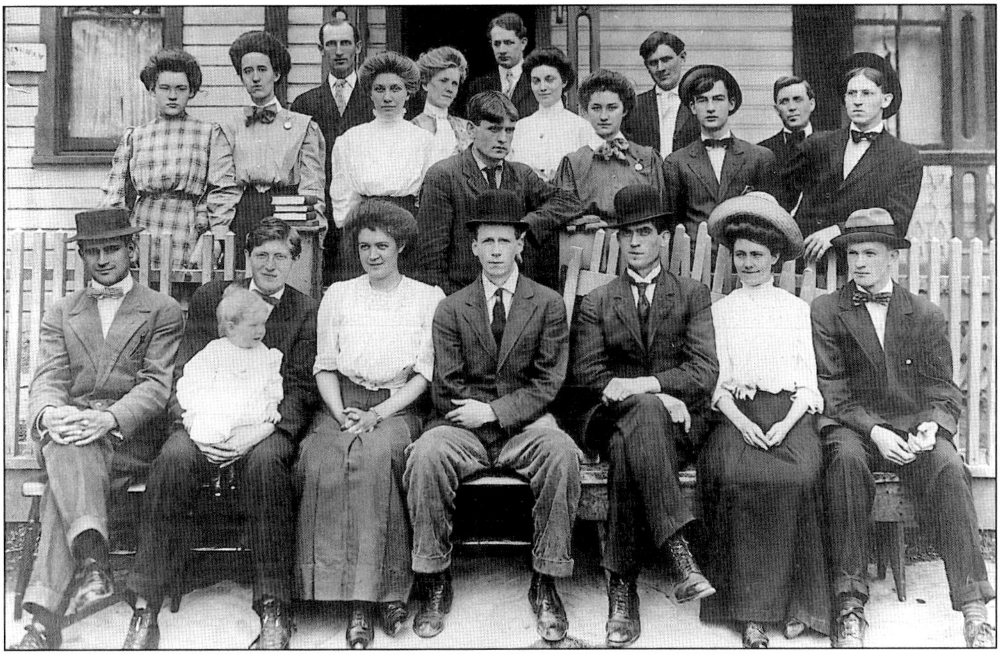

The Sayers Boarding House Gang, 1908. As with the academy, students stayed in boarding houses or hotels in the town. There were several restaurants and food stores that served these students' needs, but the town was said to be free of "saloons and other haunts of vice." In many cases two students would rent a room for $1.25 per week, bring part of their food from home, and do their own cooking.

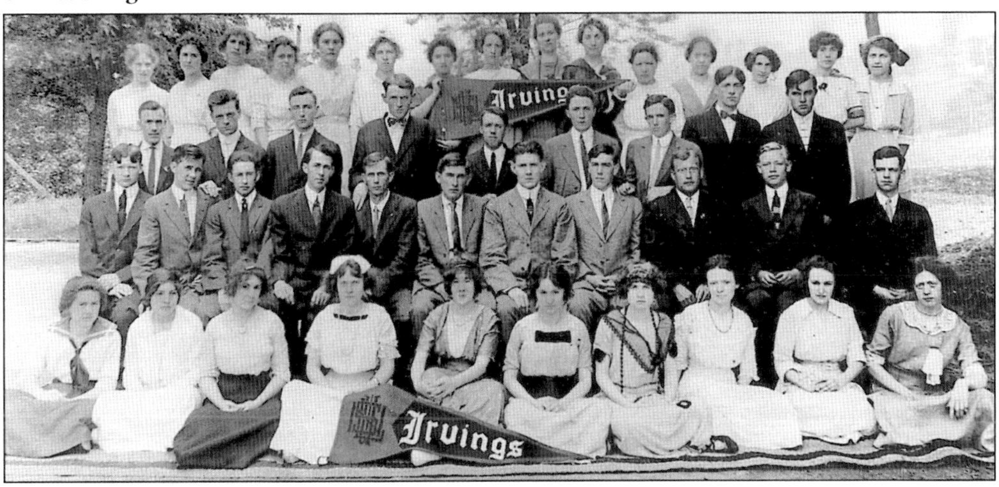

Irving Literary Society, 1914. The flowery literature of the Victorian Era led to the formation of literary societies in schools everywhere. These societies placed great emphasis on debate, oration, and essay writing. Literary societies were first formed at the normal school in 1871 but became increasingly active after 1888, when the Bryant and Irving Societies were organized. Their rivalry became so keen that the annual contest, held during commencement, often led to fist fights. Competition grew more and more bitter until the contest was discontinued in 1906. The societies continued to flourish until the development of a new style of literature that emphasized content over form. The reality of World War I also contributed to the lack of interest by students, so that by 1925, the societies were no more.

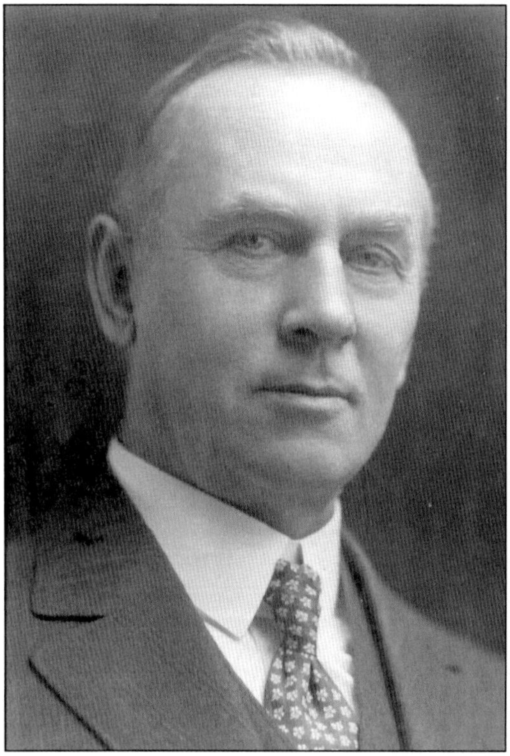

John C. Shaw. Principal John C. Shaw took office in 1908 and became the first president of the normal school in 1918. His executive ability, creative policies, and forceful personality carried the school through some difficult times, which included meager funding, lack of student housing, criticisms of the school and administration, and proposals to eliminate West Liberty and other "less efficient" normal schools.

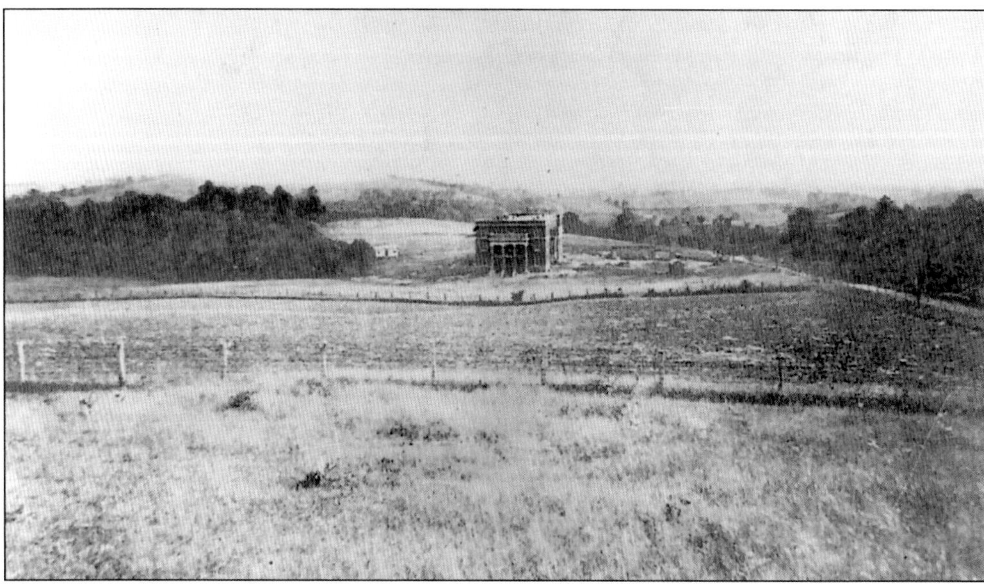

The New Campus in 1919. Shaw realized that the school could not grow in its present location because of limited space so he made an appeal for funds from the state to provide adequate housing for students. When his appeal was rejected, Shaw used his own funds to purchase and take options on 78 acres of land about a quarter-mile south of the old academy building. After a second appeal in 1915 by Shaw and friends of the school was successful, additional land totaling 102 acres was purchased and a women's dormitory was completed in 1919. This first building on the new campus, which is the present-day campus, was later named in honor of President Shaw.

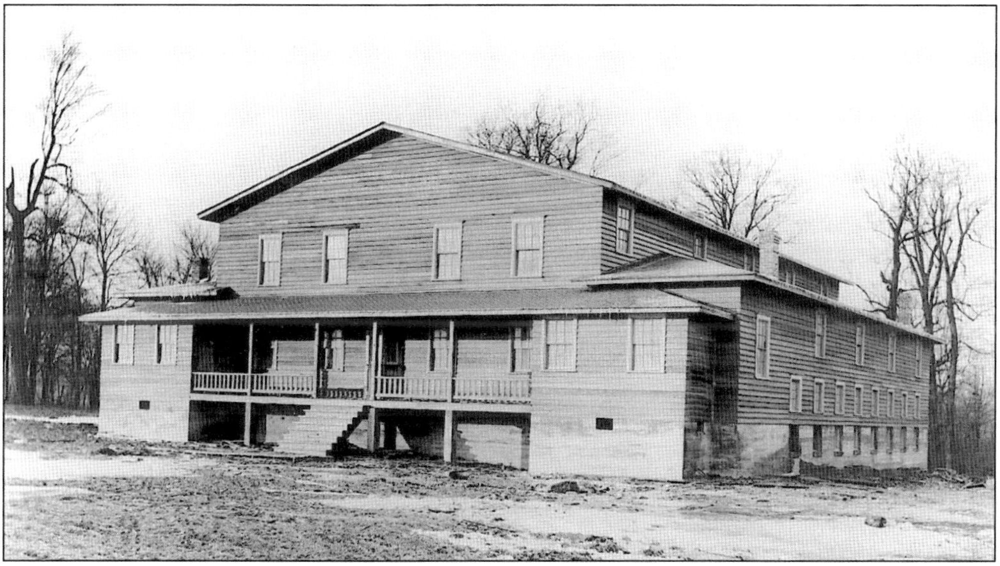

The Wood-frame Gymnasium. World War I had a number of effects on the normal school. Before the war, male students outnumbered the female students. During and after the war, the reverse was true. Large numbers of men were rejected for service in the armed forces and this led to an increased interest in physical education. The state provided funds to build gymnasiums and establish physical education programs at all the normal schools. West Liberty's Department of Physical Education was created in 1921. The gymnasium was completed in 1922.

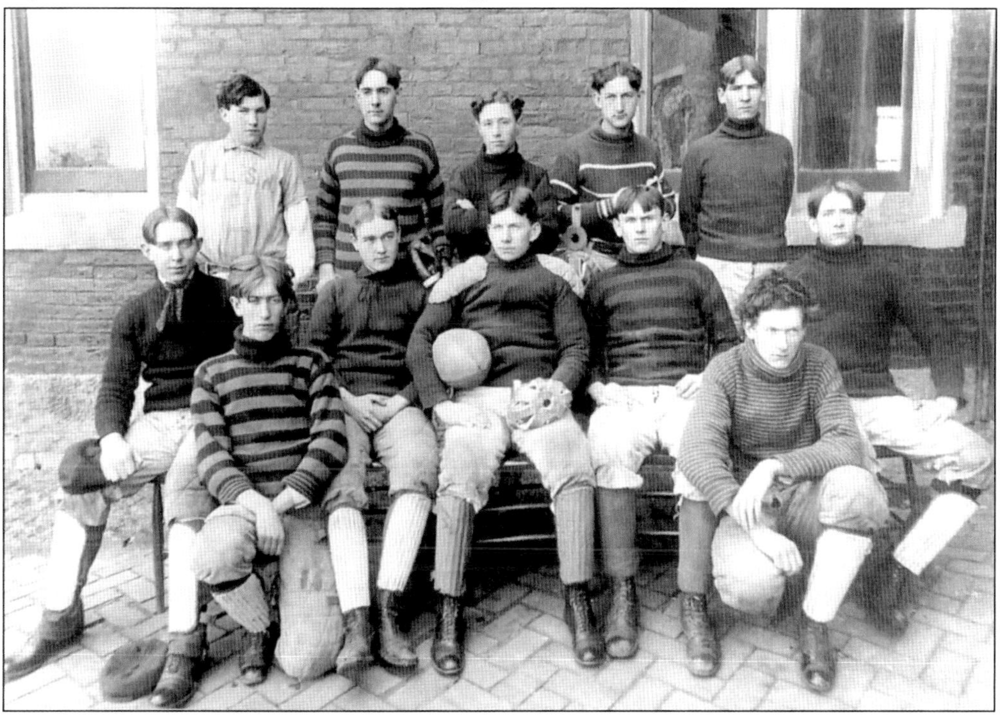

Championship Football Team, 1900. Long before a department of physical education existed, the normal school encouraged students to participate in athletics. The first organized teams were started in 1896 and the first classes in physical education began in the fall of 1901.

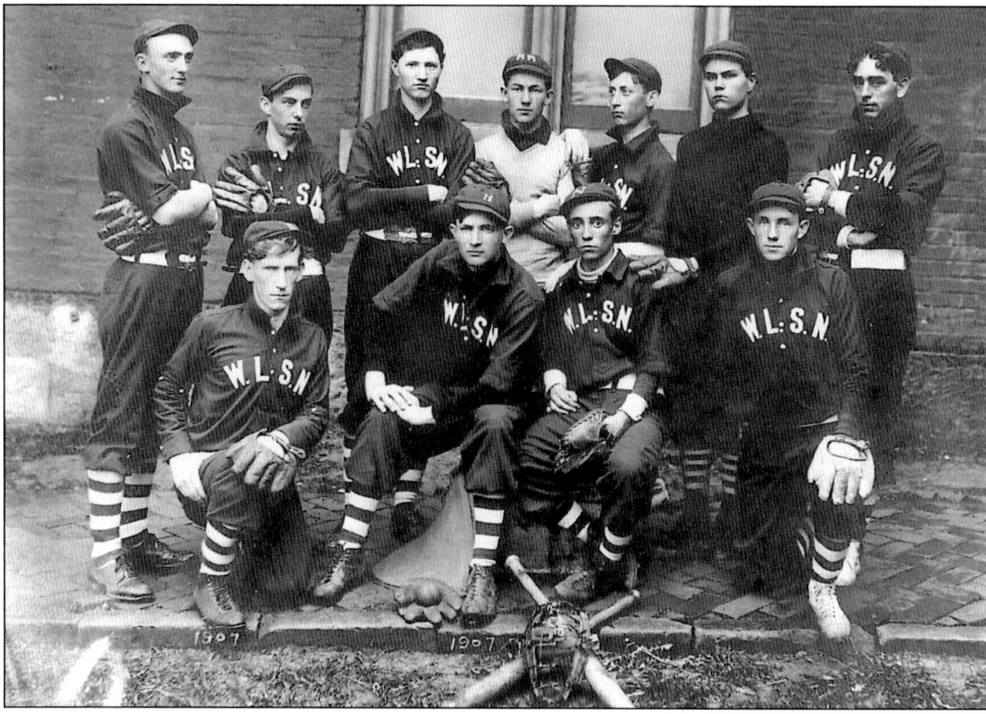

Baseball Team, 1907. Beginning in the 20th century, baseball became one of the more popular sports. Bethany and West Liberty produced surprisingly good teams and competition became very intense between the two schools. Their games drew fans from the entire northern section of the state.

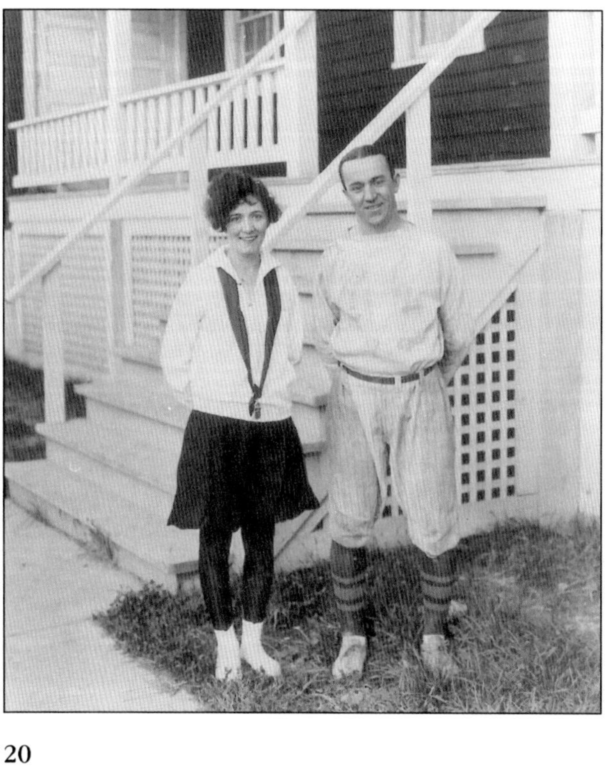

Physical Education Instructors and Coaches Florence Cary and Harry F. Sweeney. Coach Sweeney's teams won several state championships. This brought notoriety to the normal school and helped increase enrollment, which nearly doubled between 1926 and 1930.

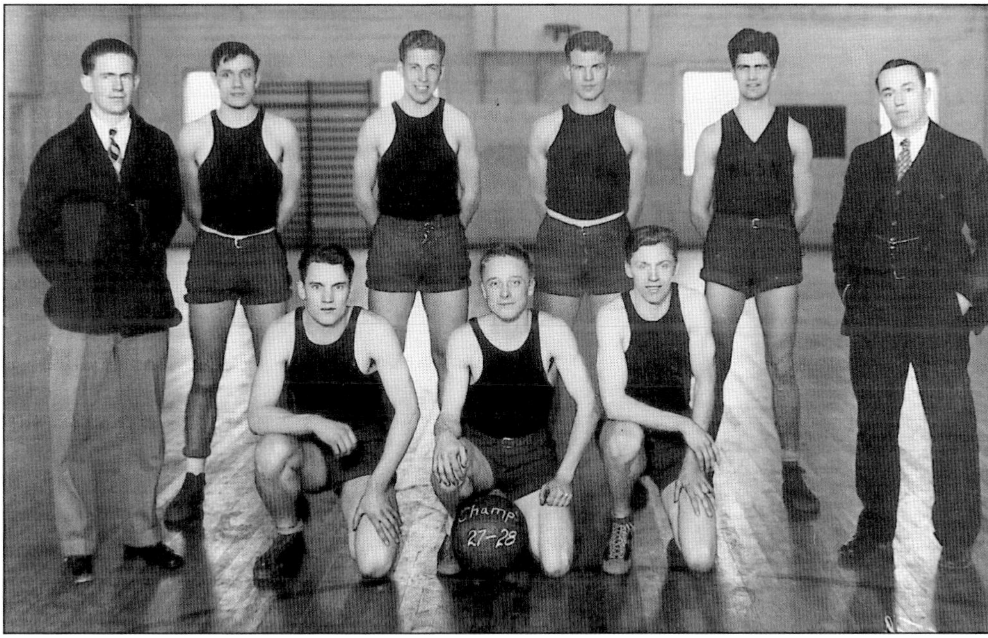

COACH SWEENEY AND THE CHAMPIONSHIP BASKETBALL TEAM OF 1927–1928. During Sweeney's seven years as coach his teams met with spectacular success in both football and basketball. The football team consistently led the state conference, and the basketball squad held the conference title for six consecutive years. "The Hilltoppers" were said to be the "terror of the state."

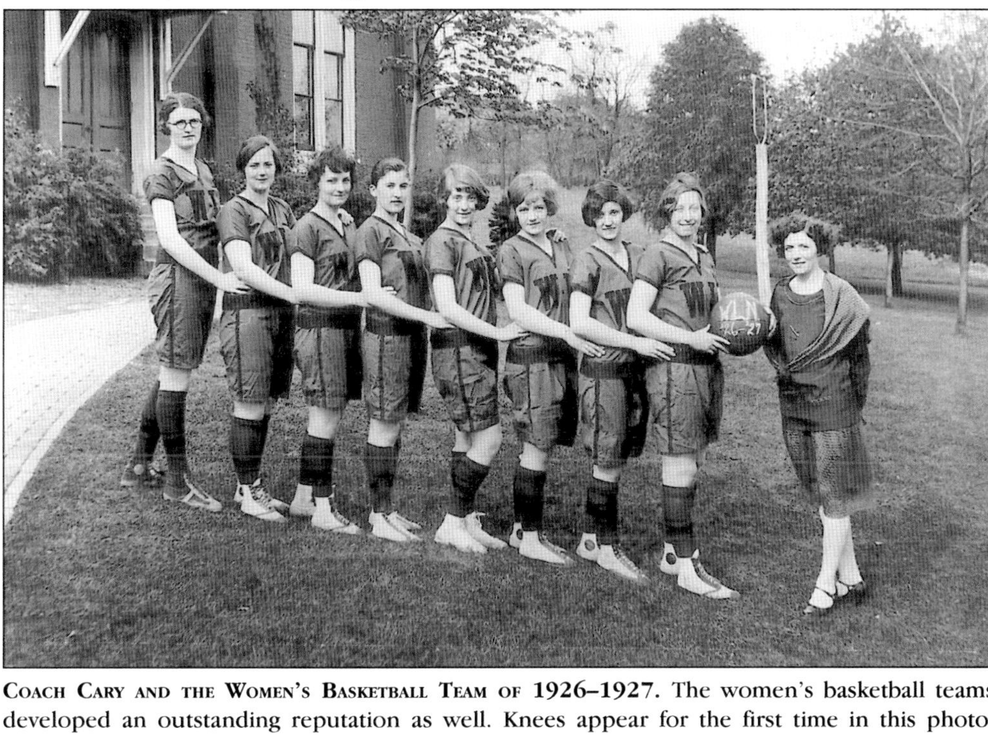

COACH CARY AND THE WOMEN'S BASKETBALL TEAM OF 1926–1927. The women's basketball teams developed an outstanding reputation as well. Knees appear for the first time in this photo. Teammates are, from left to right, Alma Millicent, Hazel Buhl, Eloise Smith, Beatrice Smoothly, Helen Hahn, Anna Sampson, Virginia Lee Kerns, Emma Kaiser, and Coach Florence Carey.

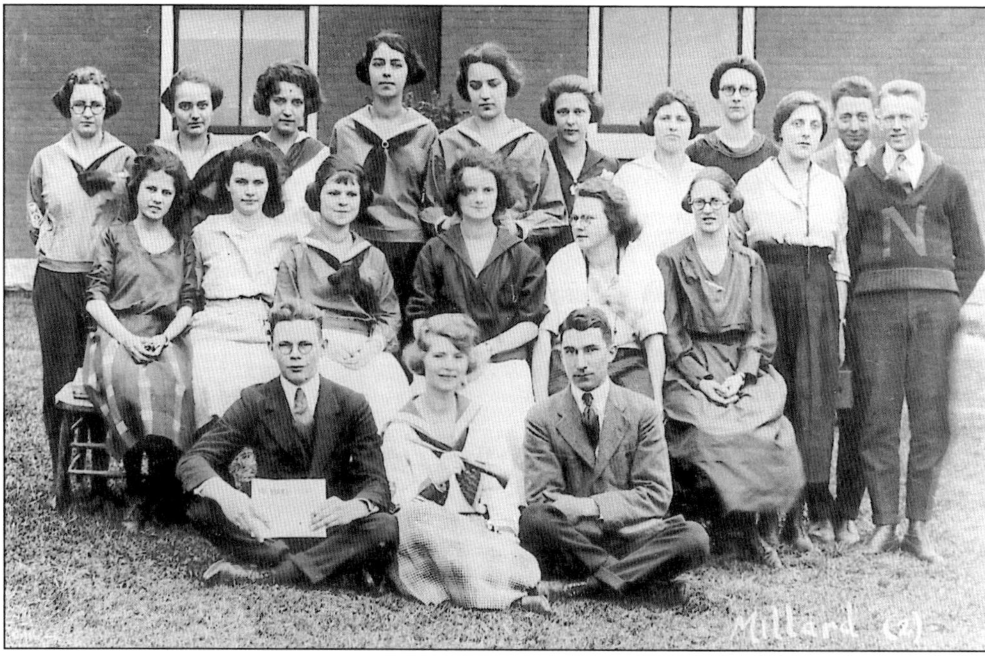

The First *Normal Trumpet* Staff in 1921. While two previous student newspapers had been published, they did not last more than a few years. The *Normal Trumpet* published its first issue on January 1, 1921. When the school changed its name the newspaper changed to *The Trumpet.* In January 2001, *The Trumpet* became, at 80 years of age, the longest-running, continuous student organization in the history of the school.

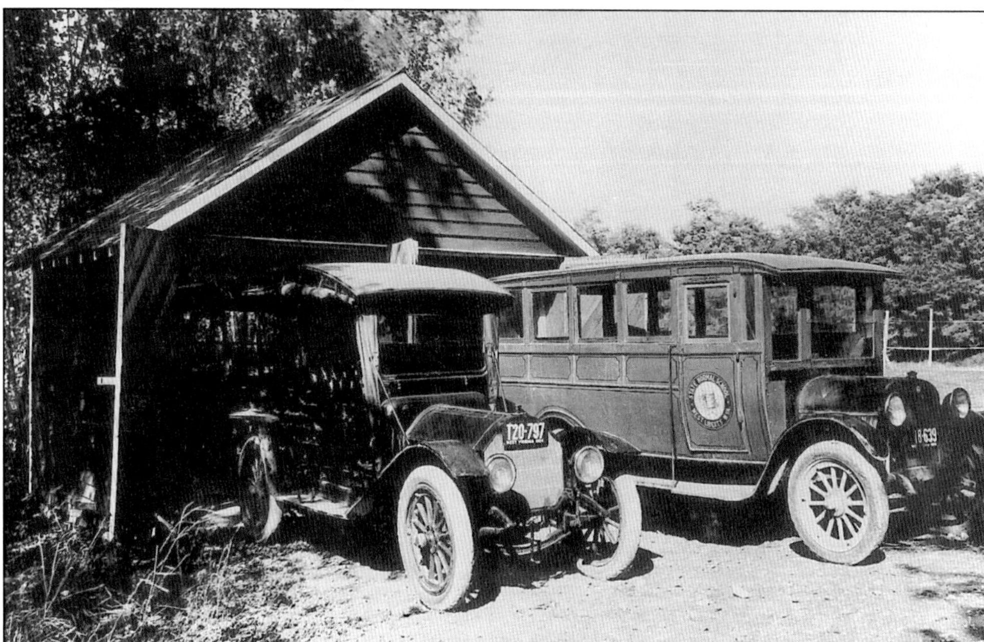

College Vehicles in 1924. The school's transportation system had come a long way by 1924. Compare this photo with those on page 14. The wooden-sided bus got frequent use. Note the normal school seal on the door.

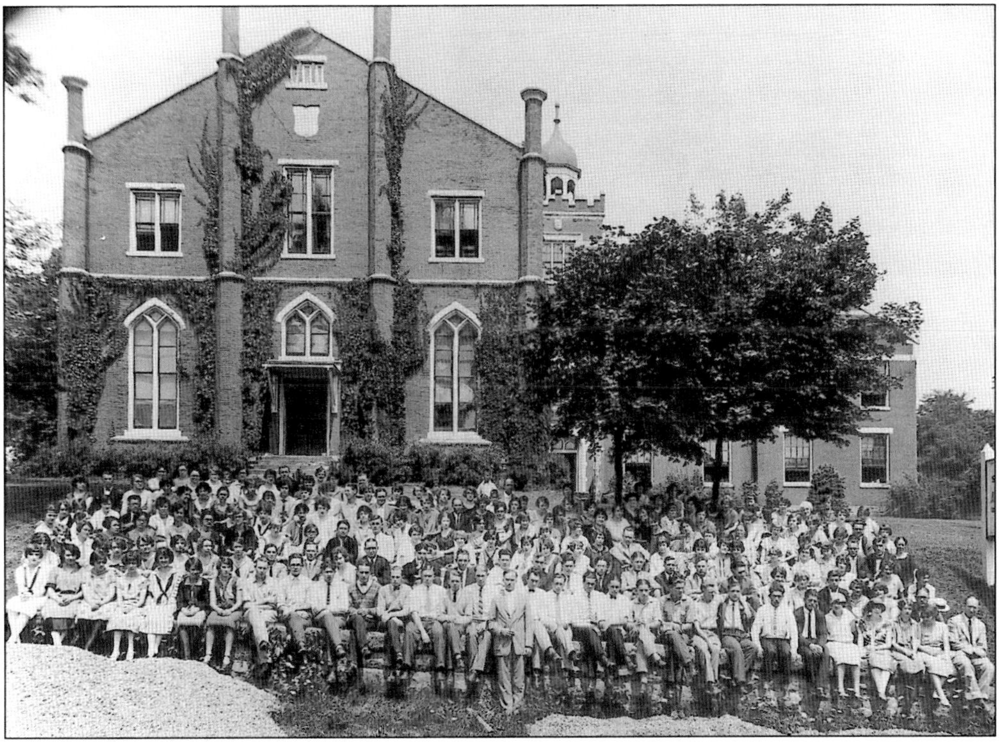

The Entire Student Body in 1924. The photograph above gives one an idea of how enrollment had grown since the academy days. Academy Hall, the annex, and the bell tower are visible in the background.

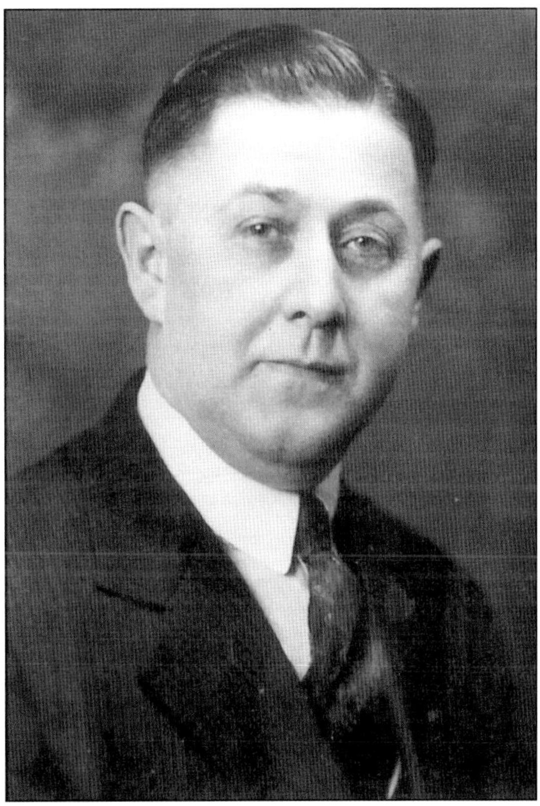

John S. Bonar. President John S. Bonar began his duties on July 1, 1926. Subsequently, he did his work so well that the normal students nicknamed him "Bonar the Builder." President Bonar was a graduate of West Liberty Normal School, held a bachelor's degree from Ohio University, and had a master's degree from the University of Pittsburgh. Bonar started work immediately to secure electricity for the school and town, and with the help of the townspeople, power was turned on in June 1927. In this same year a large dam and water filtration plant were constructed to supply adequate water for the school and the town.

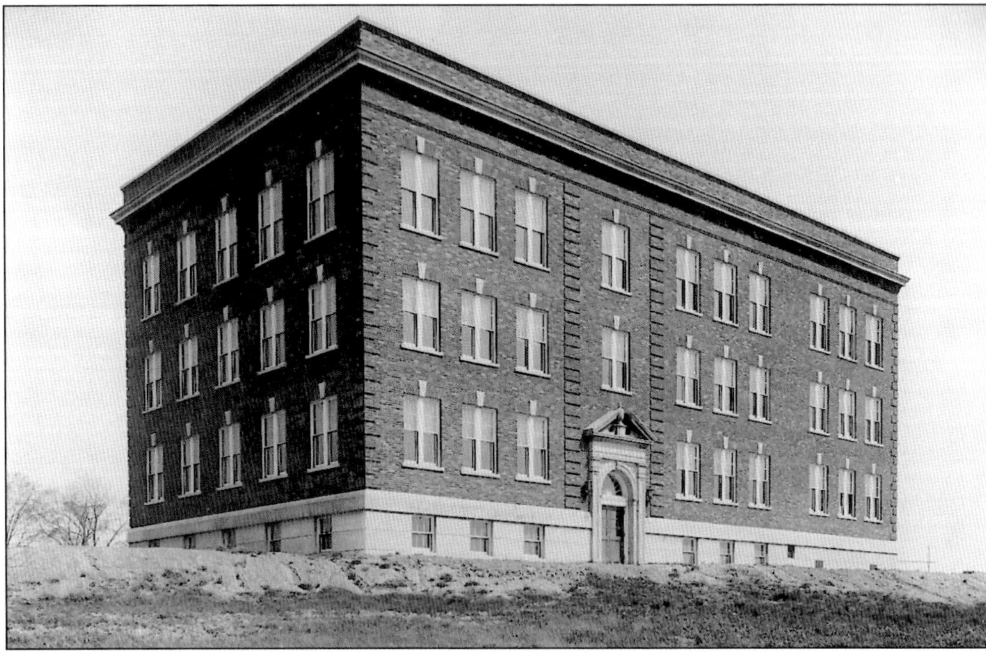

Curtis Hall in 1929. Curtis Hall was the first classroom building constructed on the new campus. This three-story structure contained the science laboratories and most of the classrooms. It was completed in 1929.

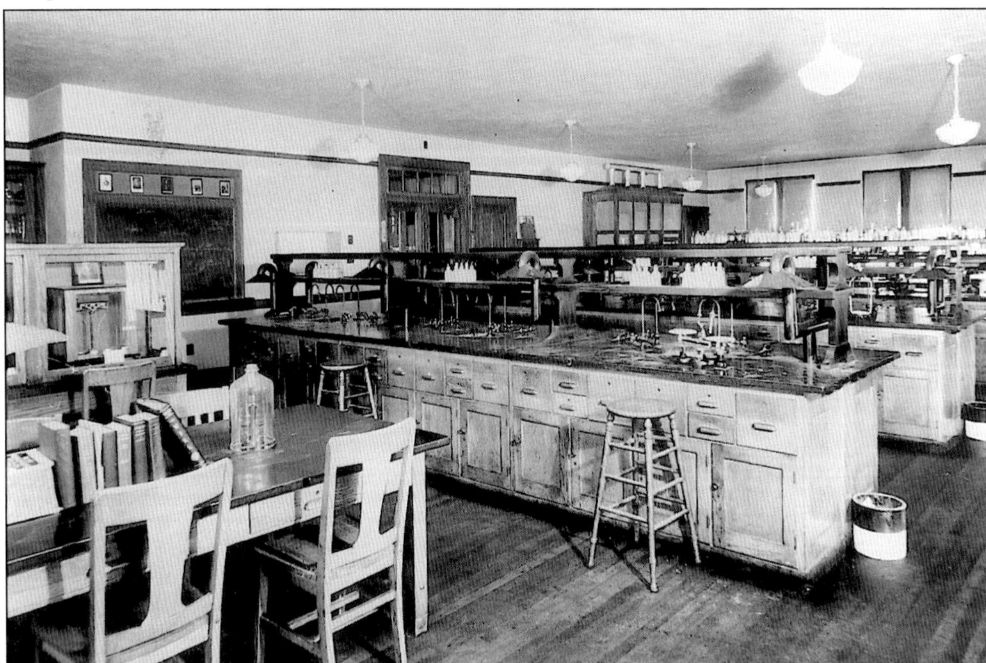

The Chemistry Laboratory, *c.* **1935.** The biology and chemistry departments were located on the top floor of Curtis Hall. This large chemistry lab, a biology lab, two storerooms for supplies, a special science lecture room, and two small "research" labs made up the departments. For over 30 years this was the location of these two departments until Main Hall was constructed in 1960.

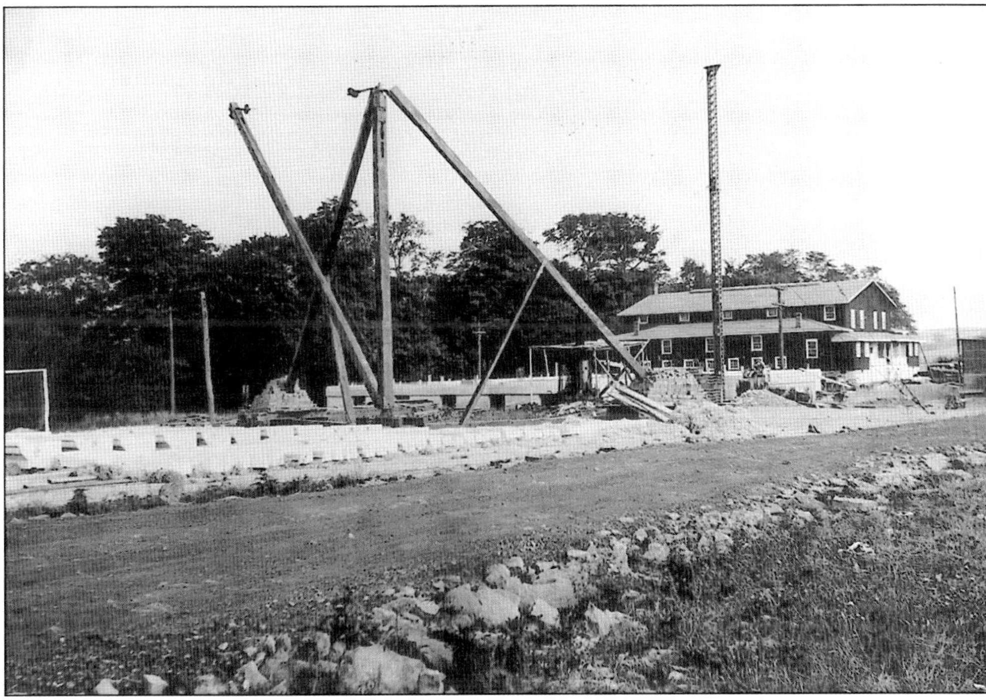

McColloch Hall under Construction in 1930. Construction began on a second building in 1930. As can be seen in this photograph, the building was near the wood-frame gym. It was planned that this building would house a much-needed library and administrative offices.

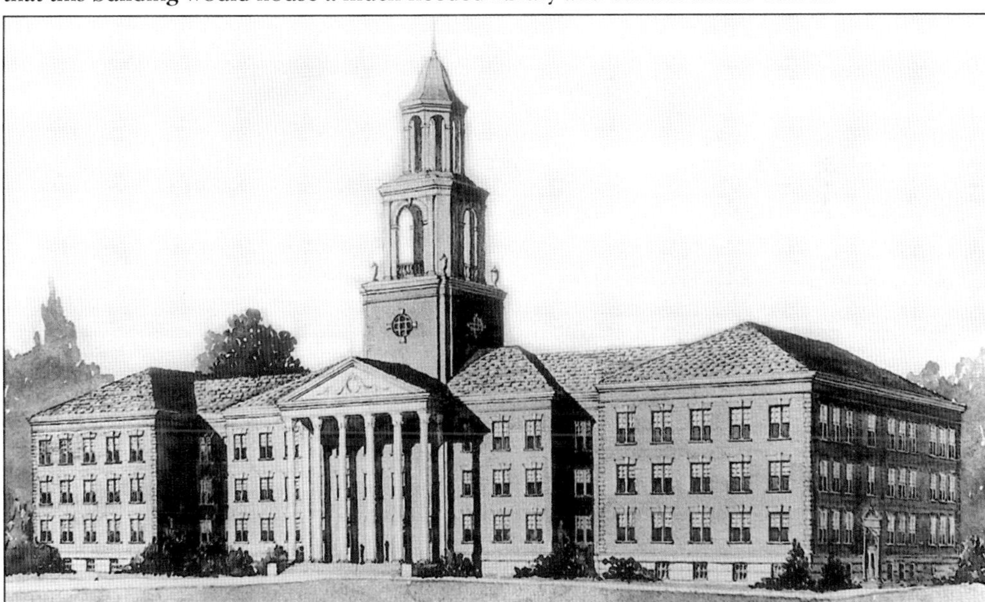

Architect's Design for Main Hall, *c.* 1928. The original plan called for Curtis and McColloch Halls to be connected by a center section. Indeed, the two buildings were in alignment and the heating plant for both buildings in the basement of Curtis Hall was designed for a larger single building. The center section was not completed until 30 years later, when architectural styles had changed. That wonderful tower in this drawing was never constructed.

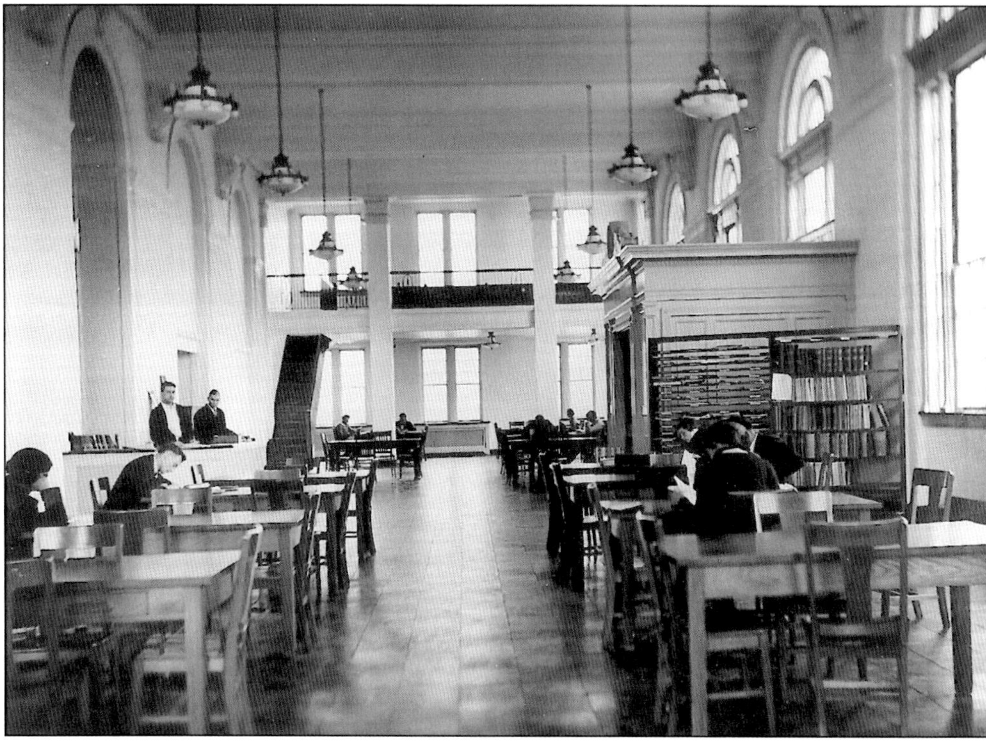

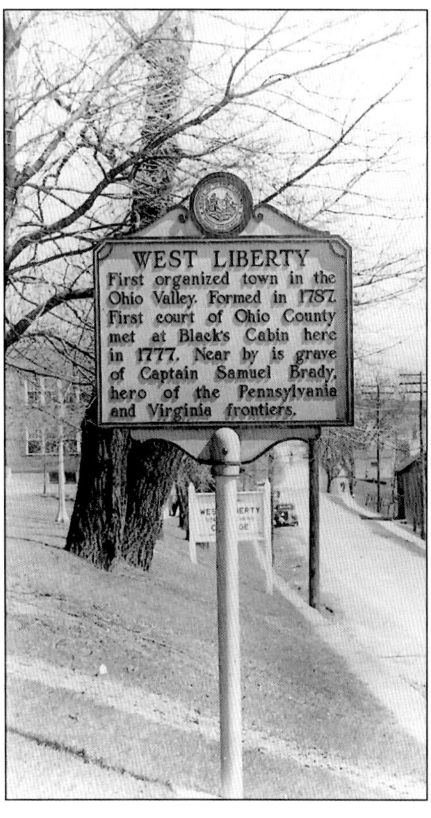

Milton McColloch Library Soon after Opening. McColloch Hall was partially completed in 1931 when the library section was opened. The stacks, located behind the main desk on the left, held many new volumes as a result of a special appropriation for books. The balcony in the background was the location of a small college museum. Later a series of historical murals were added to the walls opposite the two-story high windows on the right (see page 13).

Historical Marker and New State Teachers College Sign, *c.* 1931. From the time Bonar became president until 1930, the school's enrollment nearly quadrupled. This was probably the result of the physical improvements plus the notoriety brought to the school by Coach Sweeney's winning teams. With this record, President Bonar approached the state board of education with a request to change the status and name of the school. In March 1930, his recommendation was approved by the board. In 1931, the state legislature approved the action of the board and West Liberty Normal School became West Liberty State Teachers College, a four-year, degree-granting institution.

Three

Teachers College to State College

The Elbin Era

Dr. Paul N. Elbin became president of West Liberty State Teachers College on August 15, 1935. At 30 years old, he was the youngest president of a four-year college in the United States. Like President Bonar, Elbin's goal was to convert West Liberty into a four-year, degree-granting state college offering various programs in addition to teacher education. Elbin began by organizing a long-range plan for the accreditation of the college: advance public relations of the college, expand the physical facilities of the campus, and make easier the upgrading of academic standards and student services. Elbin recognized the necessity of making the college more appealing to prospective students. To this end he sought the best artists and musicians he could find to teach art and music. He hired the school's first professor of speech and created the position of dean of students. He hired the first trained librarian, the first dietitian, and revived the theatrical group, the Hilltop Players. So that the faculty should be involved in cultural improvement, he was instrumental in the formation of a faculty club.

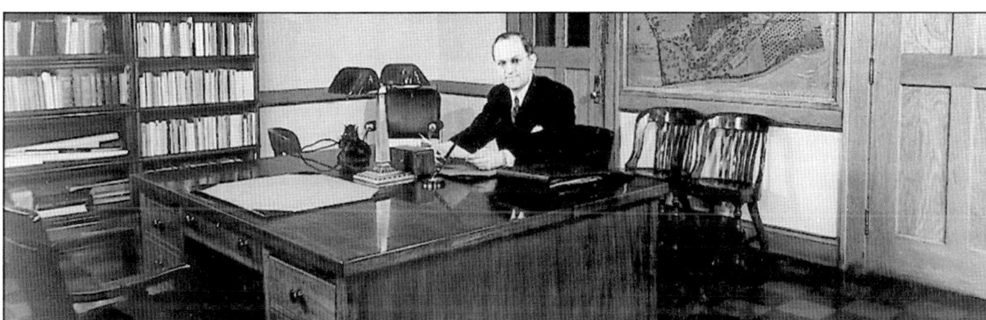

Dr. Paul N. Elbin in the President's Office in McColloch Hall, 1937. In the entire course of the school's history, no individual has had such a monumental influence on West Liberty State College as Paul N. Elbin. During his 35-year presidency, Dr. Elbin accomplished more for the reputation and the academic and physical advancement of the institution than was accomplished in the previous 98 years by the collective efforts of his predecessors. By force of his personality, Elbin fought an uphill battle to build a true college on the hilltop campus. He brought a tiny, local teachers college to the status of a nationally accredited state college.

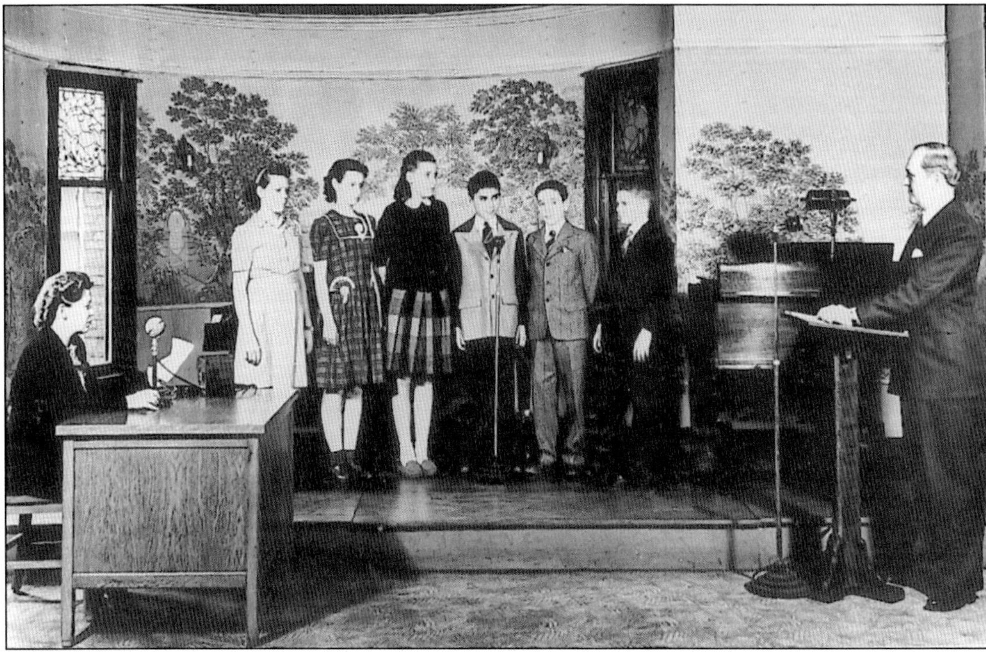

"Bible Question Bee," 1944. In order to make the public aware of the college and its degree programs, Dr. Elbin began a series of four 30-minute radio programs per week, broadcast over WWVA, in February 1936. In 1937, he began airing a live show on Saturday morning called the "Bible Question Bee." Dr. Elbin acted as quizmaster for a panel of biblical experts consisting of West Liberty students and area schoolchildren. Hundreds of letters poured in from all over the country containing favorable comments and/or submitting quiz questions. The program developed a national reputation. Pictured here are some of the contestants flanked by Helen Elbin on the left and Paul Elbin on the right.

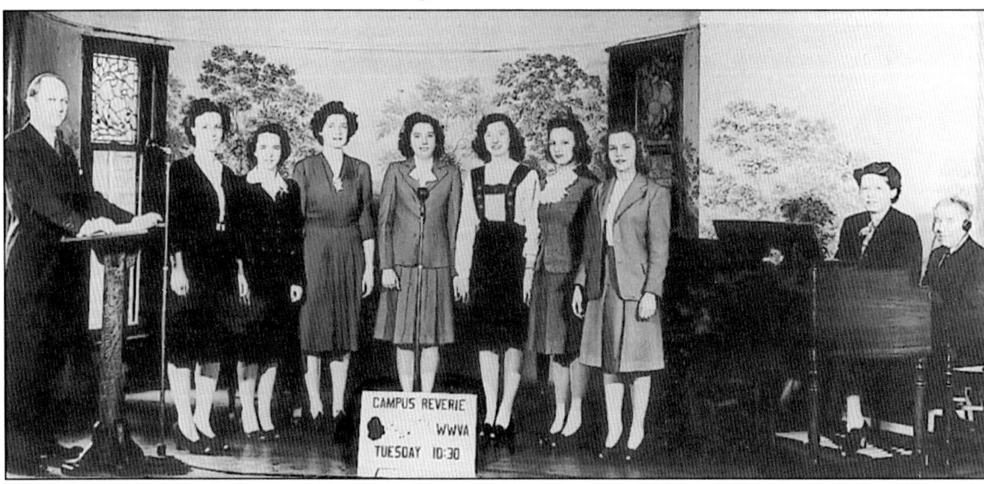

"Campus Reverie," 1938. In 1938, Mrs. Elbin, who was a voice instructor, suggested that some of the coeds interested in singing might be willing to appear on a program consisting of musical interludes and poetry. The program, known as "Campus Reverie," broadcast regularly on WWVA one evening per week at 10:30 p.m., was an instant success. Pictured, from left to right, are Dr. Elbin, Vera Cordona, Ruth Bishop, Mary Jane Nichols, Doris Schiffler, Gloria Von Berg, Mary Bea Montgomery, Alba Panico, Mrs. Elbin, and William Conrath (engineer).

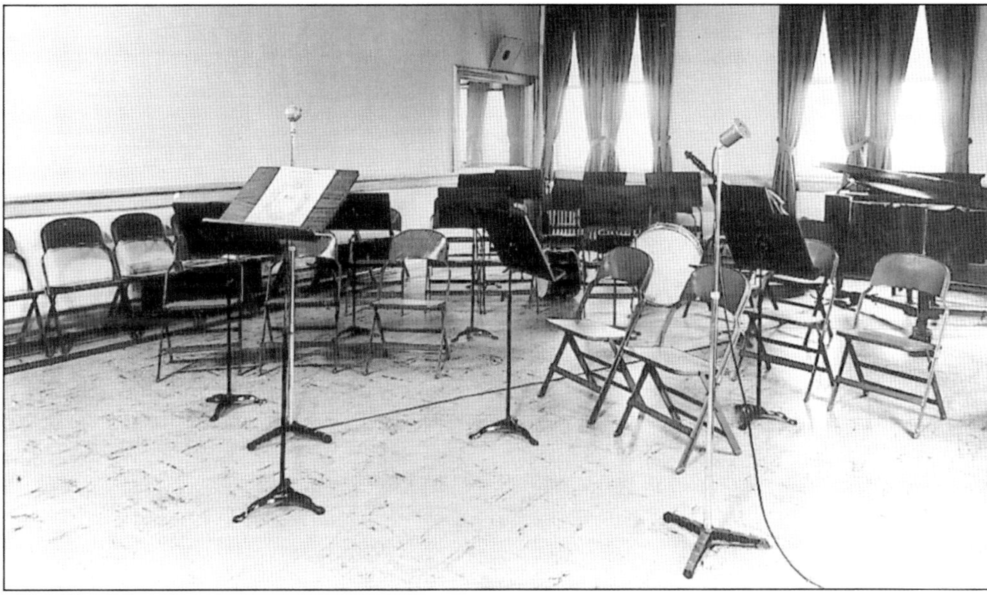

Broadcast Studio, c. 1938. The radio programs were broadcast live from the Academy Hall auditorium, the West Liberty State Teachers College Downtown Center in Wheeling, and the WWVA studios in the Hawley Building in Wheeling. In 1937, a radio studio was constructed on the top floor of McColloch Hall.

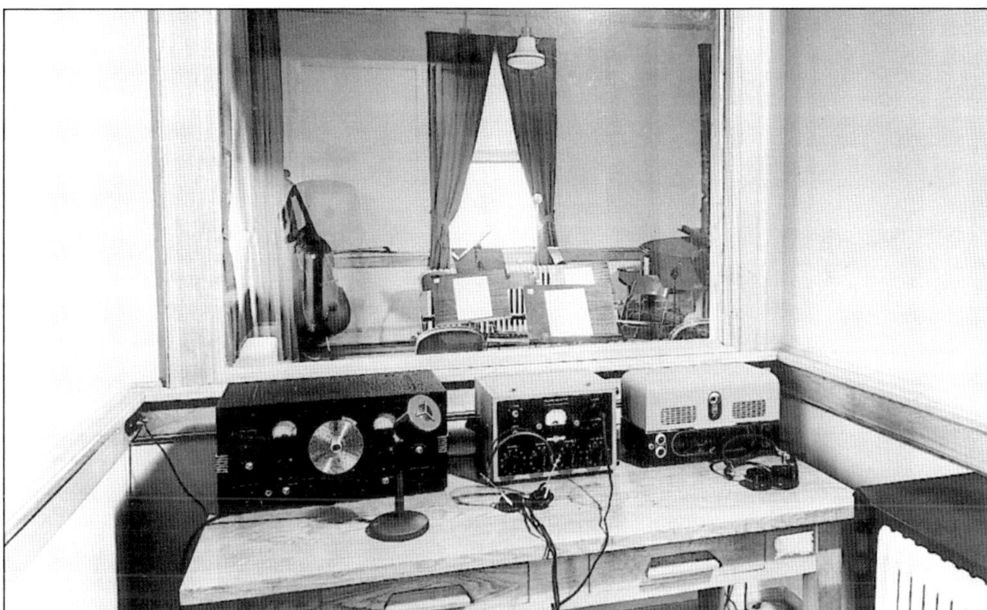

Studio Control Room, 1937. Telephone lines ran from the "control room" on the campus to WWVA's transmitter which, at that time, was located a few miles south of the college. Although the two original programs ended in the mid-1950s, West Liberty State College continued its long association with WWVA through "Music from the Campus" and "West Liberty Presents." These tape-recorded programs lasted well into the 1970s and 1980s and were produced by Professors Edward C. Wolf and Vernon Riemer, respectively. These public service broadcasts were two of the longest-running series of programs anywhere in America.

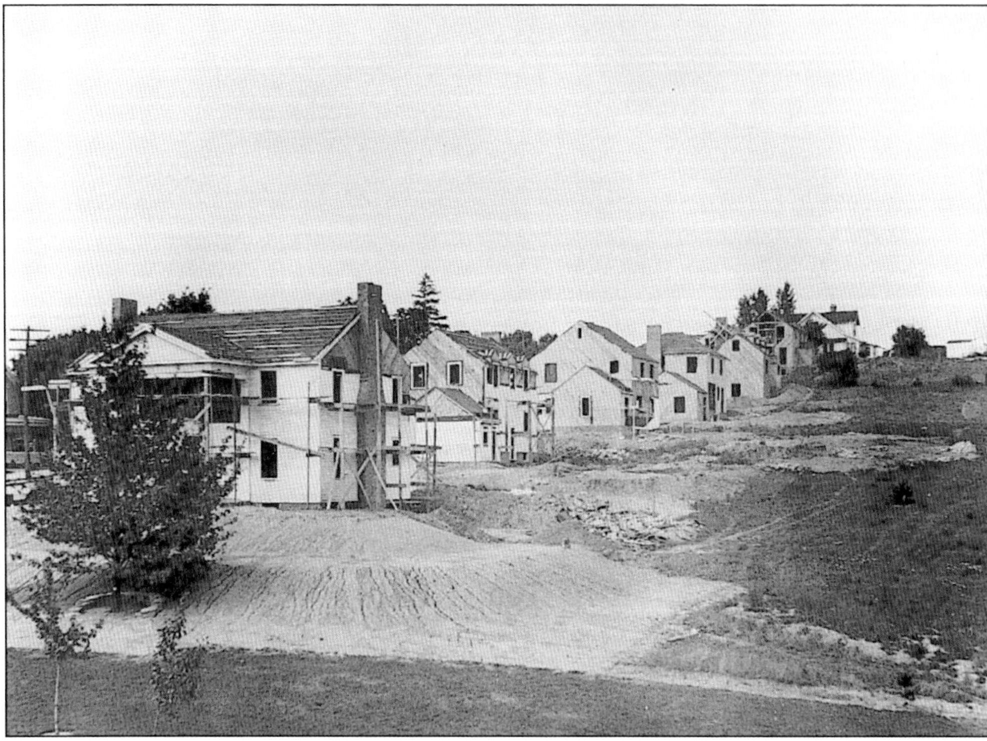

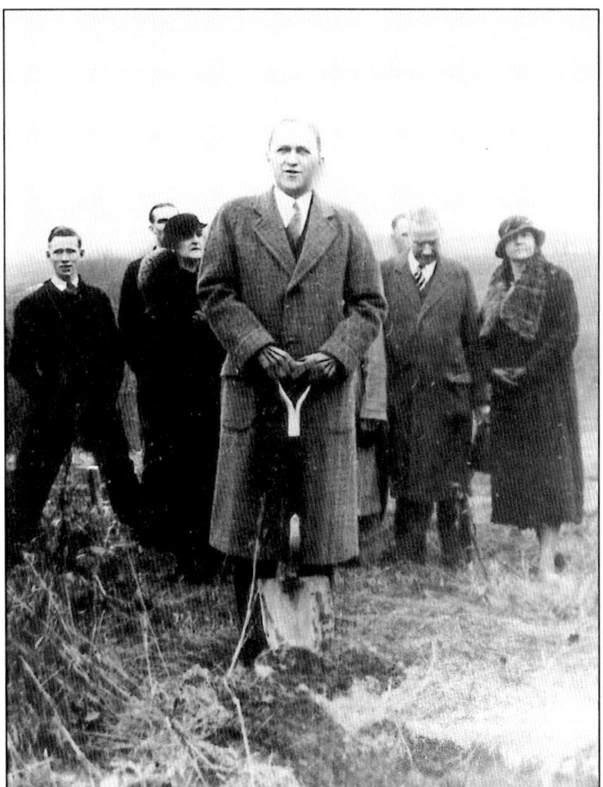

Public Works Administration Project Known as "Colonial Heights," 1937. President Elbin wished to expand the physical facilities of the campus but the economic depression had placed the state government in financial distress. Availing himself of the federal spending programs of the New Deal, he submitted a proposal for a faculty housing project. The project received federal approval and work was begun in March 1936.

Groundbreaking for "Fraternity Hall," 1936. Building a men's dormitory was President Elbin's second housing project, and again, he relied on the availability of federal funds. Although there was some opposition by townspeople, who feared loss of revenue from boarding students, the Public Works Administration approved the application.

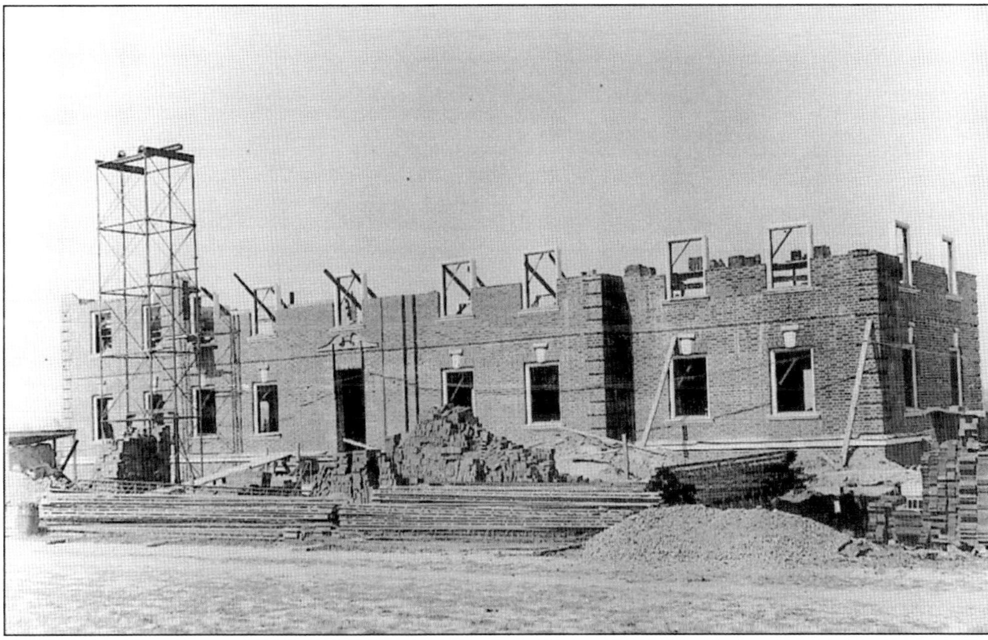

Fraternity Hall under Construction, 1936. The building was at first called "Fraternity Hall" but later renamed after Nathan Shotwell. It was completed and ready for occupancy on February 1, 1937. Thirty-six students immediately left their rooming houses in the town and moved to the campus.

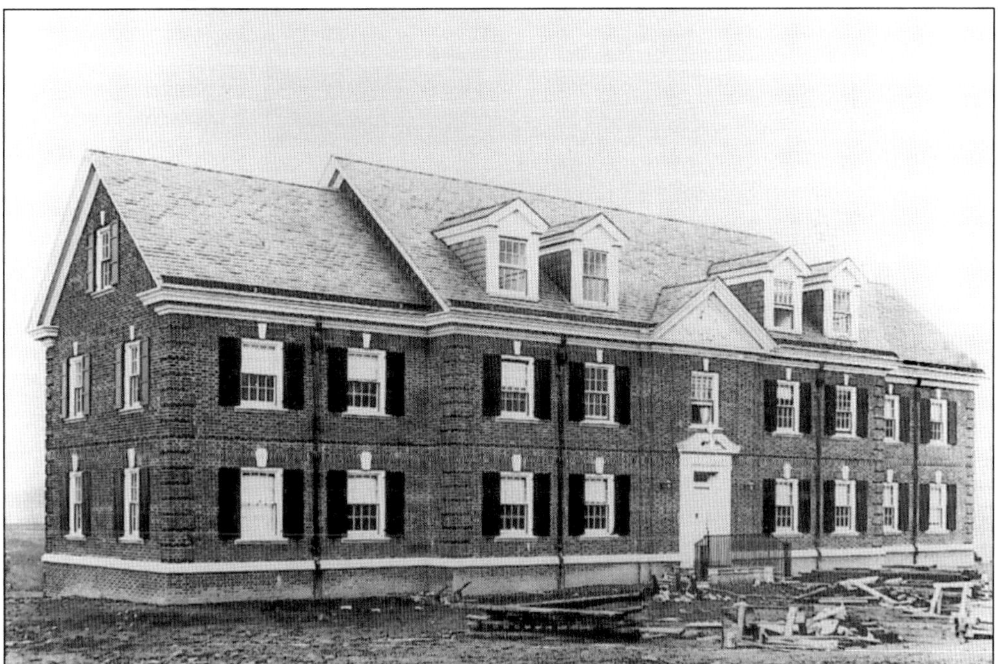

Fraternity Hall Immediately after Completion, 1937. By September 1937, at registration time, the building was already booked beyond its estimated capacity of 48. The hall continued to be occupied by students until it was converted into a faculty office building in 1968.

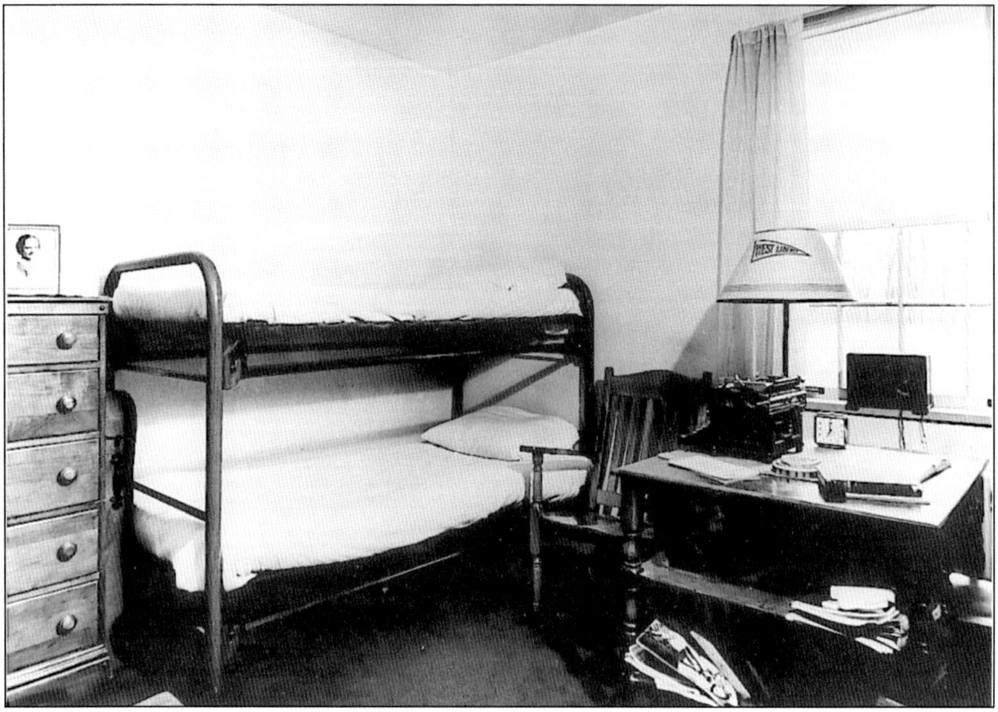

A Typical Room in Shotwell Hall, 1949. Usually two students occupied a room. Note the "modern" accessories—typewriter, AM radio, wind-up alarm clock—and, of course, a girlfriend's photo on the bureau.

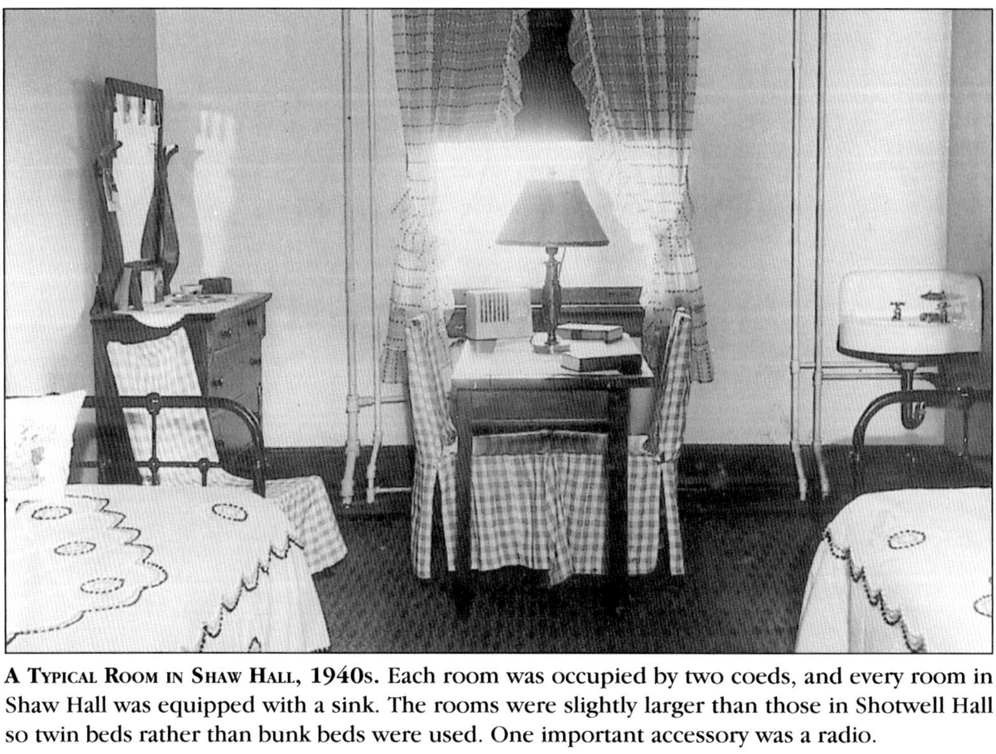

A Typical Room in Shaw Hall, 1940s. Each room was occupied by two coeds, and every room in Shaw Hall was equipped with a sink. The rooms were slightly larger than those in Shotwell Hall so twin beds rather than bunk beds were used. One important accessory was a radio.

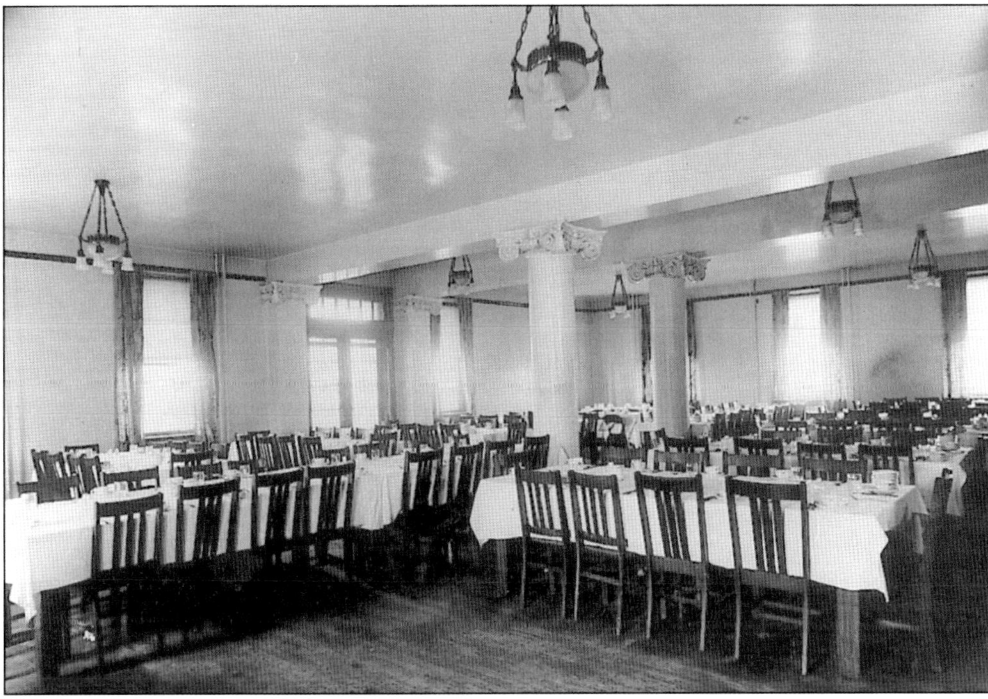

Dining Room in Shaw Hall, 1938. Both male and female students took their meals in the Shaw Hall dining room. Dress was semi-formal, and male students were expected to appear in a coat and tie. The dining room was also utilized for many years for special occasion dining until Rogers Hall cafeteria was constructed in 1959.

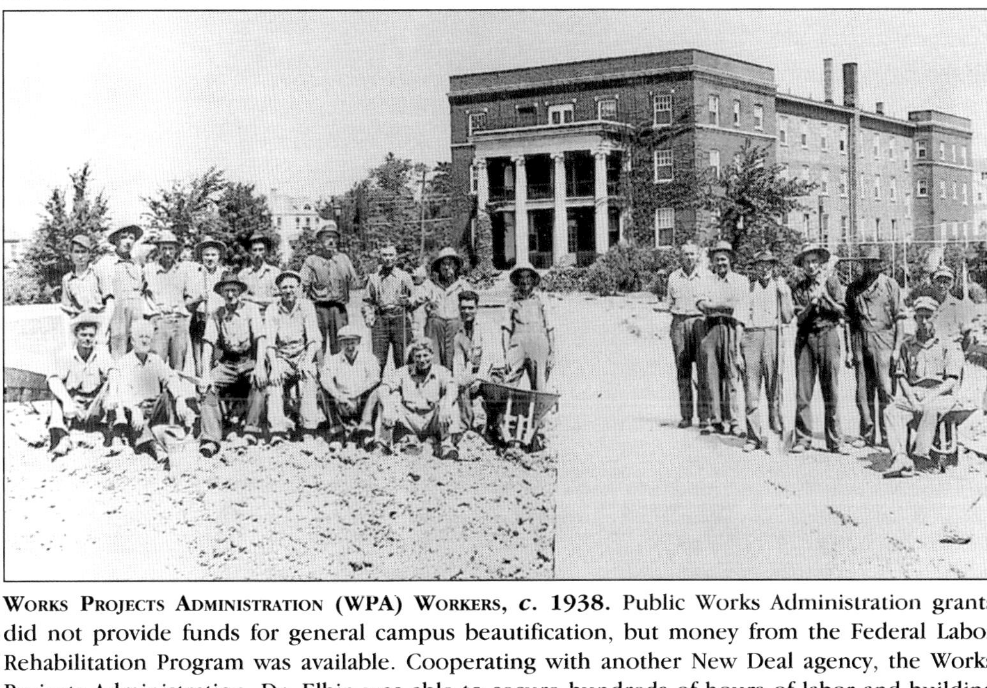

Works Projects Administration (WPA) Workers, c. 1938. Public Works Administration grants did not provide funds for general campus beautification, but money from the Federal Labor Rehabilitation Program was available. Cooperating with another New Deal agency, the Works Projects Administration, Dr. Elbin was able to secure hundreds of hours of labor and building materials for the construction of driveways, curbing, and sidewalks.

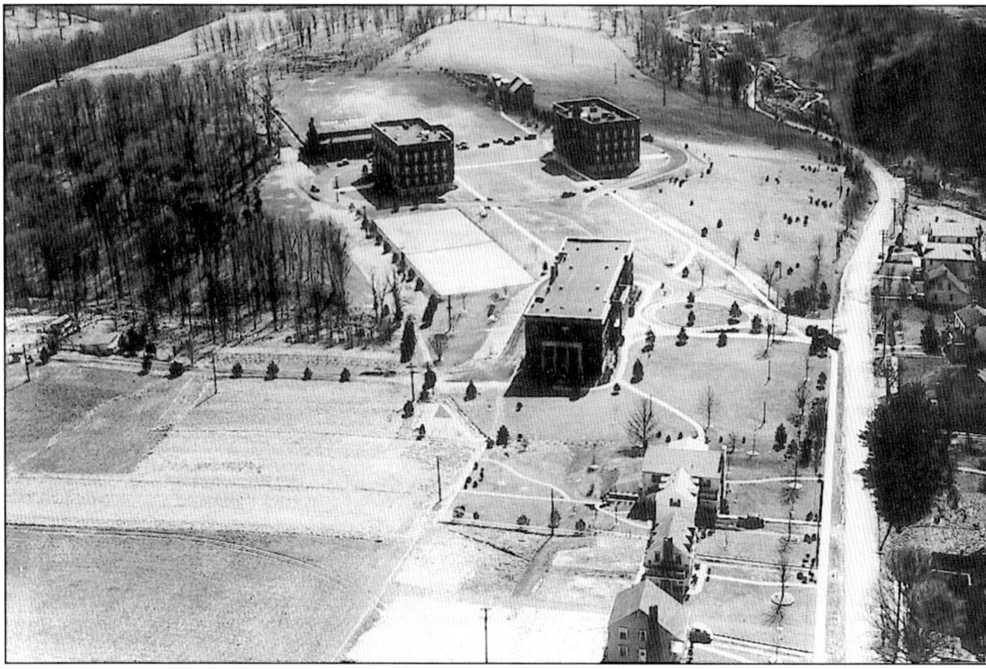

The West Liberty State College Campus, 1939. WPA labor was used for painting, cleaning up the wooded areas of the campus, transplanting trees, and improving the landscape. This aerial photo shows Colonial Heights in the foreground and Shaw Hall, McColloch Hall (left), Curtis Hall (right), the gym (behind McColloch Hall), and Shotwell Hall in the background. The sign on the roof of the gym reading "West Liberty College" helped guide aircraft to the Ohio County Airport, which was only a few miles north of the college. Notice all the young trees that were part of the landscaping. The area between Shaw Hall and McColloch Hall was a tennis court. The road on the right is Route 88.

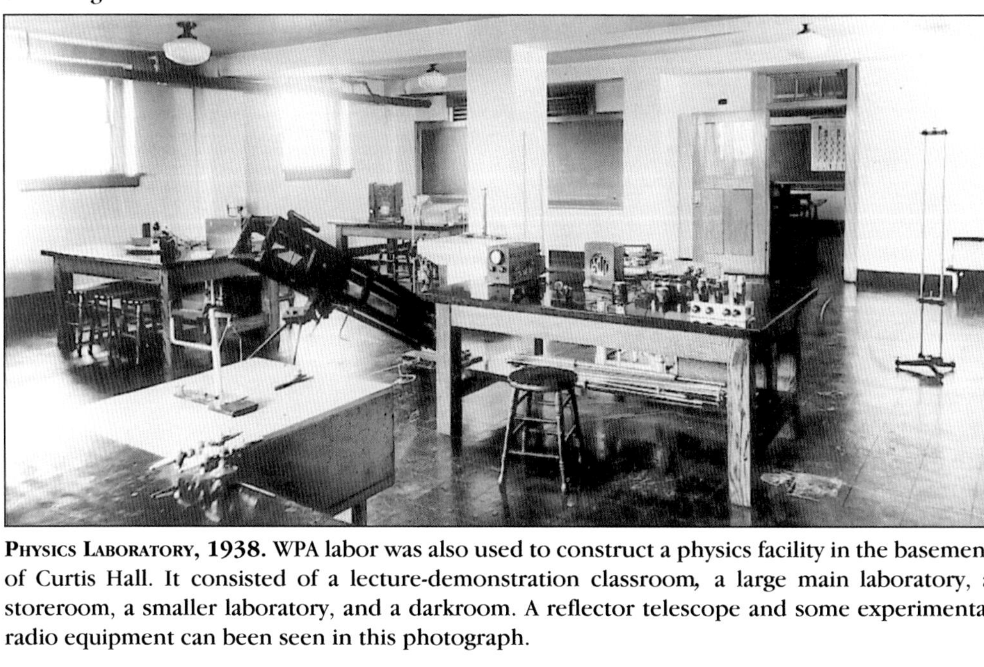

Physics Laboratory, 1938. WPA labor was also used to construct a physics facility in the basement of Curtis Hall. It consisted of a lecture-demonstration classroom, a large main laboratory, a storeroom, a smaller laboratory, and a darkroom. A reflector telescope and some experimental radio equipment can been seen in this photograph.

Letter from President Franklin D. Roosevelt. The year 1938 was, of course, the 100th anniversary of the institution and an occasion for a centennial celebration. The feature event was a 12-act pageant, using antique furniture and equipment and authentic costumes, depicting the history of the town of West Liberty, the academy, the normal school, and the teachers college. One performance was presented on June 8th in Academy Hall and another on June 9th in the amphitheater in Oglebay Park. Special radio broadcasts were presented and Professor C.C. Regier compiled a history, *West Liberty Yesterday and Today,* published in early 1939.

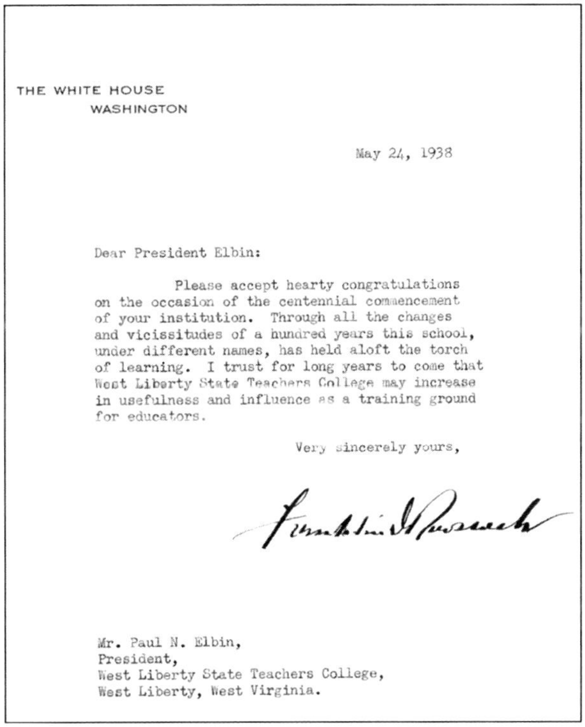

THE WHITE HOUSE
WASHINGTON

May 24, 1938

Dear President Elbin:

Please accept hearty congratulations on the occasion of the centennial commencement of your institution. Through all the changes and vicissitudes of a hundred years this school, under different names, has held aloft the torch of learning. I trust for long years to come that West Liberty State Teachers College may increase in usefulness and influence as a training ground for educators.

Very sincerely yours,

Mr. Paul N. Elbin,
President,
West Liberty State Teachers College,
West Liberty, West Virginia.

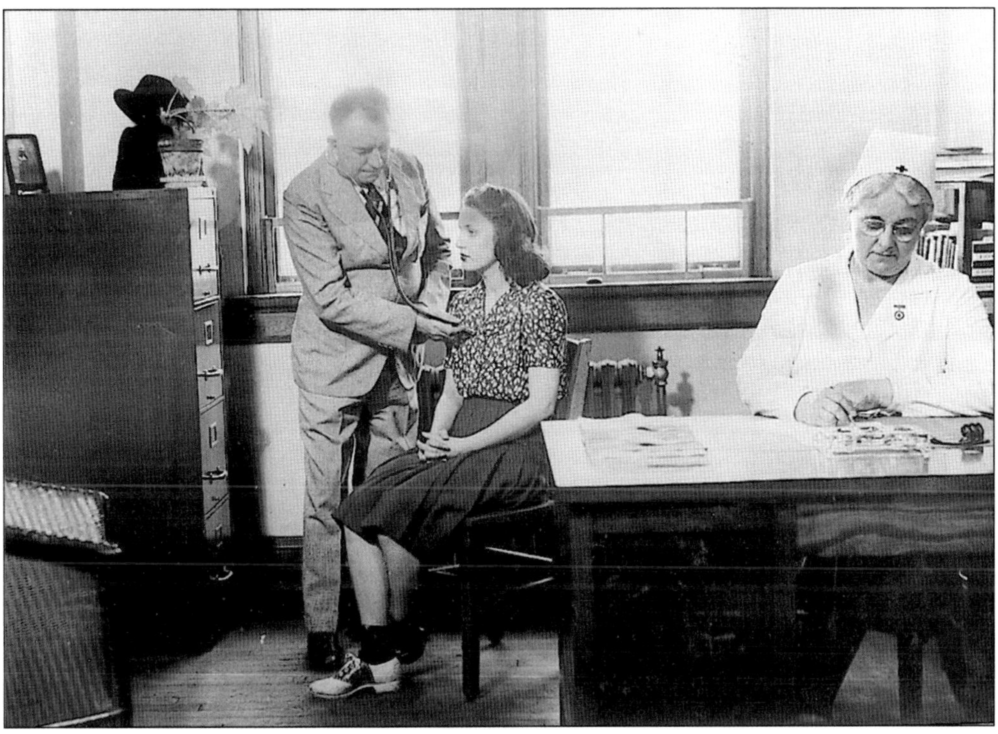

Health Staff, 1937. In June 1935, a college physician was appointed by the State Board of Education. In September 1938, a full-time registered nurse was added to the staff. Pictured here are Dr. J.W. Ruckman M.D., the college physician, and nurse Louise Korbert.

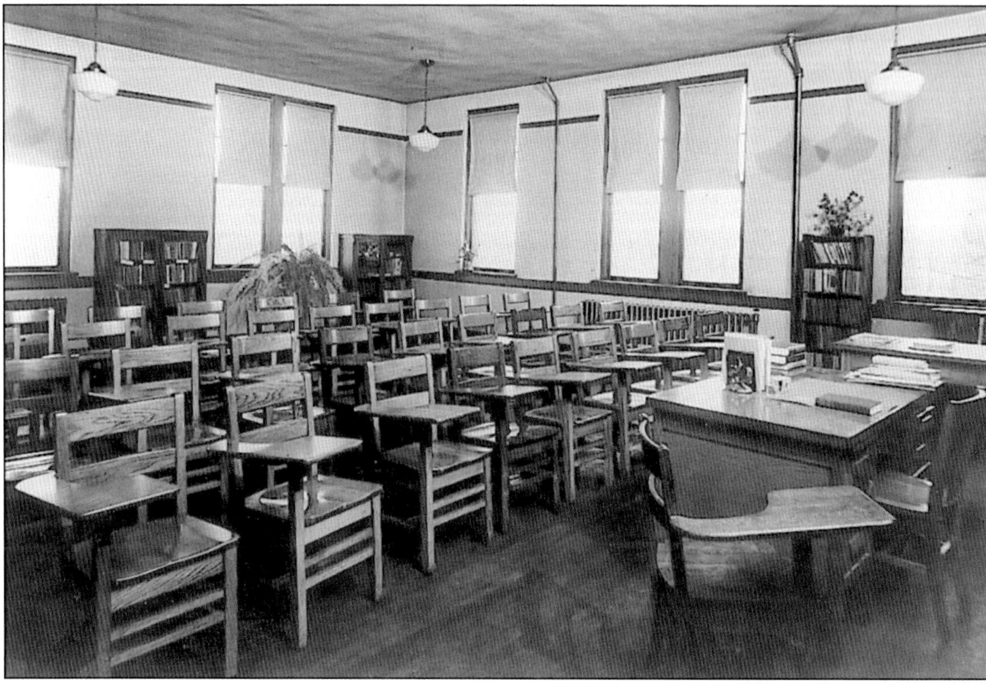

TYPICAL CLASSROOM, *c.* 1935. Paul N. Elbin never forgot for a moment his goal of national accreditation. West Liberty's McColloch Library still needed to expand the collection to meet the standards of accrediting agencies. Dr. Elbin obtained state funds and a grant from the Carnegie Foundation in New York and established a "give-a-book" campaign among faculty and alumni. Over 5,000 volumes were added to the collection.

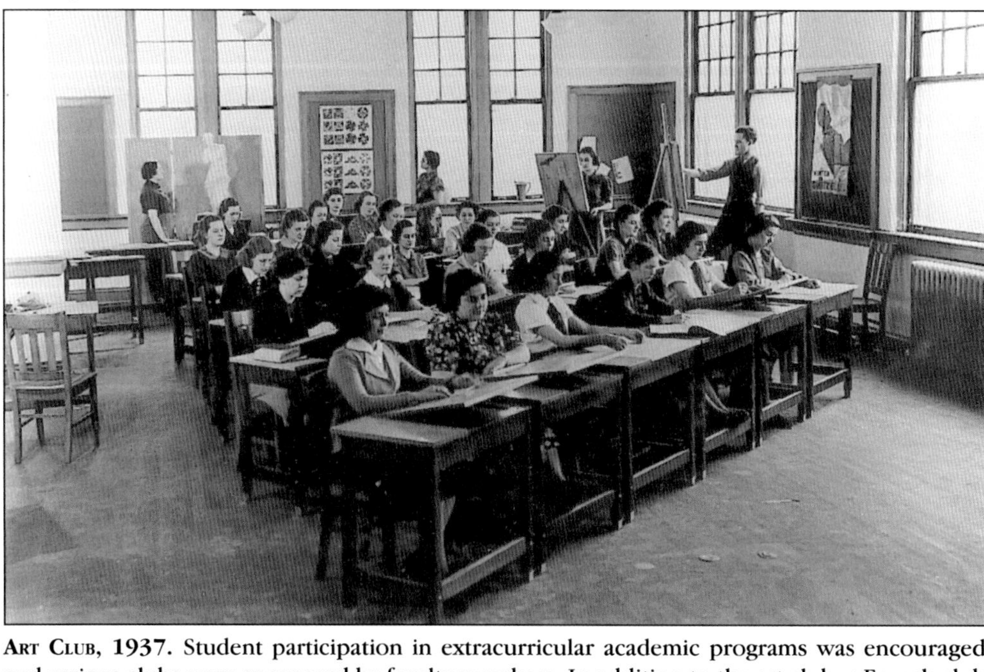

ART CLUB, 1937. Student participation in extracurricular academic programs was encouraged, and various clubs were sponsored by faculty members. In addition to the art club, a French club, Spanish club, book club, science club, and international relations club were formed.

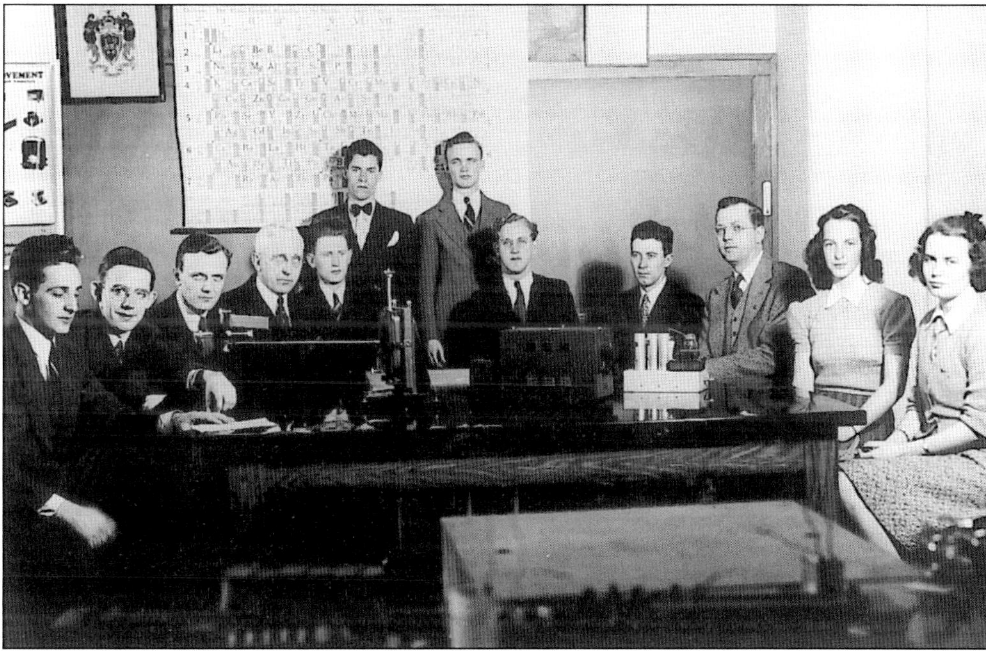

Chi Beta Phi, 1940. In 1935, the science club was chartered as the Rho Chapter of Chi Beta Phi, a national science honorary. This was the first national honorary chartered at West Liberty.

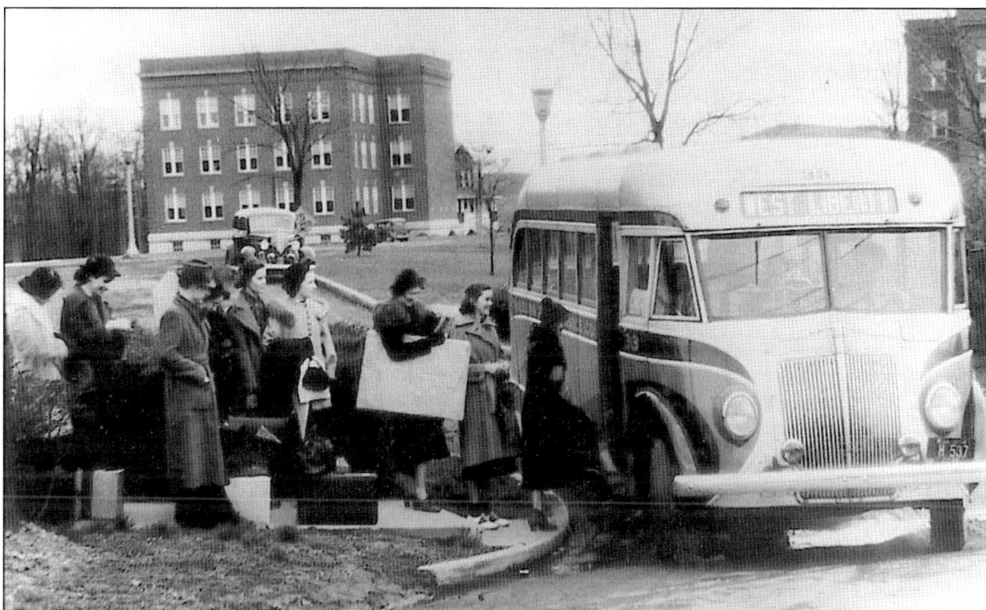

Wheeling Public Service Co. Bus Picking Up Students for a Trip to Wheeling, 1938. In December 1937, a team from the American Association of Teachers Colleges came to the campus for an inspection. Terming the recent progress at West Liberty "miraculous," they filed a favorable report. On February 26, 1938, the college was given unconditional national accreditation by the American Association of Teachers Colleges. On the following November 10th, the State Committee of the North Central Association of Colleges and Secondary Schools placed West Liberty on its approved list.

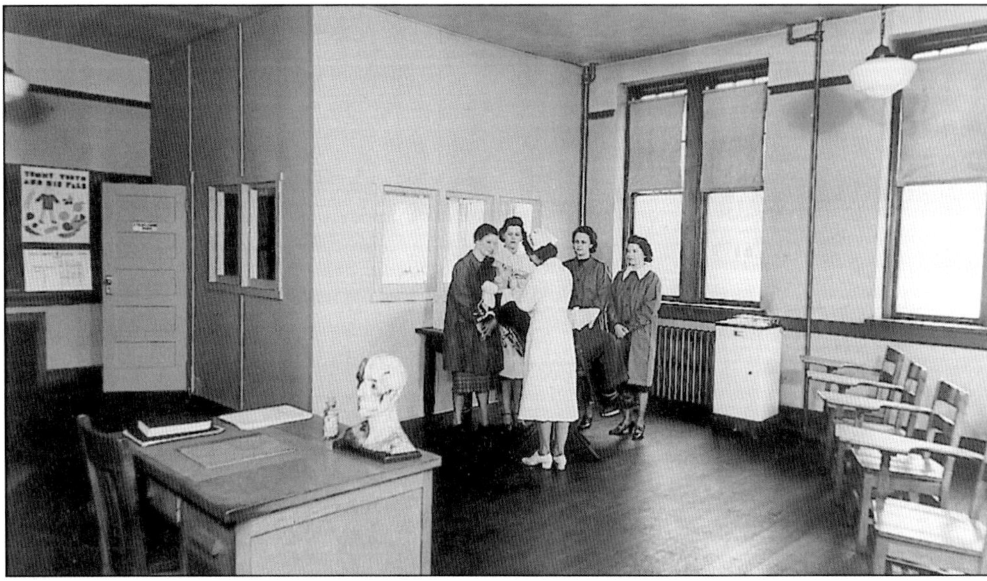

First Class in the Oral Hygiene Department, 1939. In this image, Miss Ada Resnick, an instructor, performs oral prophylaxis on student Paul Kelchak while Oral Hygiene students, from left to right, Hazel Reed, Margaritta Joliffe, Mana Mae Rogerson, and Ruth Hammond look on. As a result of Dr. Elbin's continuous search for means to attract more students to the West Liberty campus and encouraged by the Wheeling District Dental Society, Elbin established a Department of Oral Hygiene (now known as the dental hygiene program) in 1938.

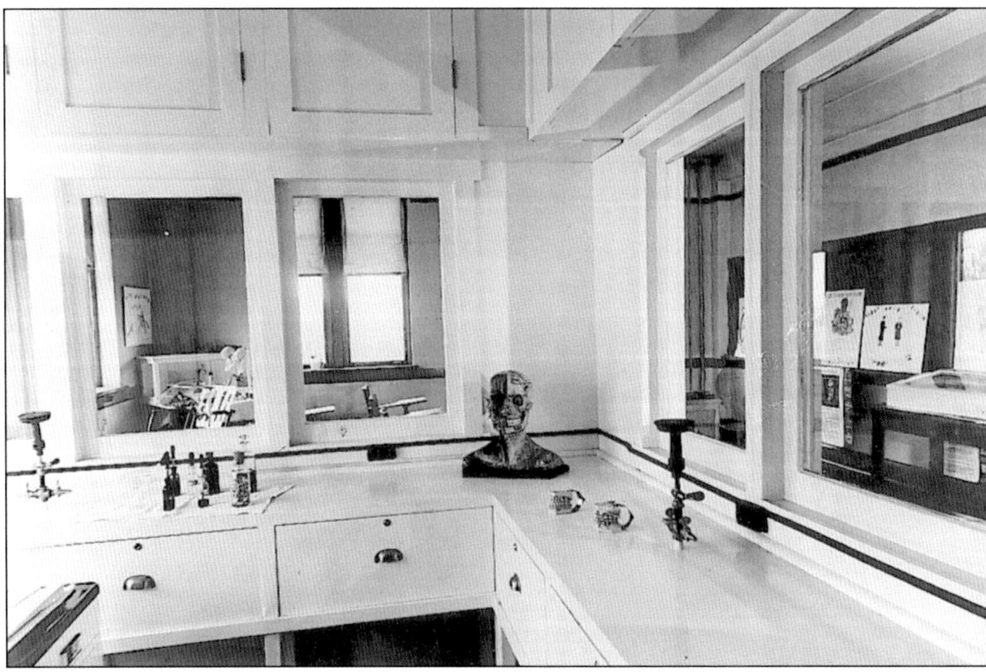

Interior of the Sterilizing Room, Department of Oral Hygiene, 1938. There were fewer than two dozen schools in the country giving adequate training in oral hygiene. Sarah Whitaker Glass, a resident of Wheeling, generously donated funds to remodel the first floor of Curtis Hall and to construct modern laboratories and a clinic.

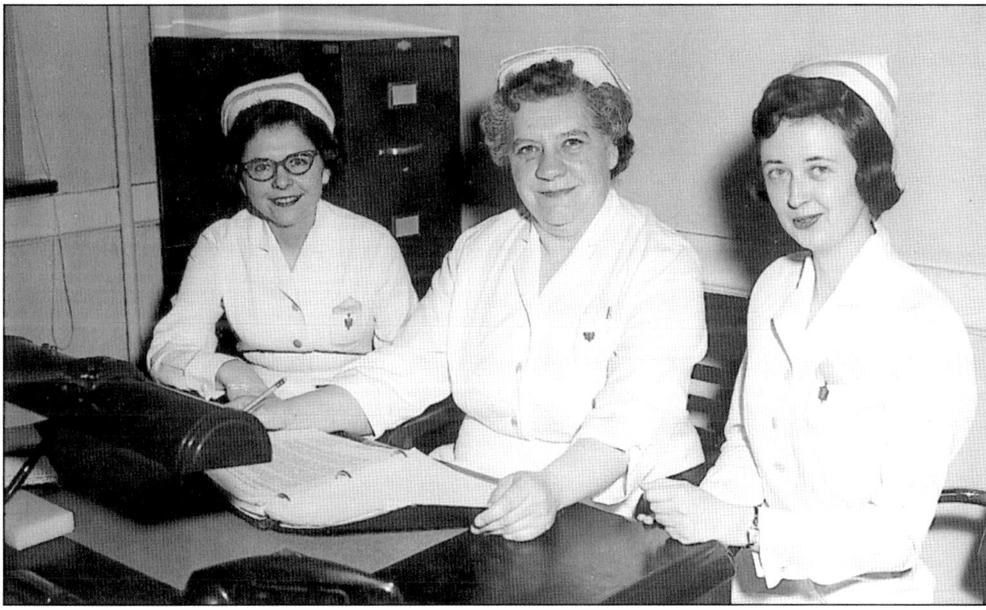

Dental Hygiene Faculty, *c.* 1956. Subsequent gifts from Mrs. Glass and her daughters, Mrs. Gibson Caldwell and Mrs. W.W. Holloway, made possible the continued expansion and improvement of the dental hygiene department. The program was a two-year course, but in 1939, a four-year course leading to the degree of bachelor of science in dental hygiene was added. From left to right are faculty members Emmajo Shearer, Roxie Stitzer (supervisor), and Eleanor Baily.

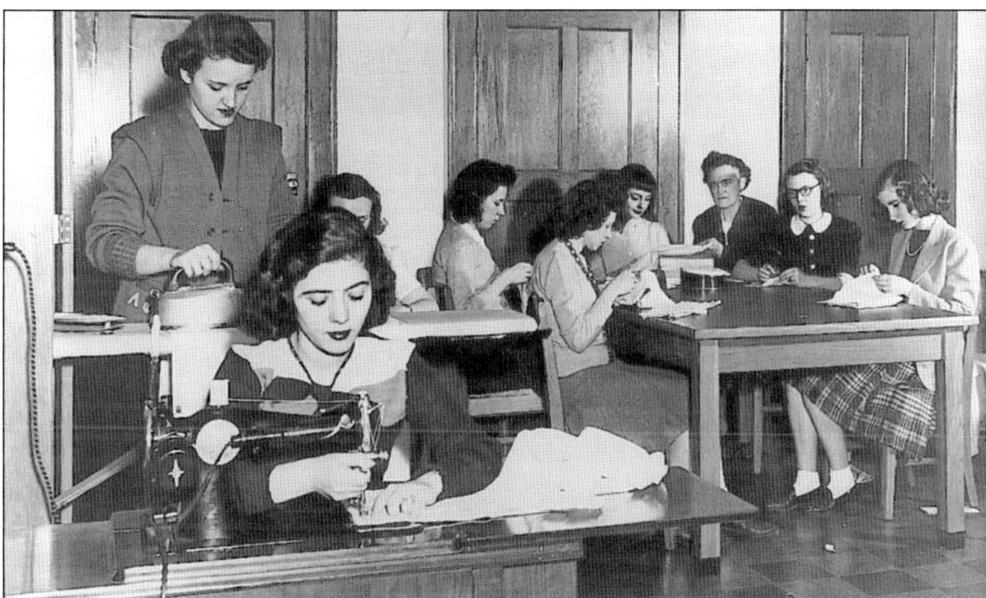

Home Economics Class, 1940. Professor Areta Hicks (at the table on the right) directed a new program for the training of teachers in home economics and a separate program in home arts for students interested in homemaking. An appropriation from the state and a WPA grant in 1939 were used to remodel the basement of McColloch Hall. A model kitchen, sewing laboratory, and practice dining room were all part of the new facility.

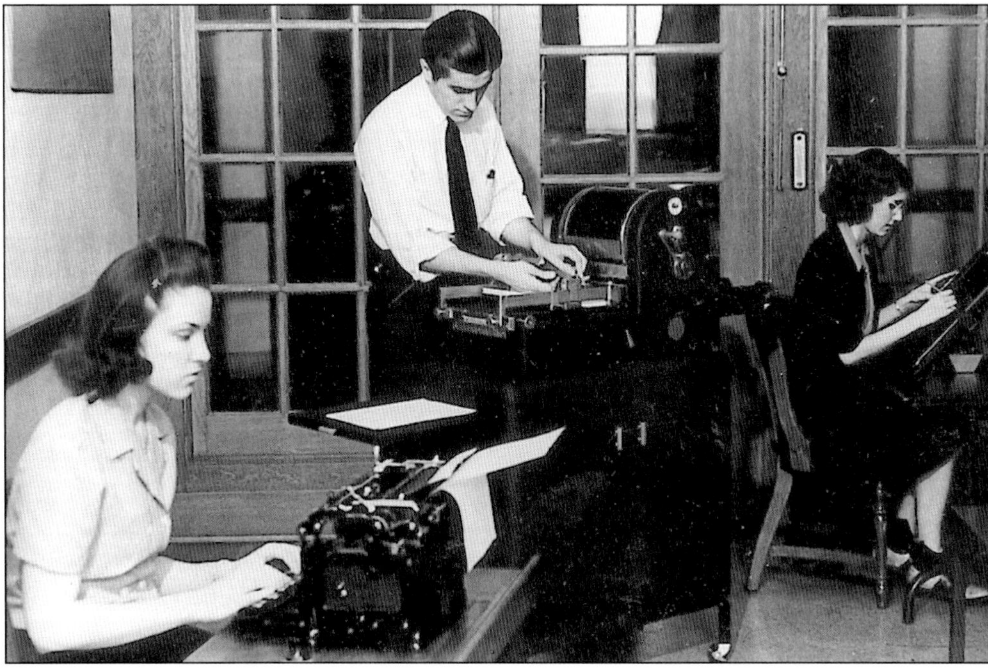

COMMERCE DEPARTMENT, 1940. The years 1938 and 1939 were important years for the expansion of the academic program. In addition to the programs already mentioned, commerce and library science programs were also added.

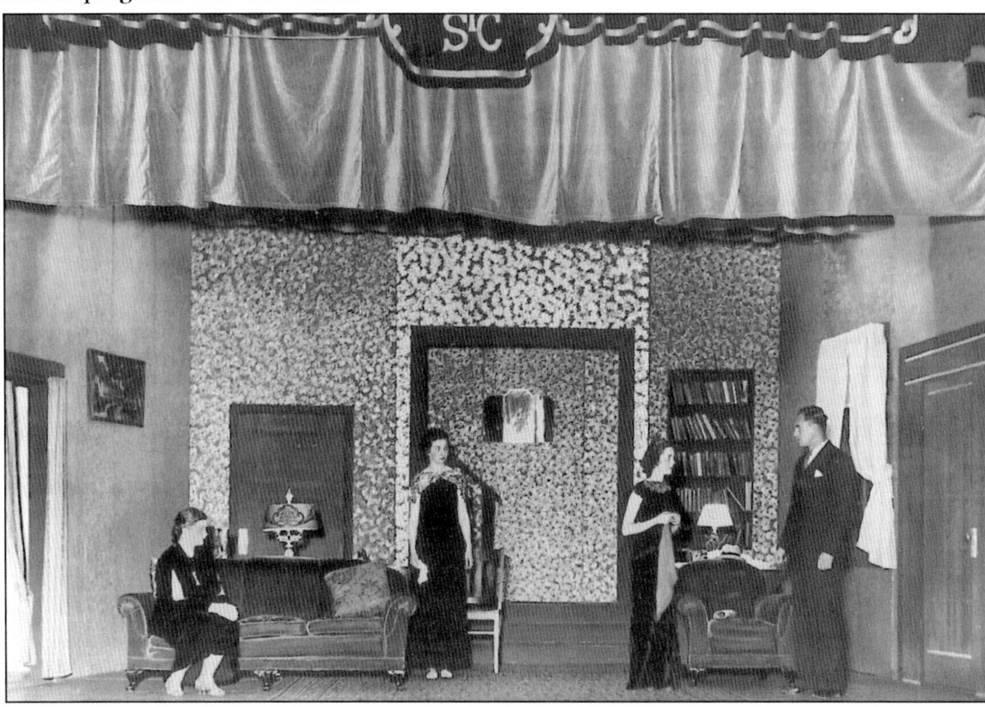

HILLTOP PLAYERS, 1940. The Hilltop Players was organized in 1926 and is the second-oldest, continuous student organization. Over the years this group has produced a multitude of student productions, including plays and, more recently, musicals.

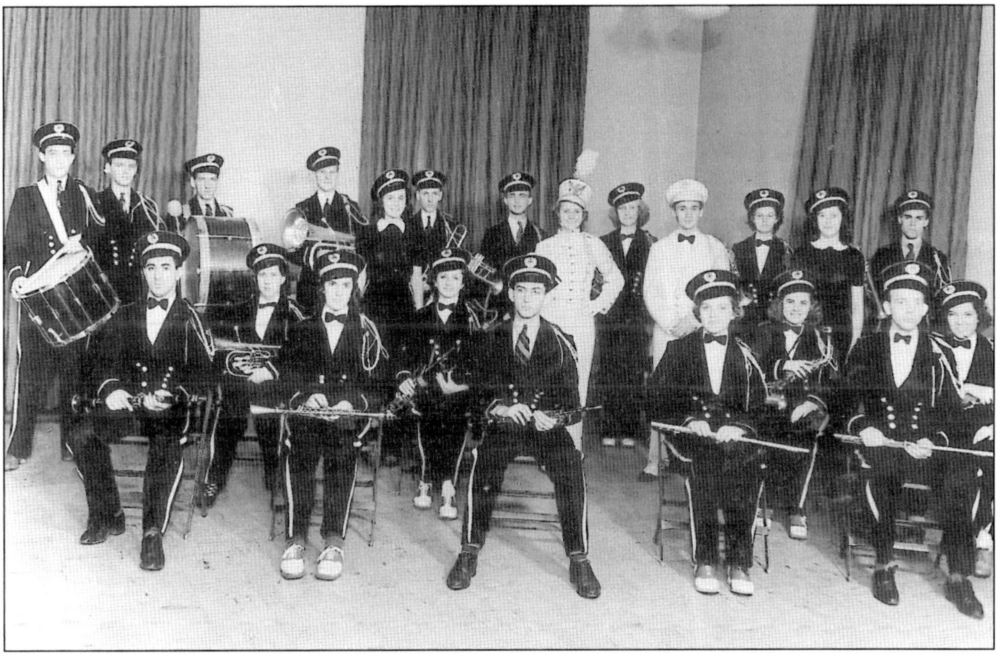

College Band, 1941. There is no record of when the first college band was formed, but the earliest records date to the late 1930s. Since then, there has always been a band, except for a short time in the 1960s. Today the college proudly boasts both a marching band and a concert band as well as several smaller musical groups.

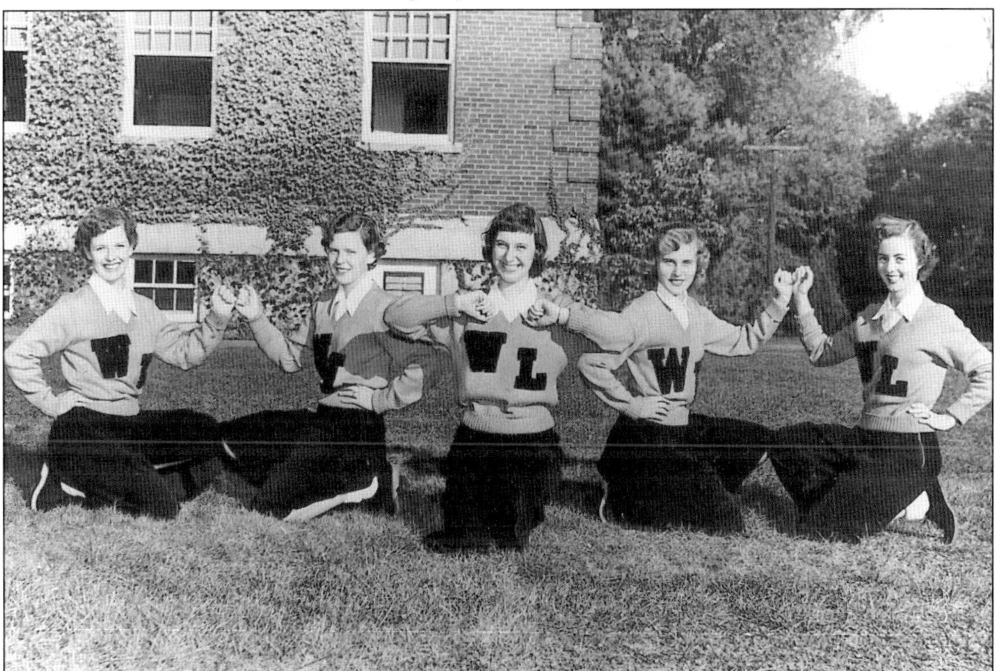

Cheerleaders, 1940. The first cheerleading squads were probably organized about the time that the first football teams were created but, again, the earliest records are from the late 1930s. These young ladies pose on the lawn in front of McColloch Hall.

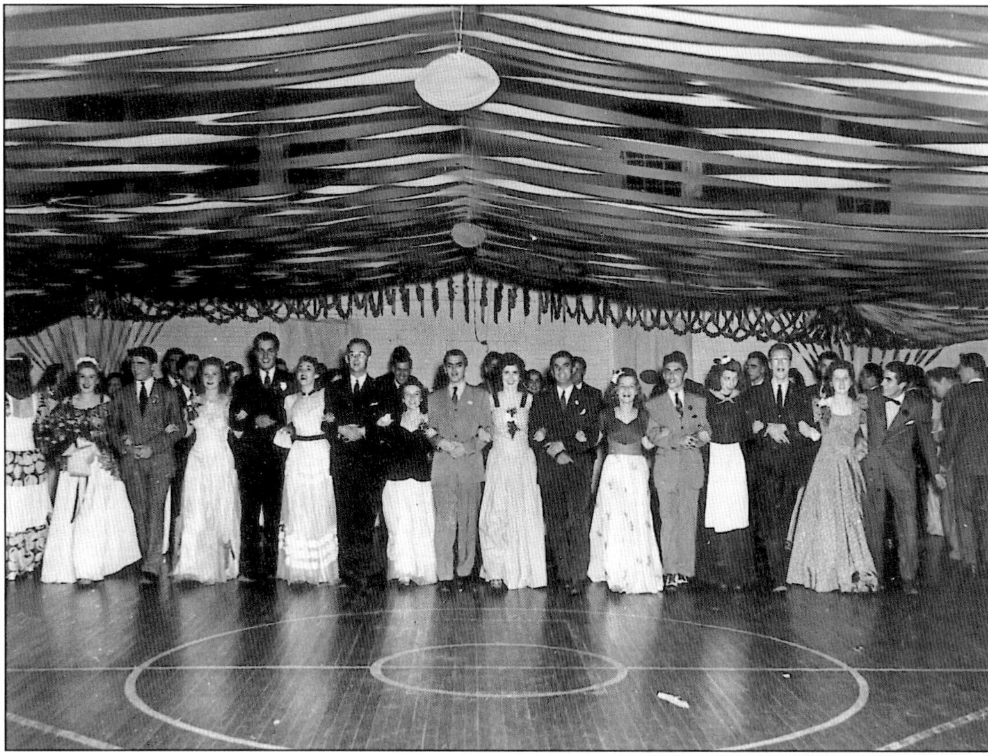

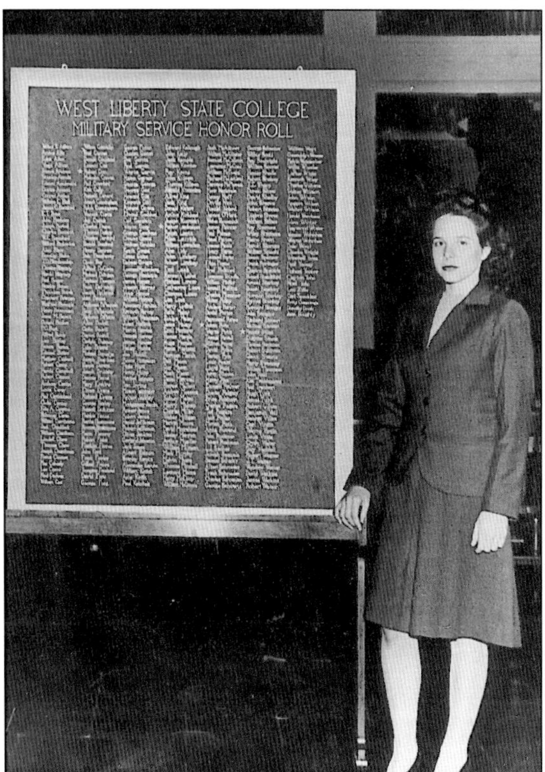

DANCE IN THE OLD GYM, *c.* 1940. Shortly after the old, wood-frame gym was constructed, students began holding dances there. Judging from the ball gowns worn by the ladies, the suits worn by the men and what looks like cardboard footballs as part of the decor, this is probably a homecoming dance.

MILITARY HONOR ROLL OF WEST LIBERTY STUDENTS AND FACULTY, *c.* 1943. Students, faculty, and staff gathered in historic Academy Hall to hear the radio address of President Franklin D. Roosevelt when he asked Congress to declare war on Japan. As it had in the past, war brought change and challenge to the institution. Enrollment diminished as students and faculty volunteered for military service, and academic life at West Liberty was put on hold for the duration. Dr. Elbin knew that the war could not last forever, so he began making plans for the return of the service men and women.

SIGN AT THE ENTRANCE TO THE COLLEGE, *c.* 1949. Working with Sen. James Paull of Wellsburg, Dr. Elbin initiated the drive to have the college charter changed to permit the institution to offer programs in addition to teacher education. This was a way to increase enrollment and meet the needs of returning members of the armed services after the war. Legislation was passed in June of 1943 that changed the name of the college to West Liberty State College and authorized it to offer "such curricula in general education . . . as the State Board of Education may direct or approve." This sign at the college entrance was installed in 1943.

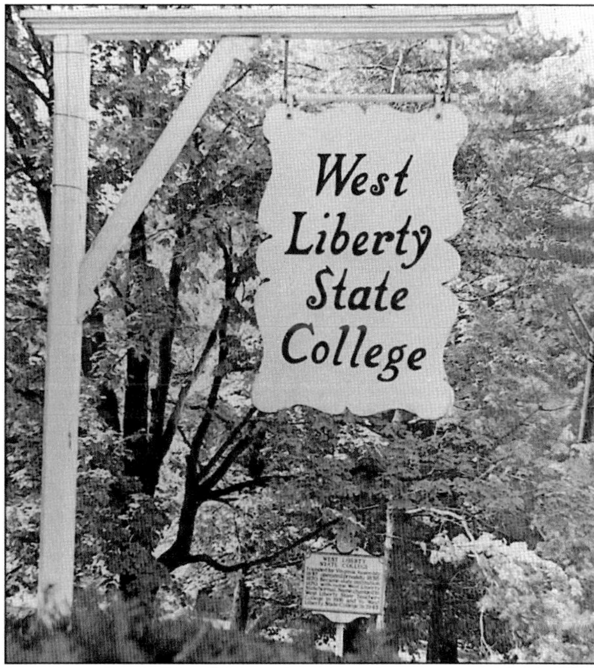

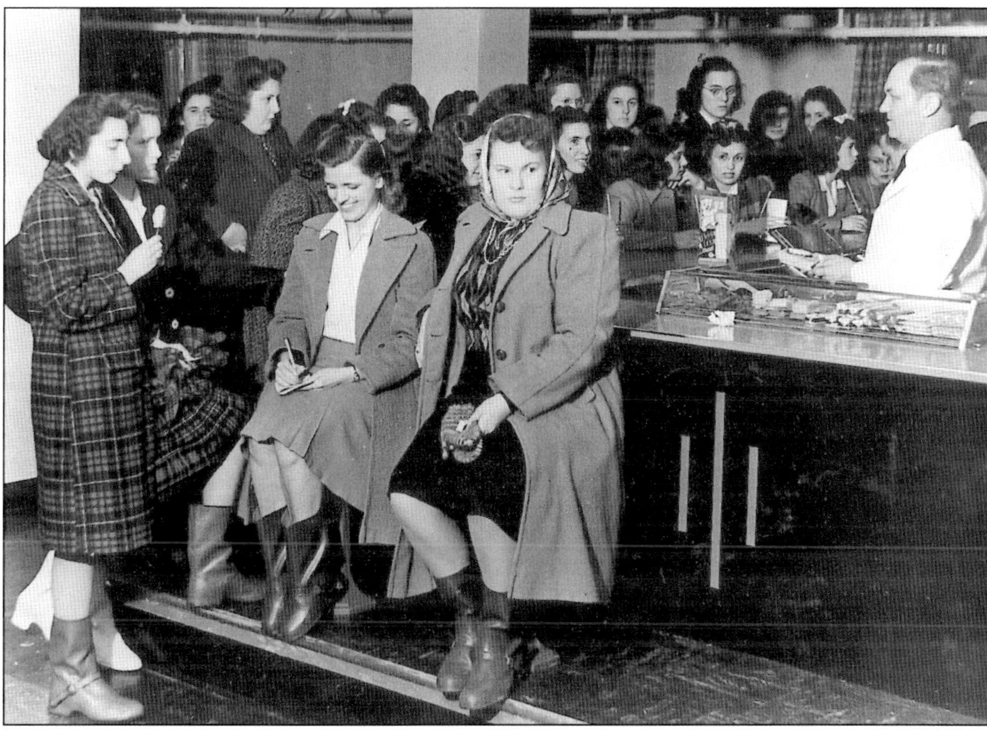

STUDENT CENTER OPENING, 1942. Despite the war, projects that were begun prior to December 1941 were continued and completed. A combination of a WPA grant and a state appropriation allowed the construction of the first student center in the state. It was located in the basement of McColloch Hall. Dr. Elbin can be seen behind the counter in this photograph made on opening day, January 5, 1942.

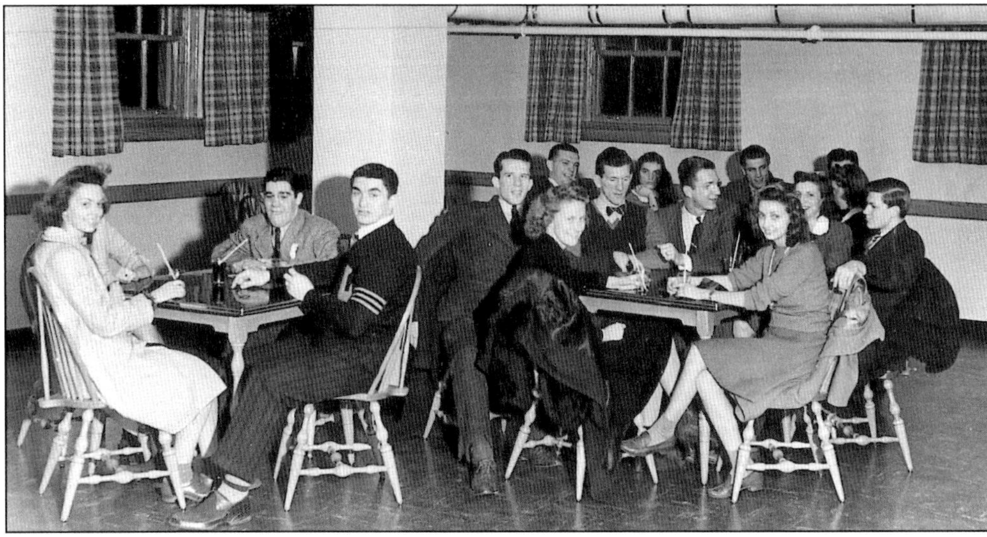

"The Center," *c.* 1942. The student center was equipped with a soda fountain, lunch counter, tables, dance floor, and jukebox. On opening day, students enjoyed dancing and free ice cream served to them by Dr. Elbin working as "soda jerk."

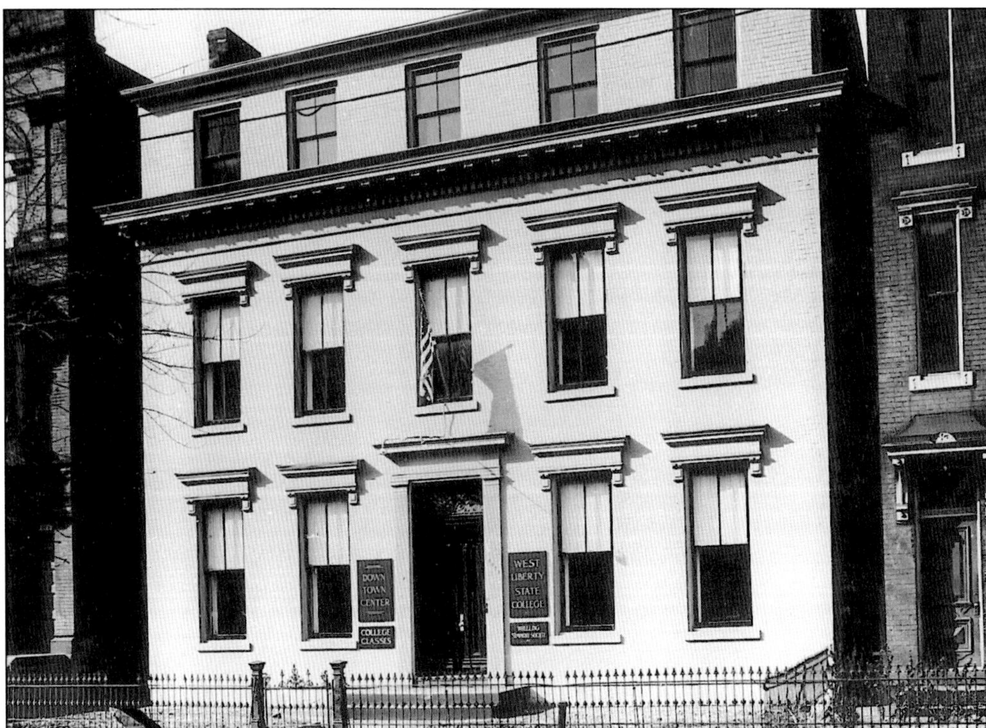

Downtown Center, 1948. West Liberty State College opened the Downtown Center at Wheeling High School in 1938. Enrollment grew and, in 1942, a large Victorian residence at 2227 Chapline Street in Wheeling was made available for the joint use of the college and the Wheeling Symphony Society. Thirteen years before the U.S. Supreme Court decision outlawing school segregation, Dr. Elbin directed that African-American students be admitted to Downtown Center classes. Credits earned would be recorded at West Virginia State, a segregated black college.

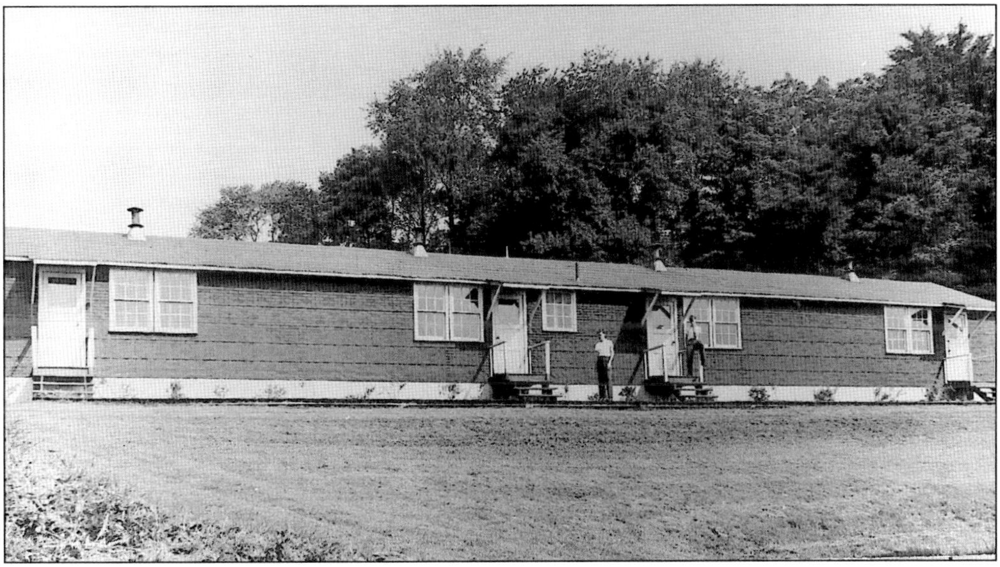

A Barracks Unit, 1946. The war's end in 1945 brought serious problems to the college; the most immediate challenge was a tremendous influx of students. Between 1945 and 1946 the enrollment increased by 218 percent. In order to help solve the housing problems, five war-surplus barracks were erected in 1946–1947 to house veterans.

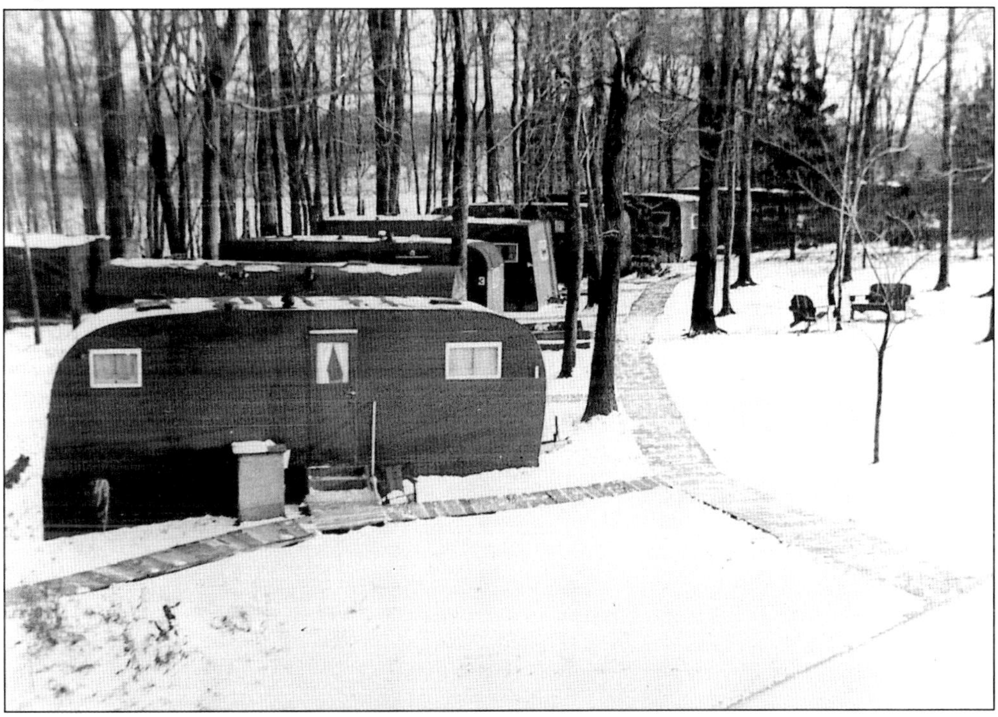

Trailer Court, 1947. Married veterans were housed in 12 army residence trailers, but there were many shortages. Not only housing but classrooms, food services, books, and faculty had to be increased. Even water and toilet paper were in short supply. Tank trucks from Fort Meade, Maryland brought in water, and students were asked to bring their own supply of toilet tissue from home.

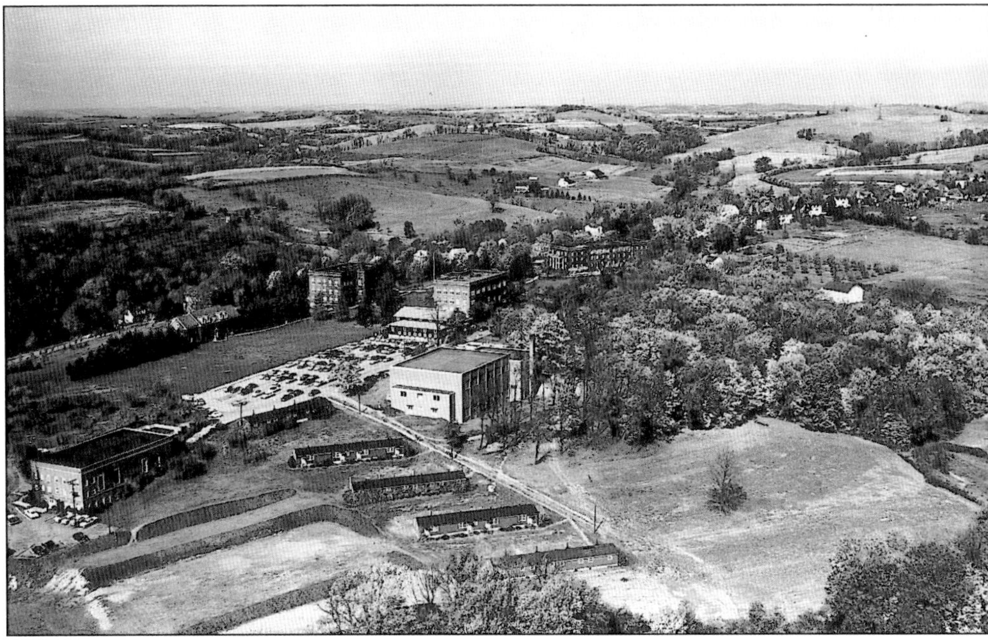

The Campus, c. 1956. Through the cooperation of the Federal Works Agency, a theater from Camp Patrick Henry, Virginia was donated to the college. Although the work of erecting the building on the campus was started in 1948, it was not completed until 1950. The theater, named College Hall, can be seen on the far left in this photo. The five barracks are to the right of College Hall.

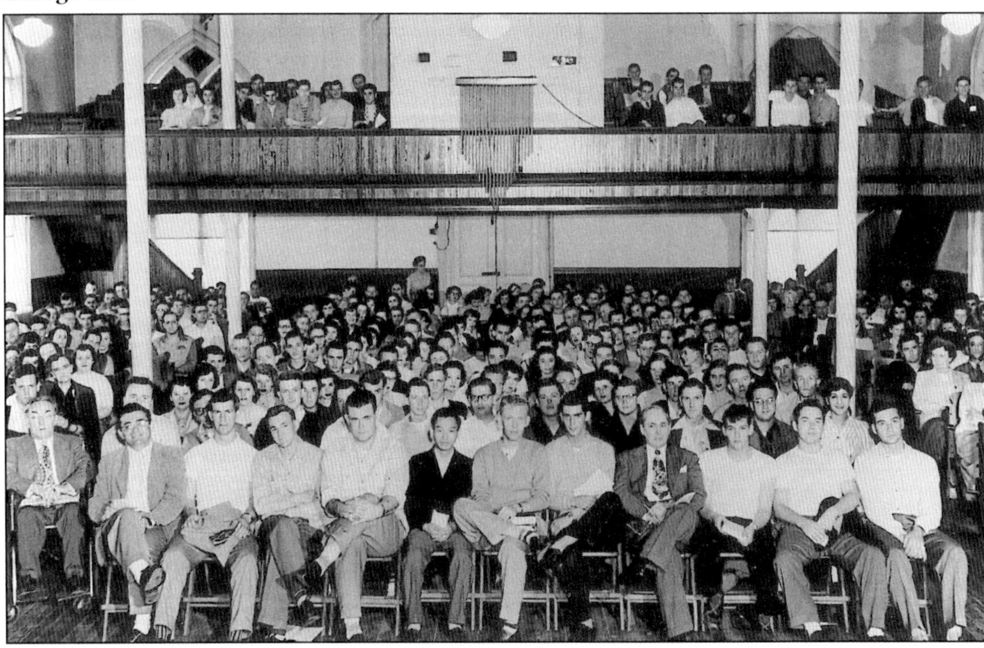

Last Assembly in Academy Hall, May 1950. West Liberty's pattern of weekly student and faculty assemblies originated with the daily chapel services of the normal school. After College Hall was completed, assemblies were held there. Assembly programs usually consisted of lecturers, artists, musicians, scientists, operatic and dance groups, as well as documentary films.

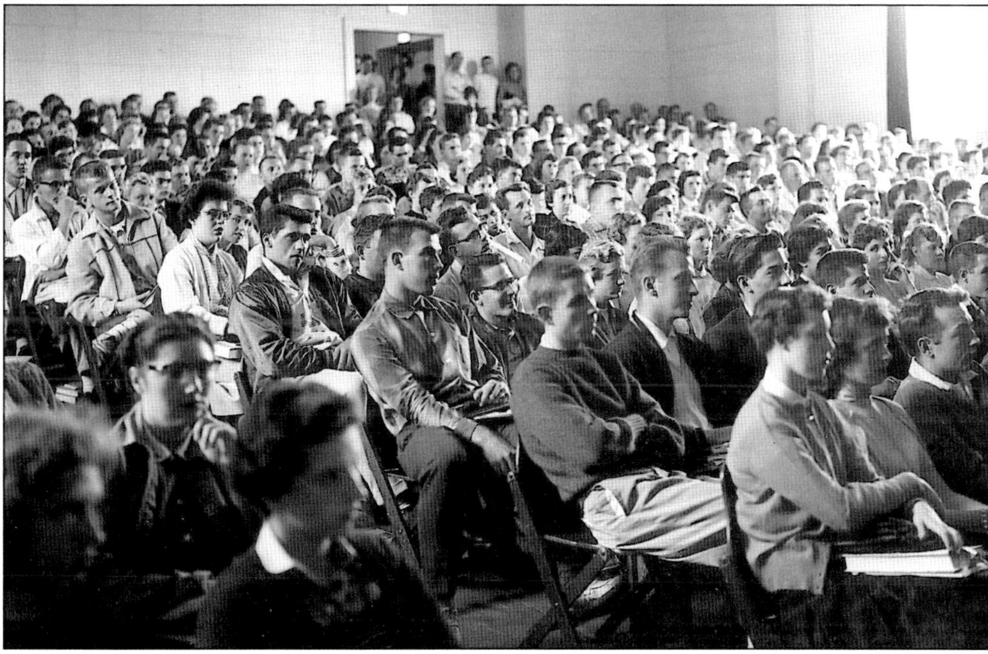

Students at an Assembly Program in College Hall, c. 1957. Required attendance at assembly programs was finally discontinued in the 1960s. Other special programs, such as the honors assembly and the Hughes Lecture Series—named after Professor Raymond G. Hughes who established a trust to bring prominent individuals to the campus—continue today.

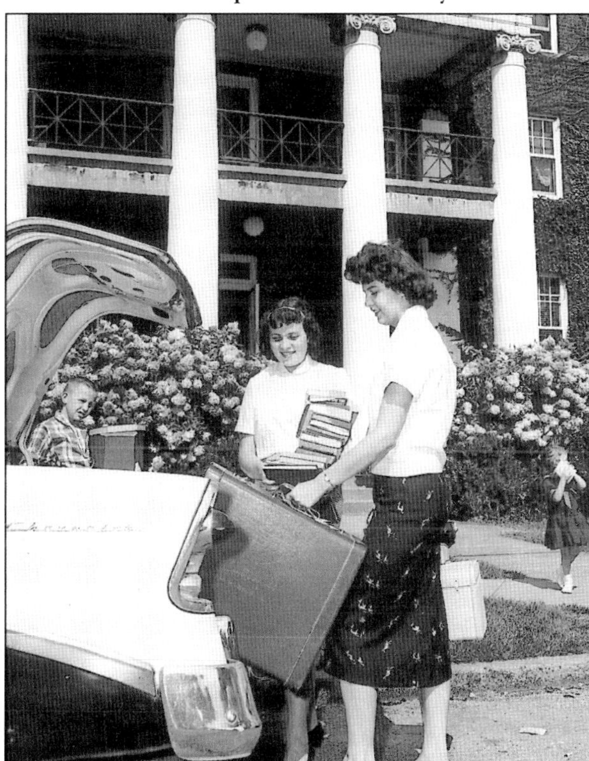

Moving In, c. 1956. The decade of the 1940s saw a swelling of enrollment by World War II veterans and, then in the 1950s, by veterans of the Korean War. These coeds are moving into Shaw Hall.

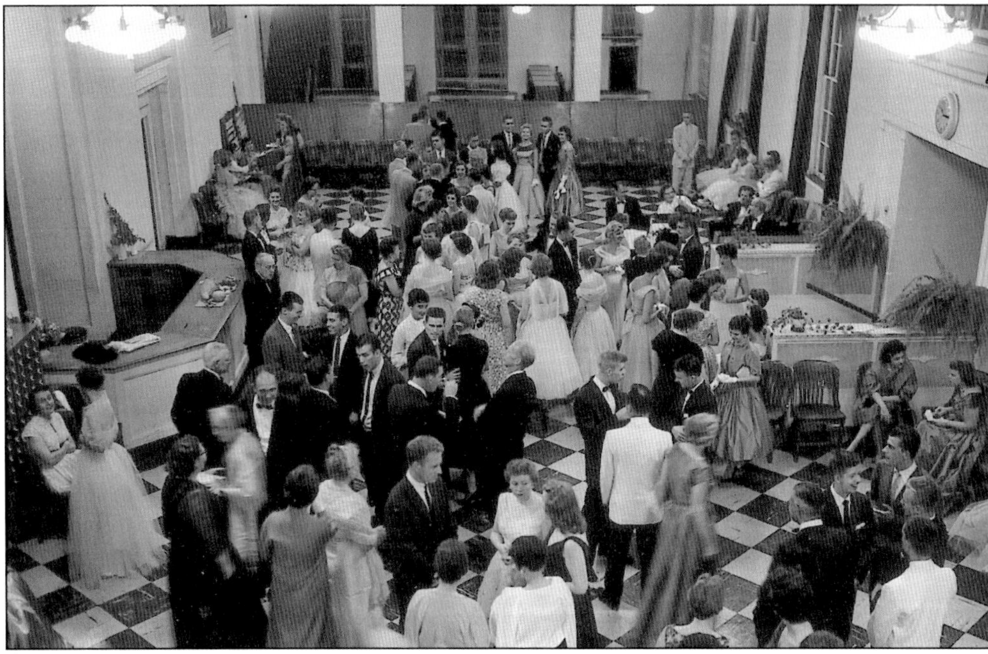

Formal Faculty Reception, c. 1956. The first major event of the school year was the formal reception held in the McColloch Library. Every member of the faculty and administration stood in a receiving line to greet each incoming student.

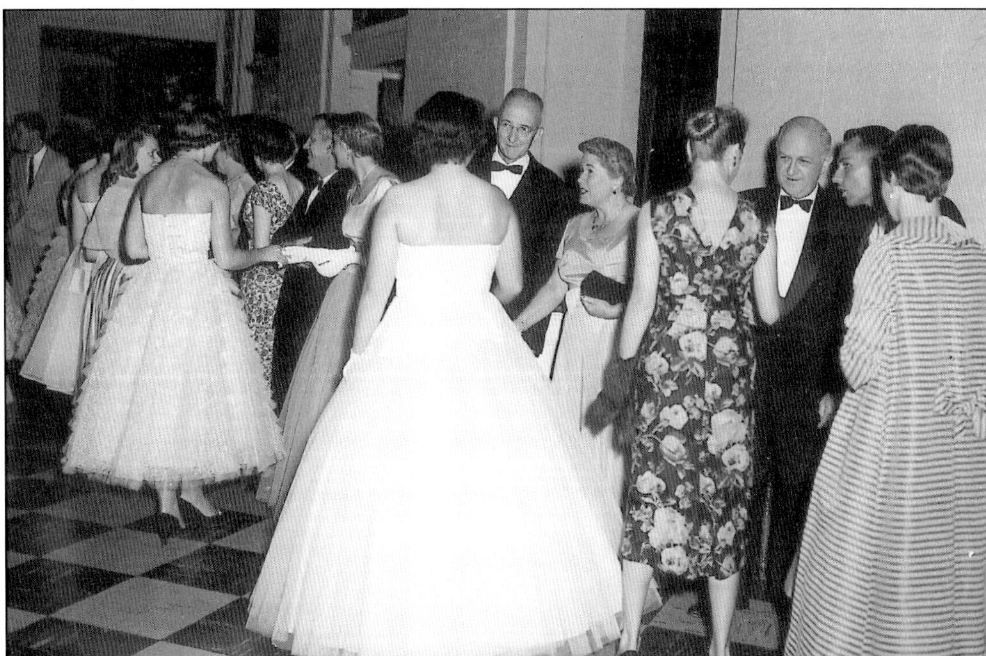

Formal Reception, 1957. Ball gowns and tuxedos were worn by faculty and administration, including, from left to right, Joseph Bartell, Denver Arnett, Helen Elbin, and Paul Elbin. The music department supplied a string quartet. Refreshments were punch and cookies prepared by home economics students.

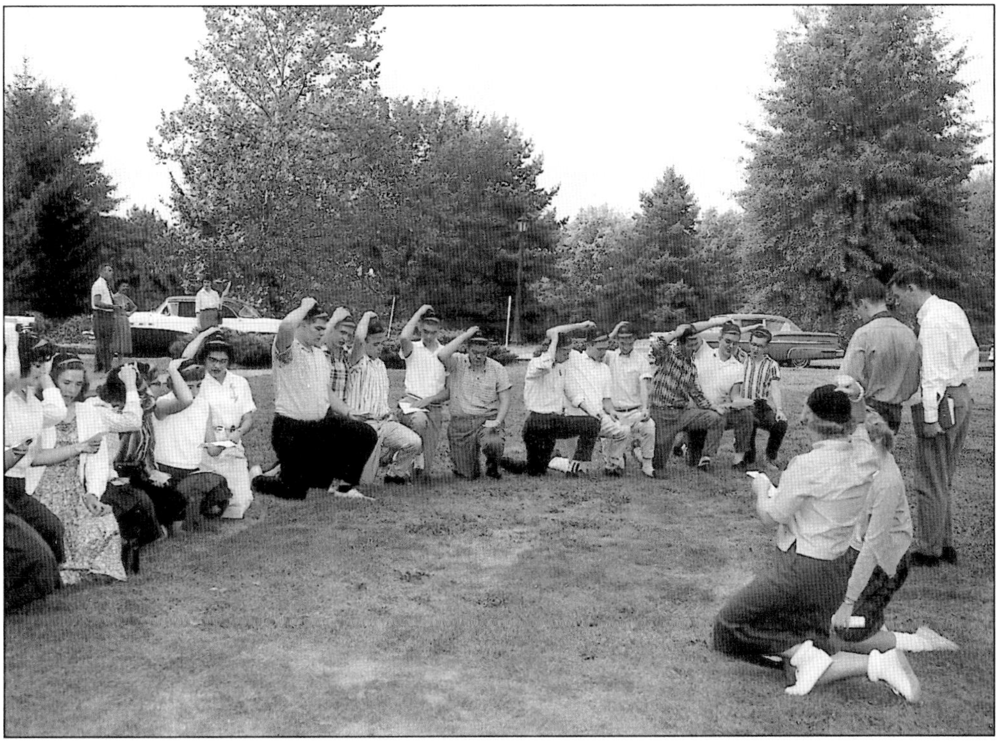

Button, Frosh!, *c.* 1959. Freshmen were required to wear a beanie and kneel and touch the button on top at the request of an upperclassman. Freshmen were also required to be able to sing the alma mater upon request. The hazing of freshmen was eventually discontinued, probably because veterans refused to participate.

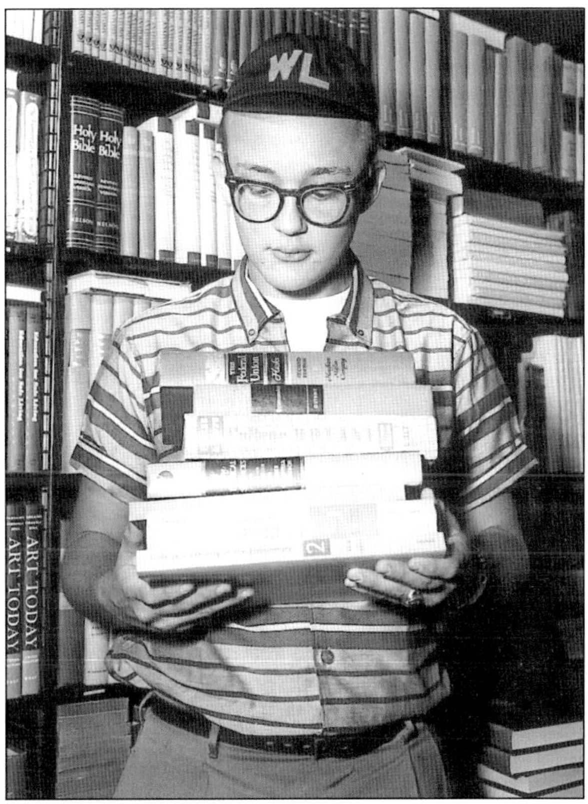

Freshman in the Bookstore, *c.* 1957. Trying to buy all the books needed was an ordeal, and this freshman seems to be loaded down with his required textbooks. Freshmen were required to wear their "dinks" (beanies) everywhere, including in bed and in the shower.

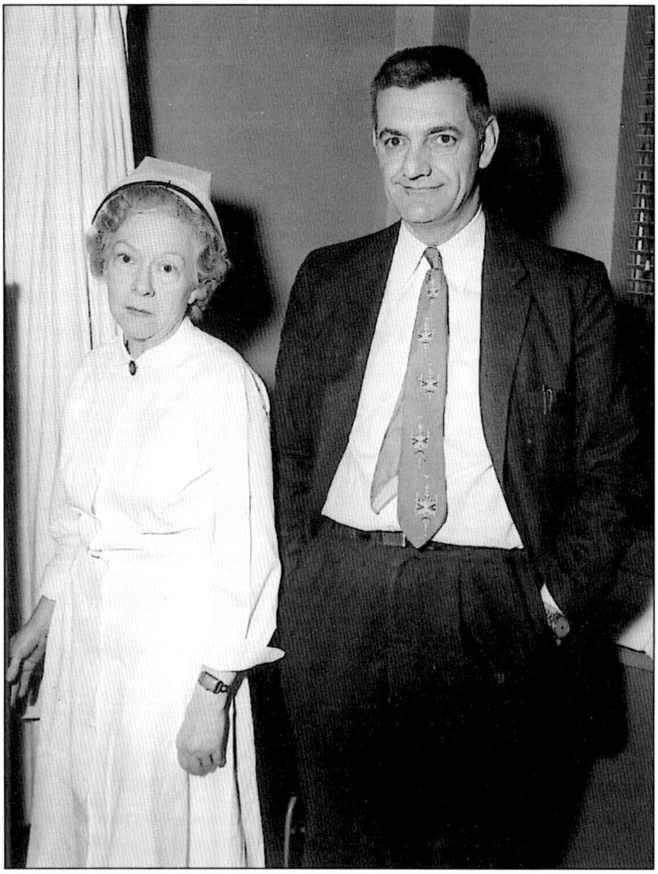

NURSE FRANCES PARRIOTT AND DR. FRED D. LARGE, C. 1956. Physical exams were required of every incoming student. The college health service was available to both students and faculty, and Nurse Parriott ("Nursie"), who lived on campus, was available whenever needed.

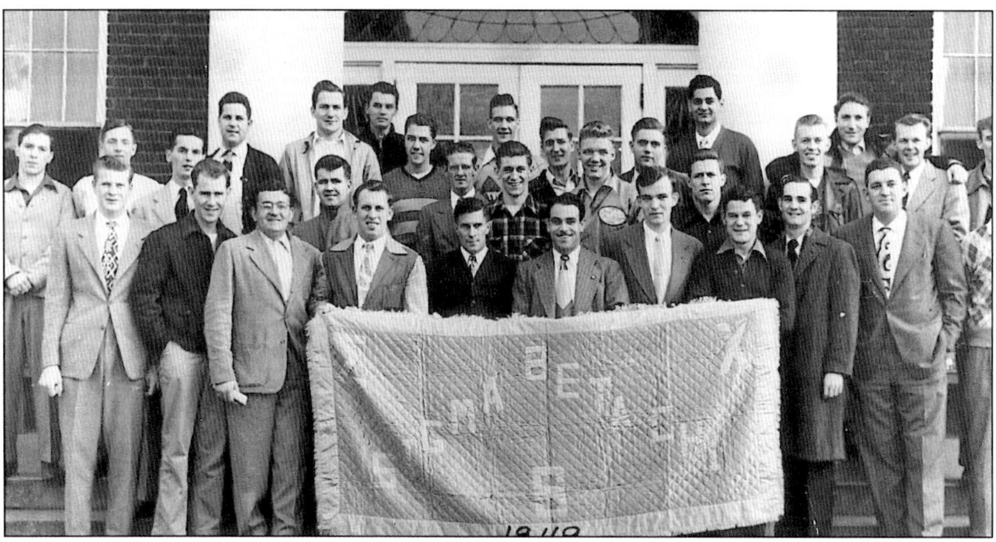

SIGMA BETA CHI, 1949. Student social life was centered around local fraternities, sororities, clubs, and other organizations. Sigma Beta Chi was the college's first social fraternity. Pictured here are Rudy Mumley (first row, left), L.A. Orsini (first row, fourth from left), and Al Blatnik (first row, eighth from left).

FRESHMEN COEDS, 1959. The 1950s were the last years when students and faculty had an especially close relationship. The student body was still small enough that everyone knew everyone else. Student dances were still chaperoned by the faculty, dress codes were enforced, and men and women visiting each other in the dormitories was not permitted.

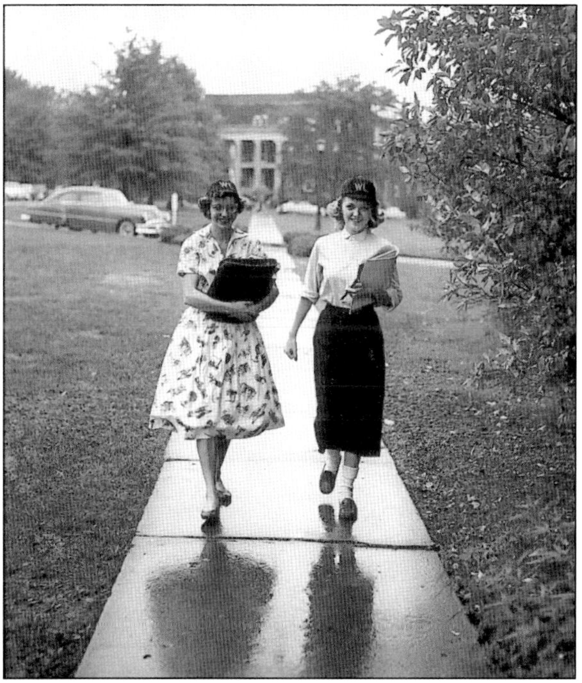

DRUM MAJORETTES, 1950. Students were involved in all sorts of extracurricular activities. The drum majorettes in this photo are, from left to right, (front row) Patty Jo Shaver and Miriam Bowden; (back row) Marion Simpson, Rhea Reitter, and Ilene Mahon.

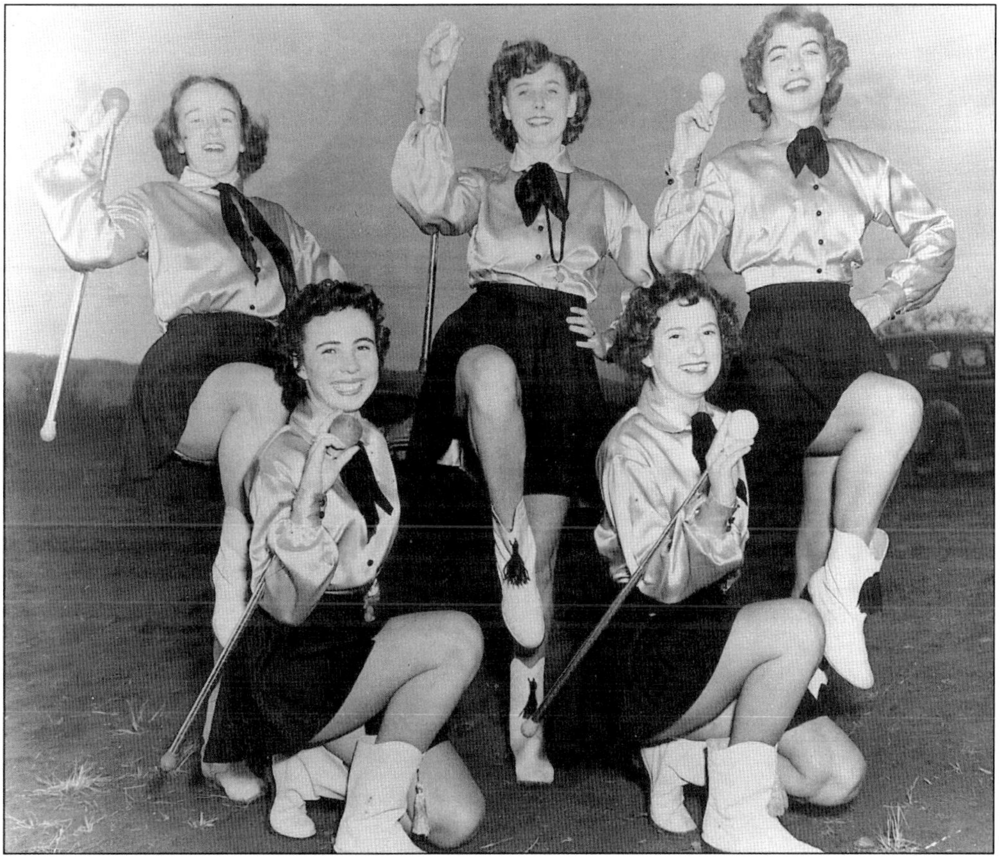

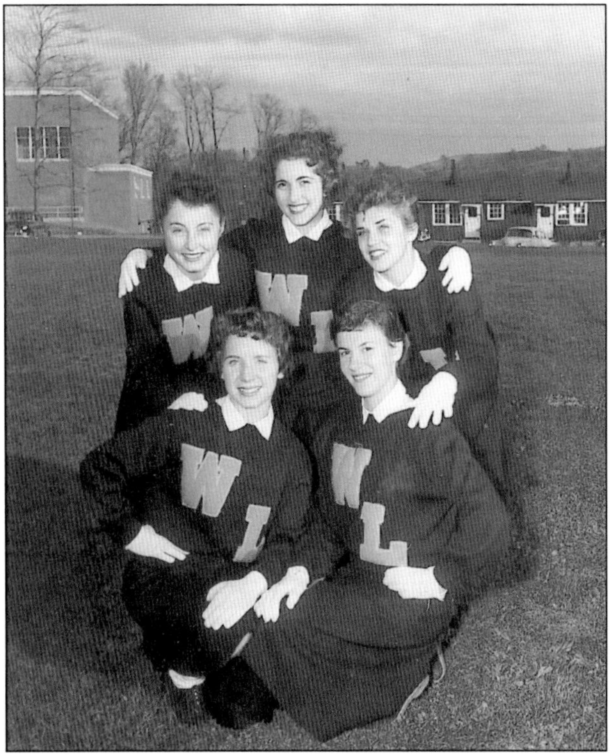

CHEERLEADERS, **1957**. The barracks can be seen in the background. There were many special-interest student groups that formed the basis of campus social life.

COLLEGE CHORUS, *c.* **1957**. Although music majors were members of the chorus and band, this was not a requirement. Many students belonged to more than one group.

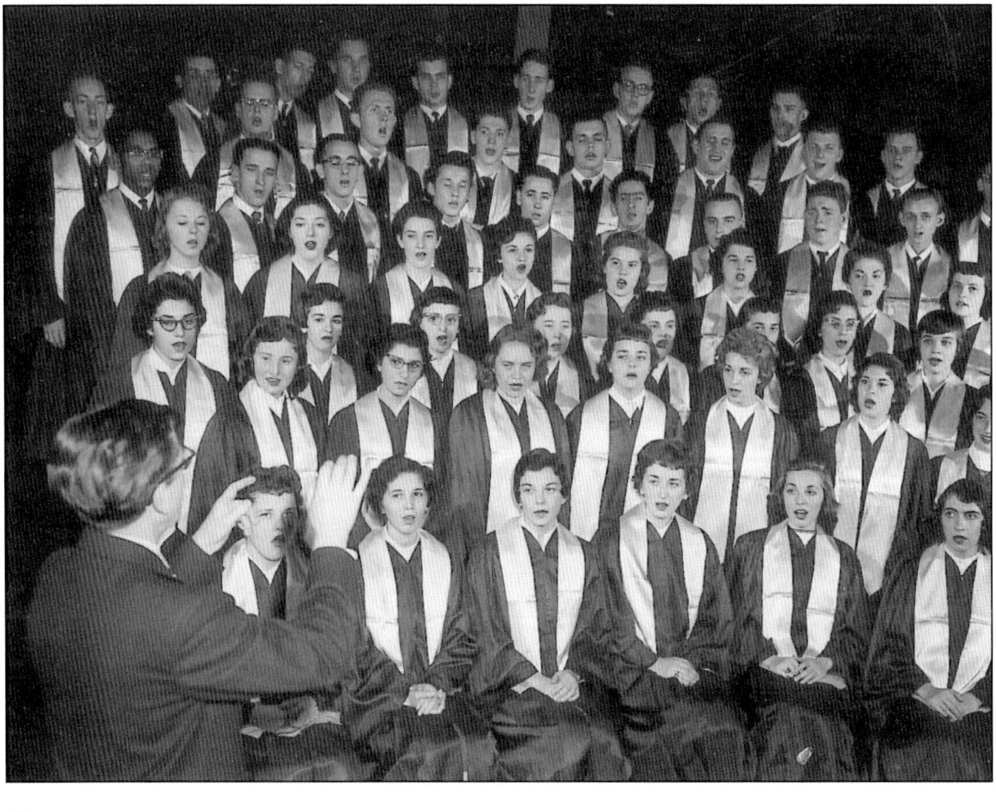

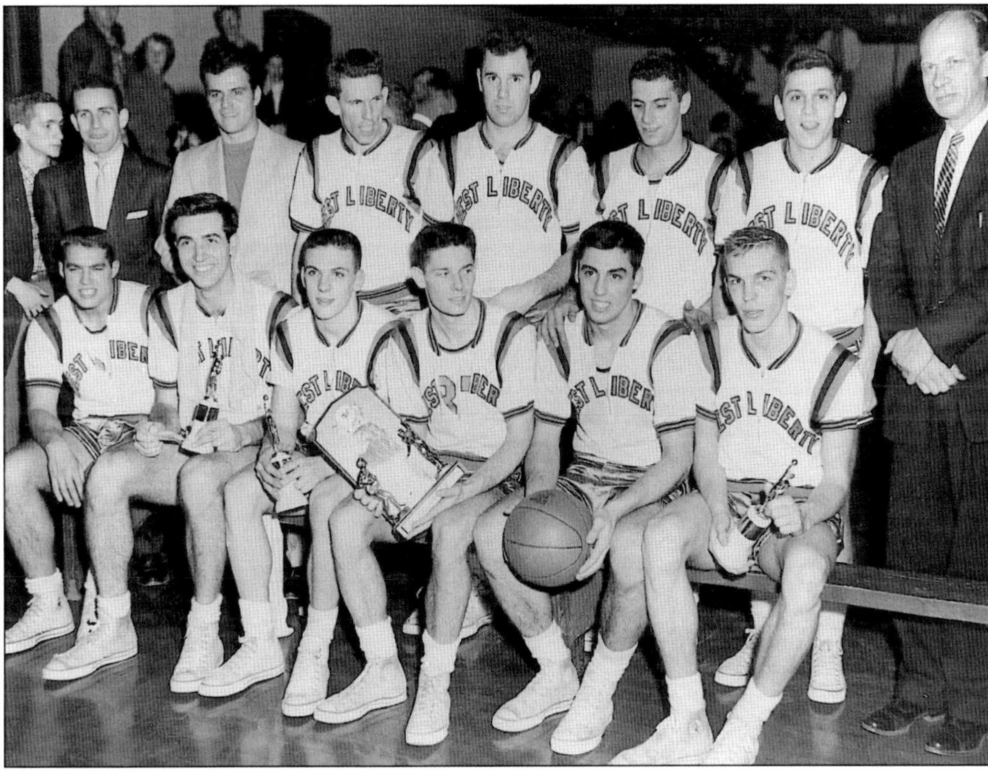

Men's Basketball Team and Coach Ollie Olsen, 1950. Basketball and football games provided both entertainment and opportunities for socializing.

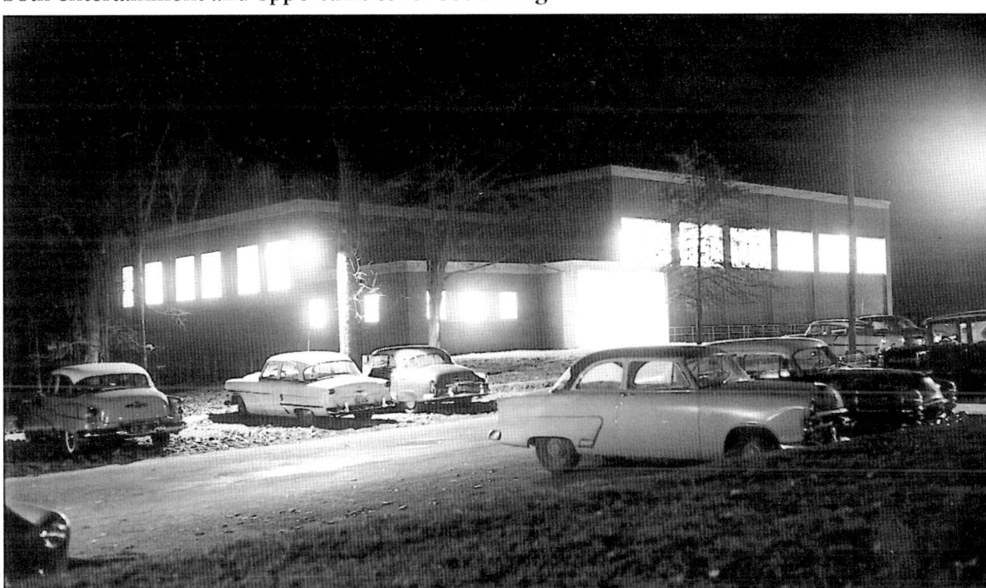

New Gym, 1956. West Liberty State College was the only state college that had not replaced its old wood-frame gym with a modern structure. Dr. Elbin repeatedly requested funds from the legislature for a new building. Finally, in 1956, the project was funded. An additional amount was appropriated to build a much-needed classroom wing.

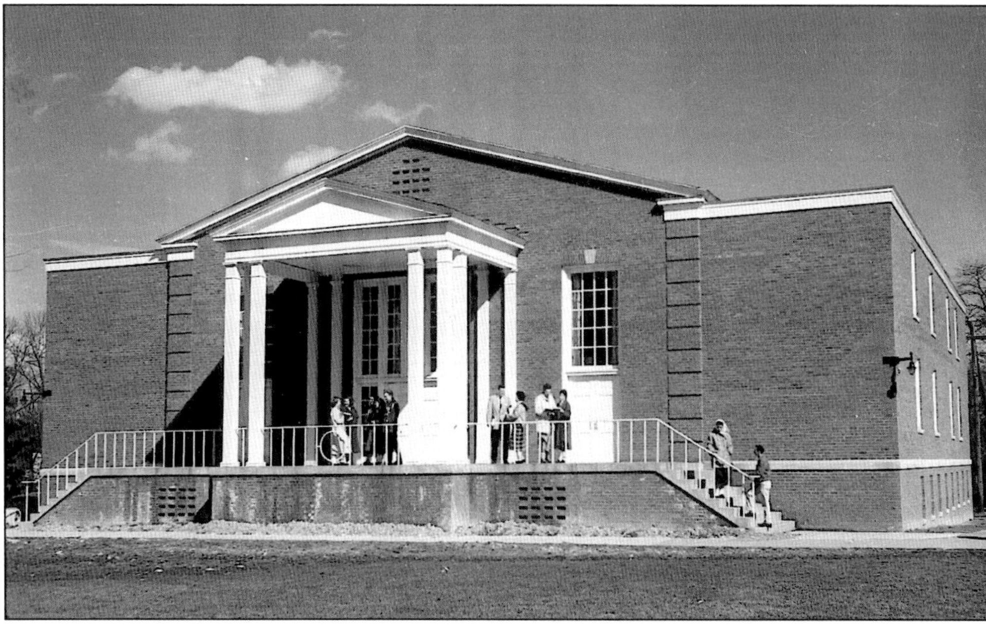

New Student Center, 1959. The old wood gym was not torn down or wasted. President Elbin obtained a loan from the Federal Housing and Home Finance Agency to completely remodel the old gym into a modern and attractive student center. The building, finished in 1959, was fitted with a red-brick surface and colonial facade to match the other campus buildings.

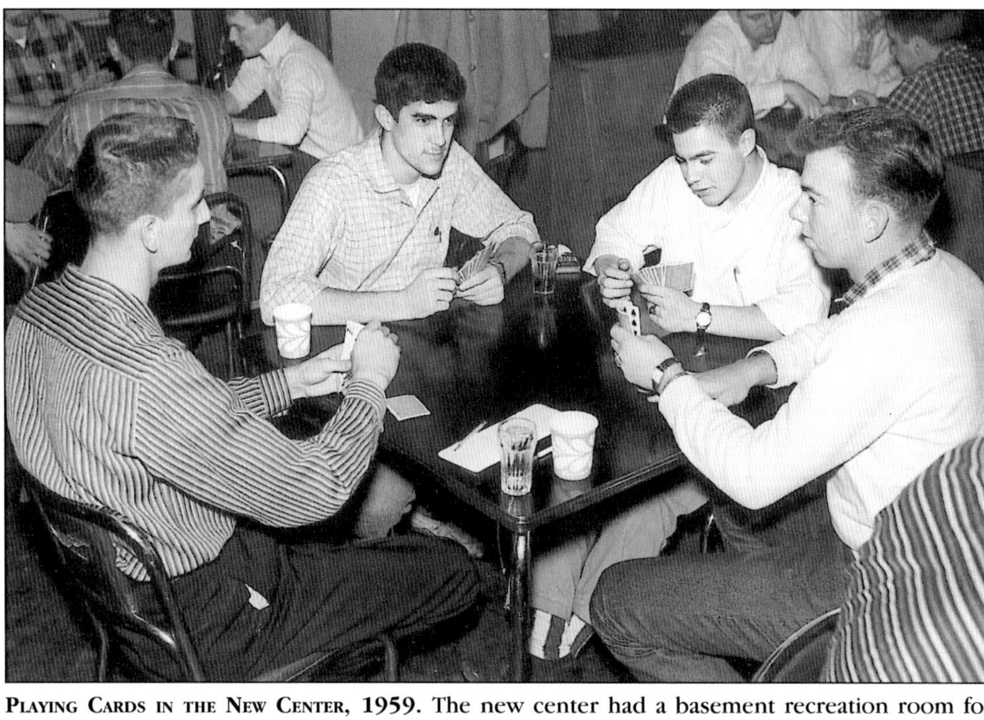

Playing Cards in the New Center, 1959. The new center had a basement recreation room for cards, pool, ping-pong, and television. Upstairs there was a cafeteria, dance floor, two faculty lounges, and three meeting rooms. Students took to the new center immediately. It quickly became a meeting place between classes and, like the old center, a home base for commuters.

Coach Joe Bartell and Football Players, c. 1957. Football games were major student events involving not only the team, but also the marching band, the halftime show, and, of course, the cheerleaders. Dr. Bartell also served as dean of men.

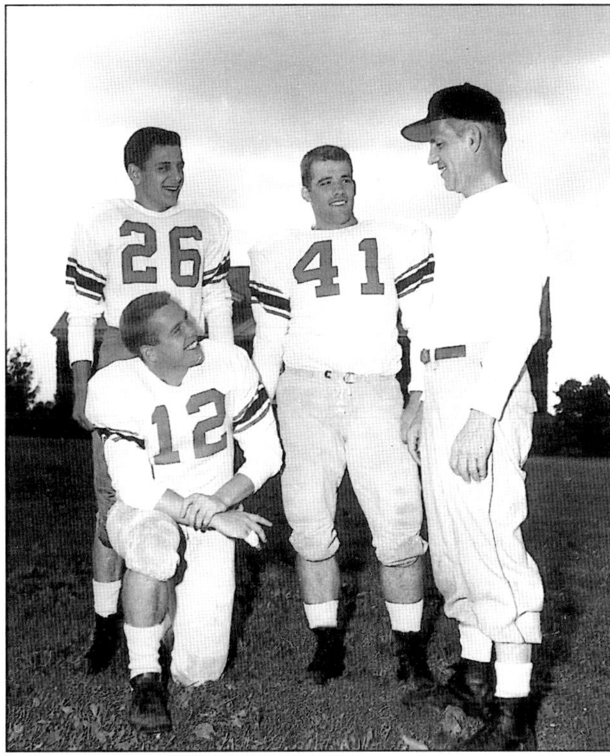

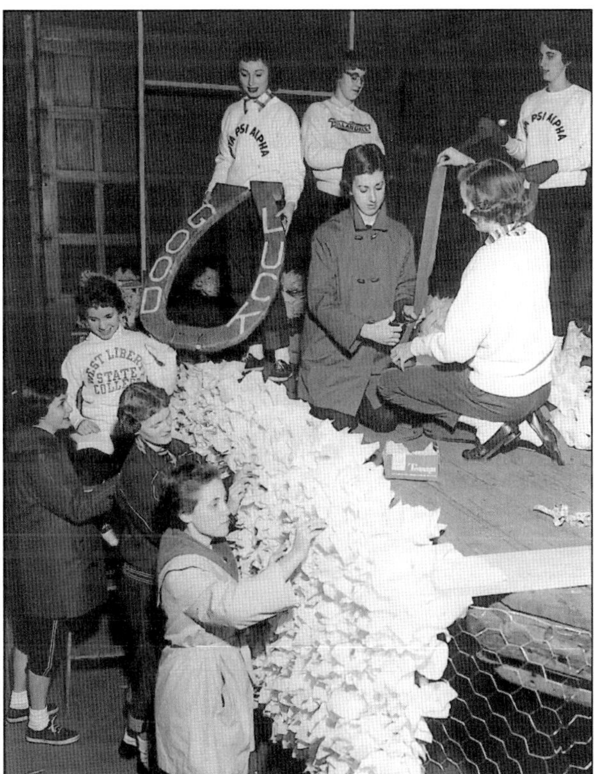

Building a Float, 1959. The biggest game of the year was the homecoming game. Fraternities, sororities, and other organizations would build floats for the big parade; sometimes two groups cooperated on one float. Float construction was often a social event and an occasion for a "date."

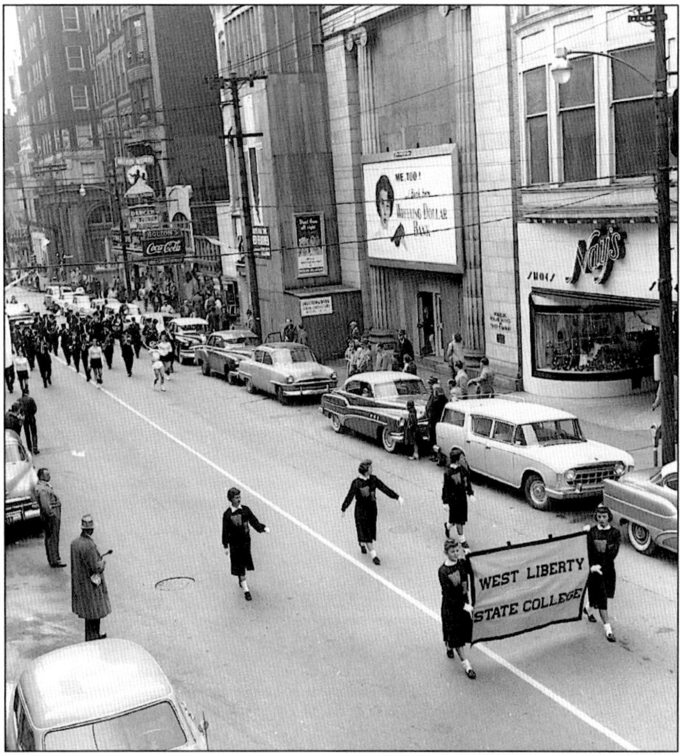

WLSC Marching Band in the Homecoming Parade, *c.* 1957. In the 1950s the homecoming parade was held in downtown Wheeling. The parade is seen here just passing Sixteenth Street and moving north on Market Street. The building pictured with the ionic columns is the Wheeling Dollar Bank.

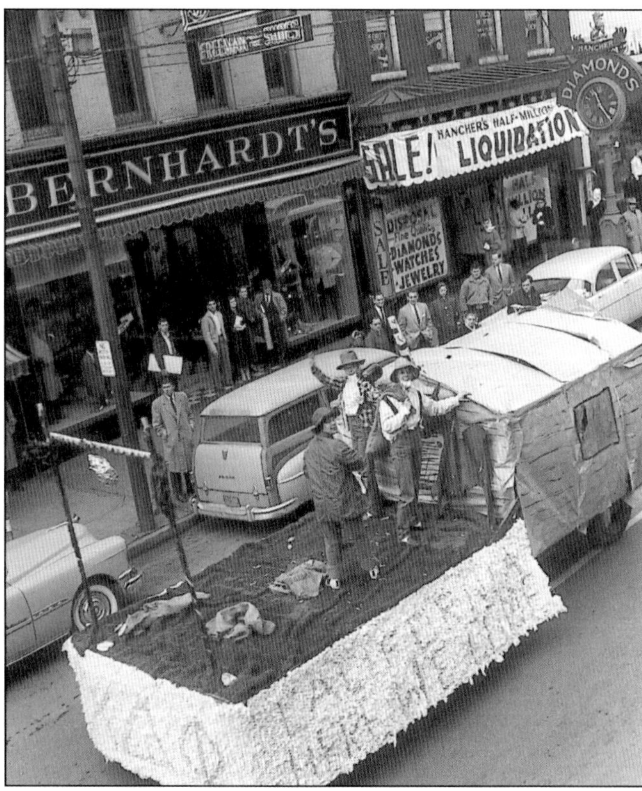

The Kappa Delta Phi's Float Passing Bernhardt's on Market Street, *c.* 1957. Competition was fierce for the prize for the best float. Many of the floats were constructed largely of chicken wire stuffed with tissues.

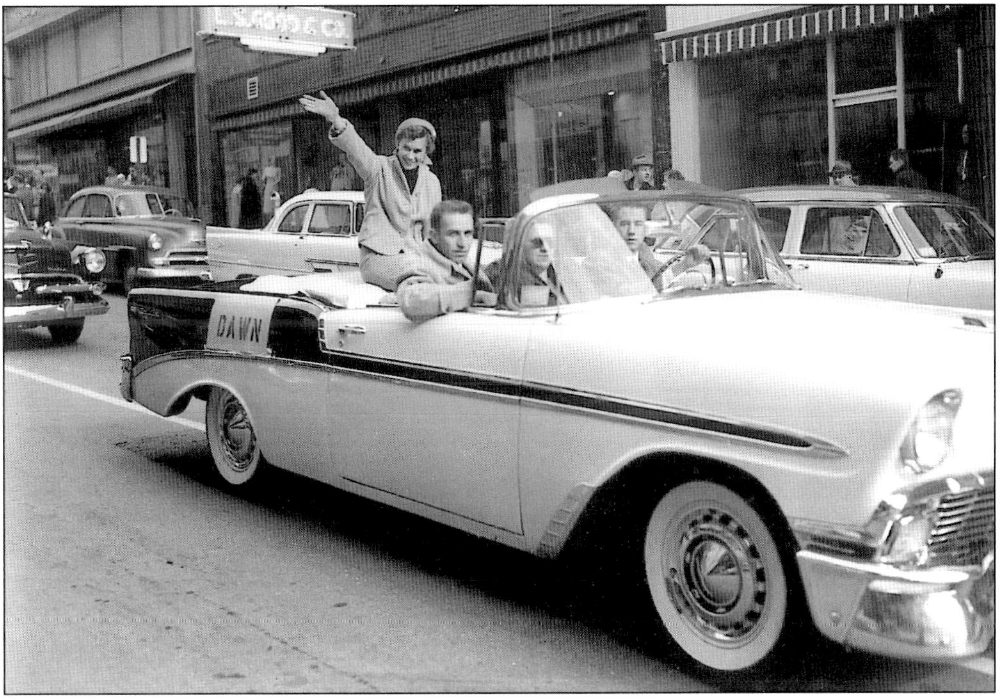

Queen Candidate Dawn Brainard, Waving to the Crowd, 1956. Dawn, a dental hygiene student, was elected homecoming queen in 1956 and crowned at halftime. The location is Main Street, approaching Twelfth Street, opposite Good's Department Store. Queen candidates were sponsored by campus organizations.

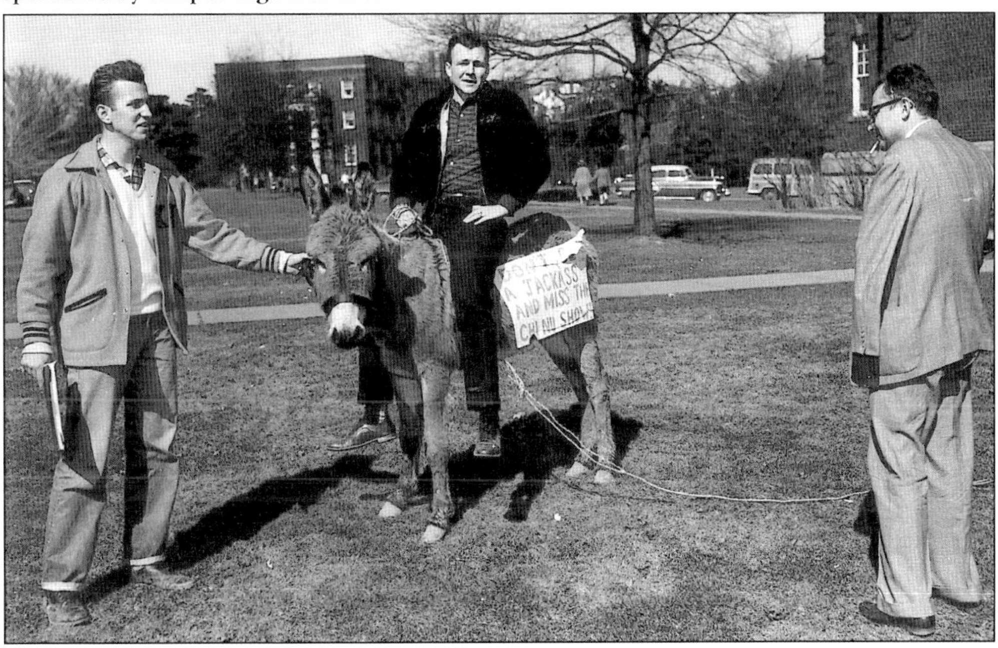

Chi Nu Advertising Their Annual Show, 1957. Fraternities, sororities, and other campus groups held annual shows in order to raise money. Everyone tried to attend the Chi Nu show on the first night since it was usually canceled after one run due to excessive raunchiness.

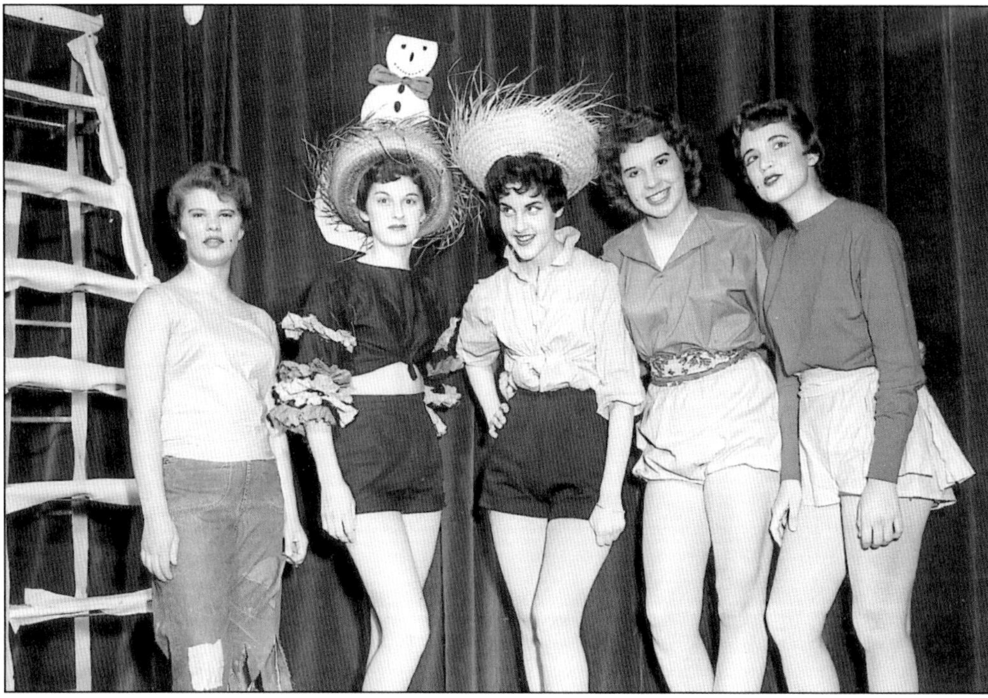

A Scene from the Dental Hygiene Show, 1957. The Dental Hygiene Department show was popular since it featured lots of pretty young ladies with very bright smiles.

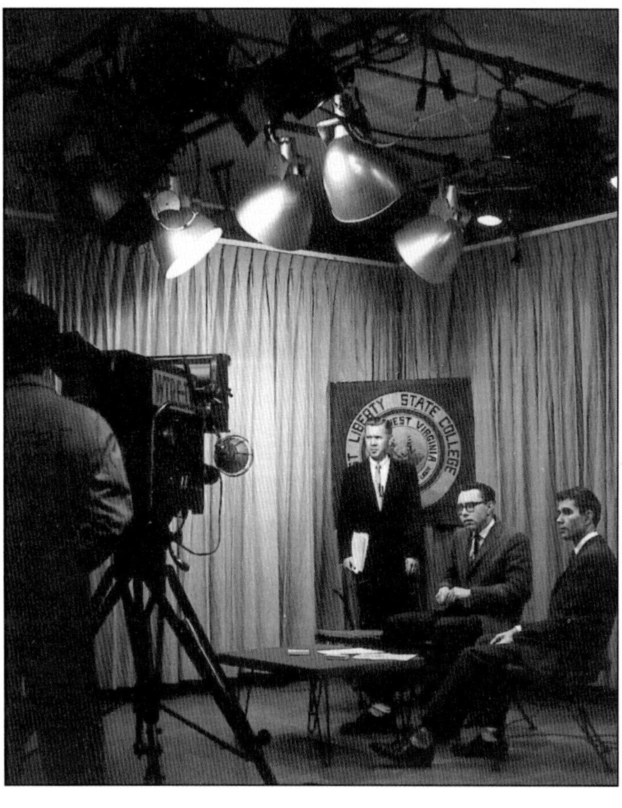

"West Liberty Presents" WTRF-TV, *c.* 1957. When television came to the area, the college produced a series of live shows broadcast over WTRF Channel 7 in Wheeling. The series was hosted and directed by Professor Vernon D. Riemer (standing). Physics professors Kenneth Rarey (left) and Robert W. Schramm (right) were featured on this show. Note the early black-and-white television camera.

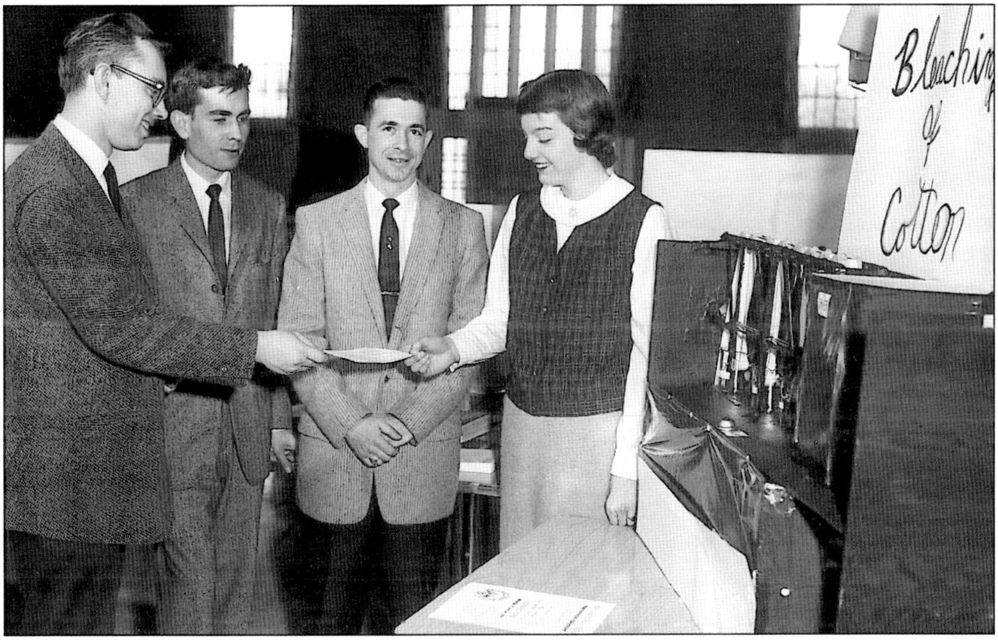

The First WLSC Regional Science Fair, 1959. Professors Schramm and Rarey organized the first regional science fair in the area. The fair stimulated numerous local fairs whose award winners competed at West Liberty. After Professor Rarey left to work in industry the following year, Professor Schramm directed the fair for the next 30 years.

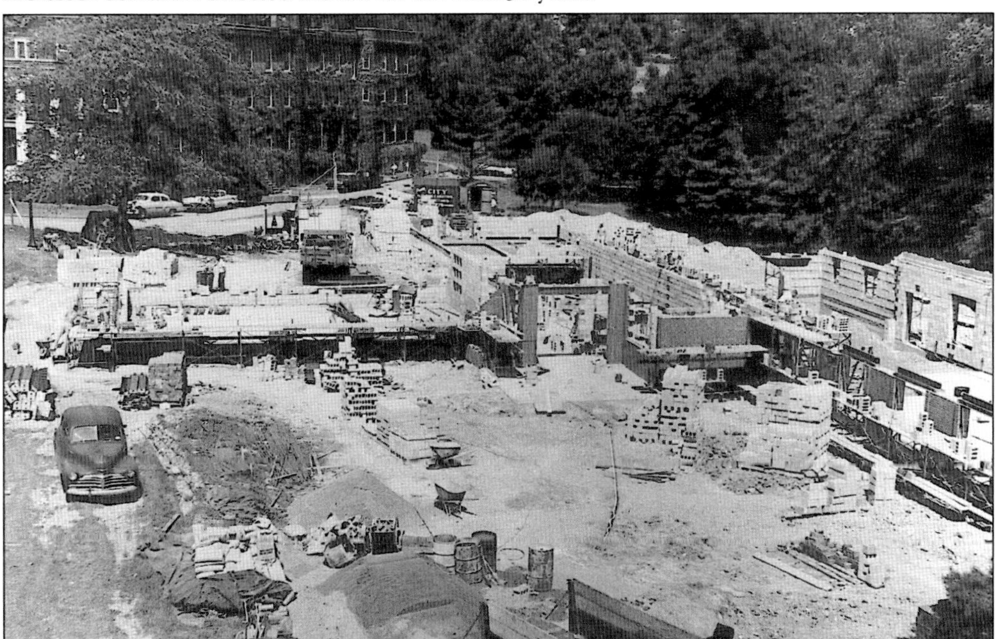

Rogers Hall under Construction, 1958. Enrollment was increasing and student housing had to be provided, especially for women. Shaw Hall was seriously overcrowded. Rooms originally designed for two women were occupied by three or four. In 1958, the college secured a federal loan for the construction of a modern women's dormitory.

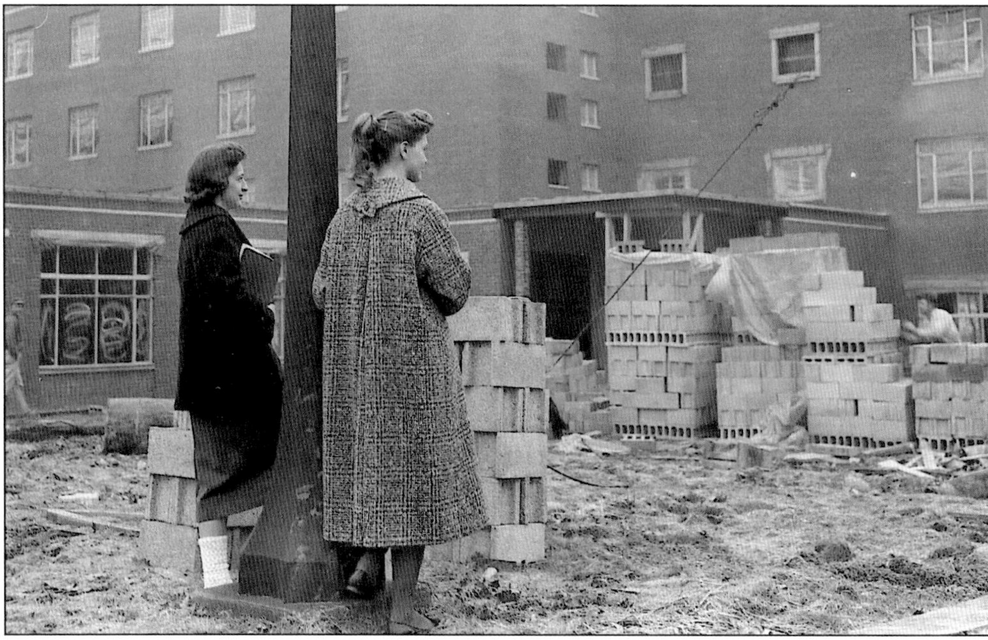

Coeds Watching the Construction of Rogers Hall, 1959. Rogers Hall was named in honor of Mrs. George Rogers, the dean of women from 1937 to 1952. The building was completed in 1959. Rogers Hall contained a modern, cafeteria-style food service center that replaced the Shaw Hall dining room.

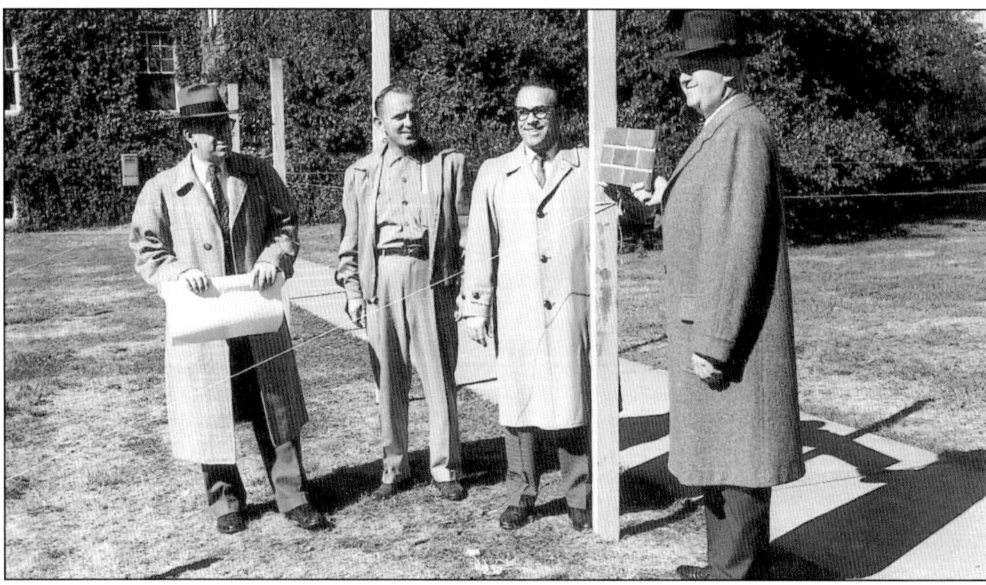

Selecting Brick Pattern for Main Hall, 1959. Pictured here are, from left to right, Fred Farris, architect; Tom Myers, superintendent of buildings and grounds; L.A. Orsini, business manager; and President Elbin. The middle unit of the administrative-classroom building had been promised in 1925, but funds were never made available, although the president requested money from the state yearly. A long process of cajoling, pleading, fighting, and even the submission of student petitions to the legislature finally paid off, and funds were appropriated in 1959.

Main Hall Groundbreaking, April 6, 1960. This is the author's favorite photograph of Paul N. Elbin. He is holding the ceremonial shovel that has been used to break ground for every major construction project on the new campus. The look on Dr. Elbin's face tells the story.

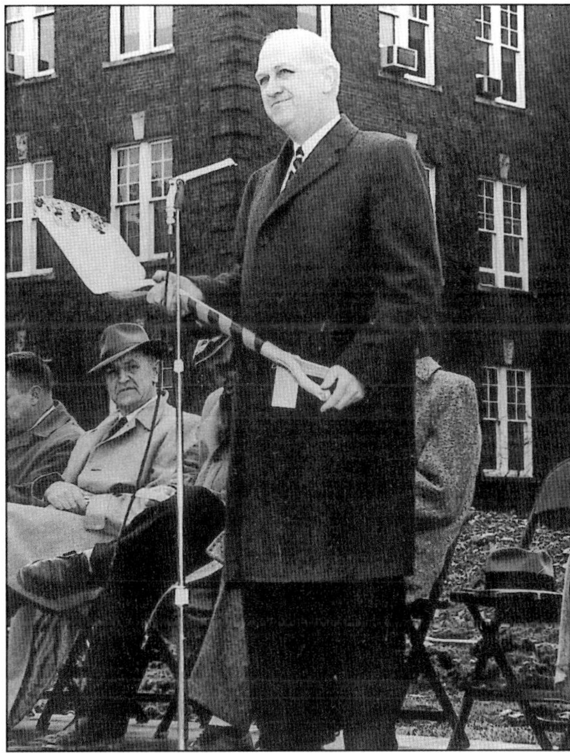

The Start of the Construction of Main Hall, 1960. Once down to bedrock, the construction company had to blast through about eight feet of solid limestone to reach the basement level of the new building. Cutting through the exterior walls of McColloch and Curtis Halls was extremely difficult. McColloch Hall (left) and the new center (right) can be seen in the background.

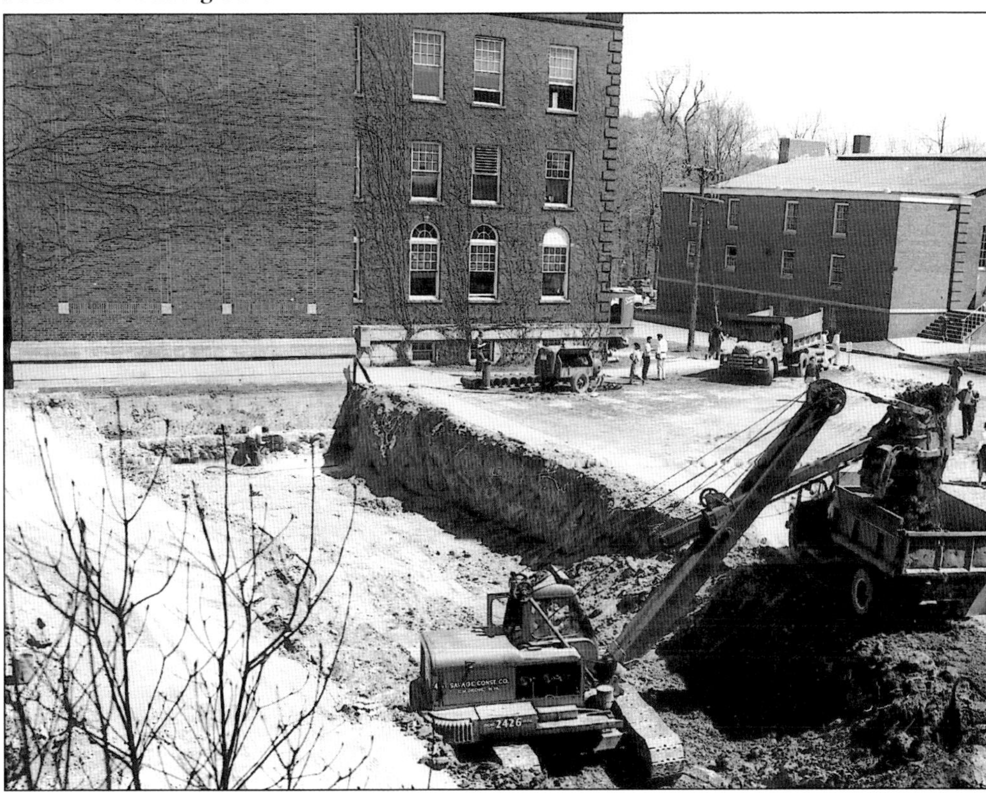

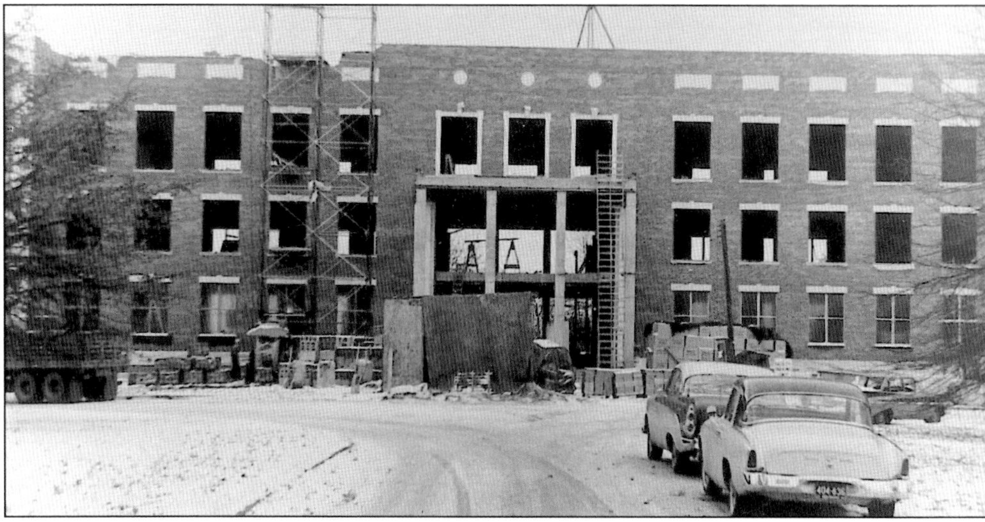

MAIN HALL UNDER CONSTRUCTION, WINTER 1960. The middle unit, or Main Hall, as the entire structure came to be known, was completed in 1961. The building housed modern biology, chemistry, and physics laboratories; two science lecture rooms; standard classrooms; faculty offices; administrative offices; a book store; a post office; and conference rooms. A distinctive feature of the building was an open arcade through the main floor ("The Promenade"), which provided an unbroken, north-south view of the campus.

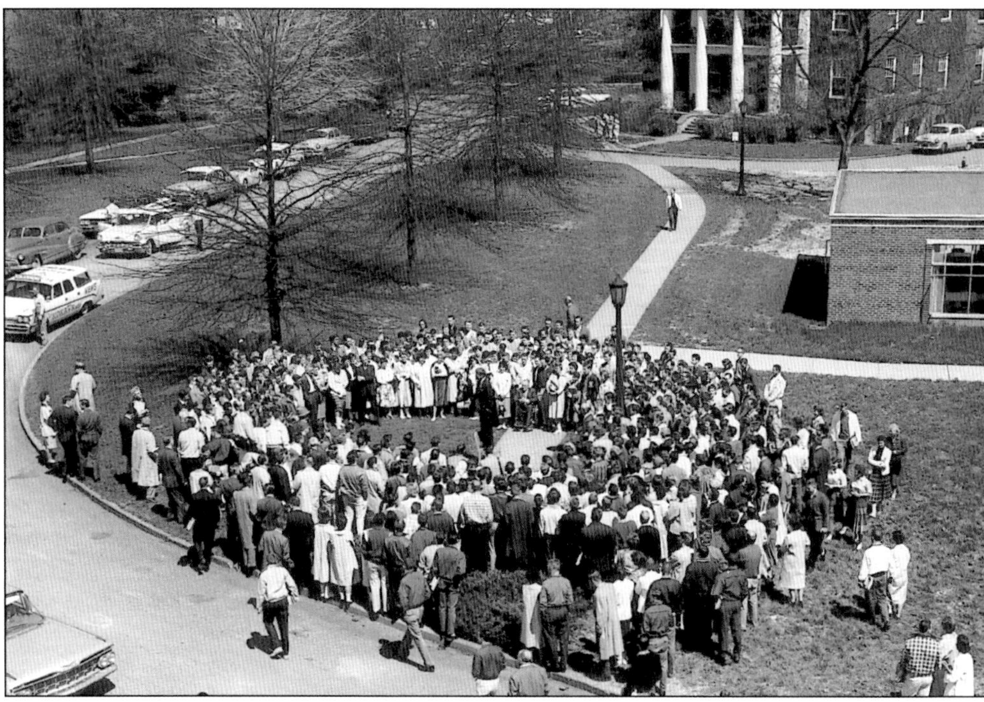

JOHN F. KENNEDY VISITS WEST LIBERTY, APRIL 1960. While the construction of Main Hall was going on, Sen. John F. Kennedy visited the campus. Standing on a chair outside Rogers Hall, he addressed the students, faculty, and administration. Dr. Raymond Hughes, Dr. Joseph Bartell, and Professor M.H. Berry can be seen in this photo. Note the KDKA Radio News car on the left. Shaw Hall is in the background.

Sen. John F. Kennedy, Dean Joseph Bartell (Center), and Dean Denver F. Arnett (Right). At the time this photo was made, those who were in attendance probably did not anticipate that Senator Kennedy would become the next president of the United States, but it has been noted by spectators that when they heard him speak, they were aware that they were in the presence of a potentially great leader.

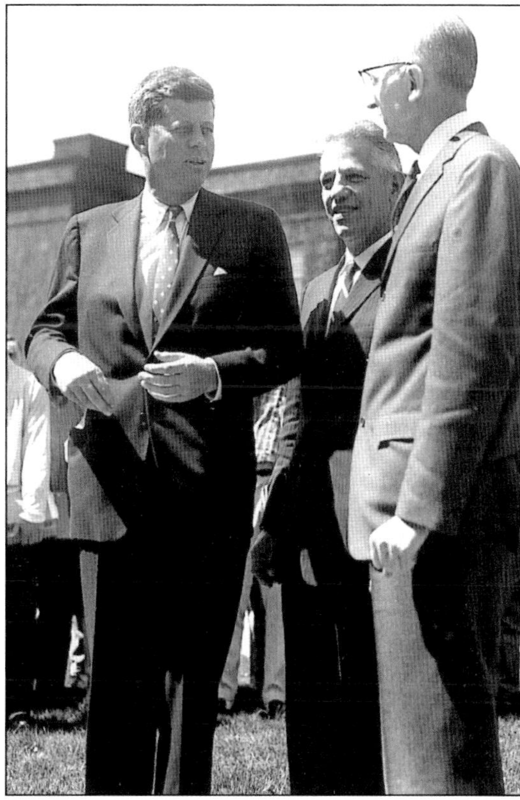

Students on the Quad, 1960s. The 1960s brought major social changes to the campus. As the baby boomers went to college, the enrollment at West Liberty tripled between 1960 and 1970. In the 1963–1964 period alone, three new dormitories were constructed: Boyd, Curtis, and Bonar. The 1960s students were activists. They demanded changes in the curriculum and more students' rights. As a result, student representatives were appointed to almost every committee.

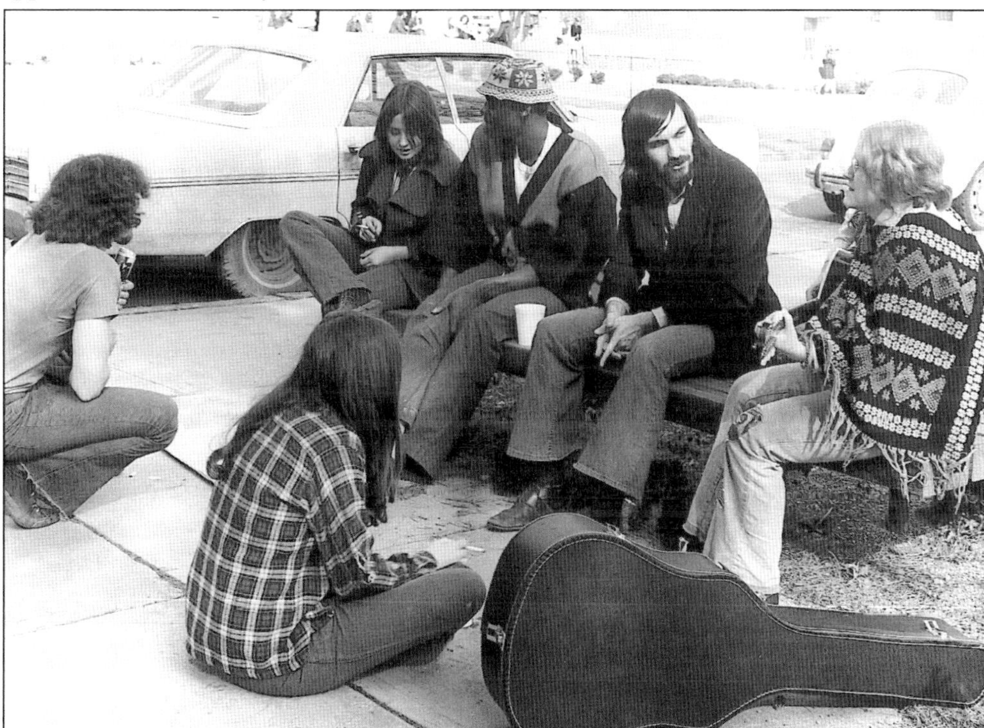

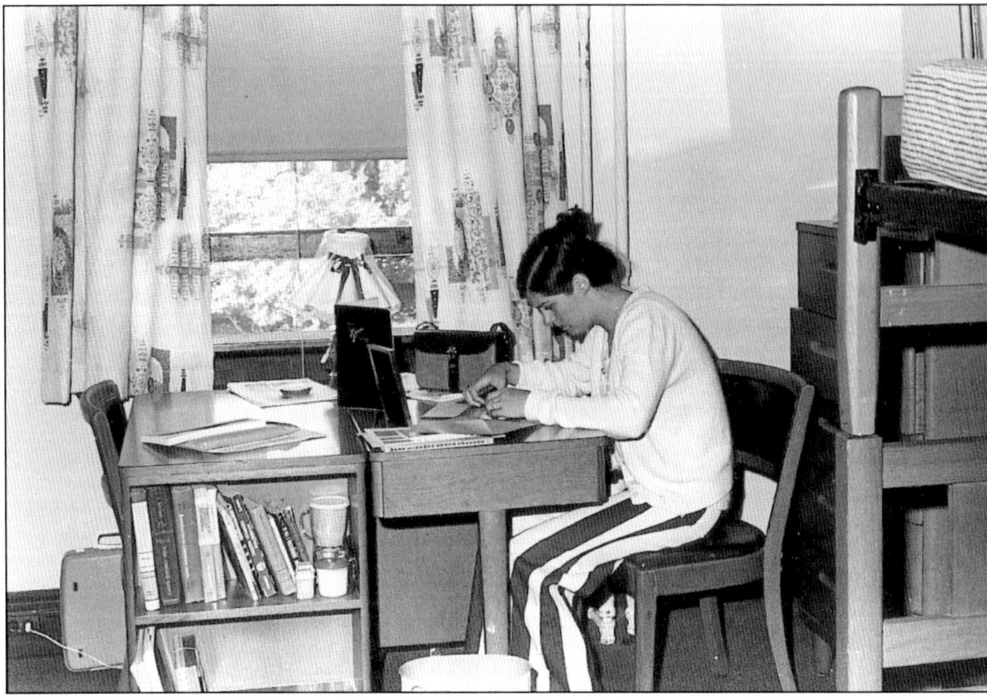

Women's Dorm Room, 1960s. The "peace and love" generation was characterized by liberal views concerning sex, drugs, clothing, and behavior. The old rigid code of conduct and the segregation of the sexes were discarded. The "visitation" of dorm rooms by members of the opposite sex was allowed. The old doctrine of *in loco parentis* was no longer the rule.

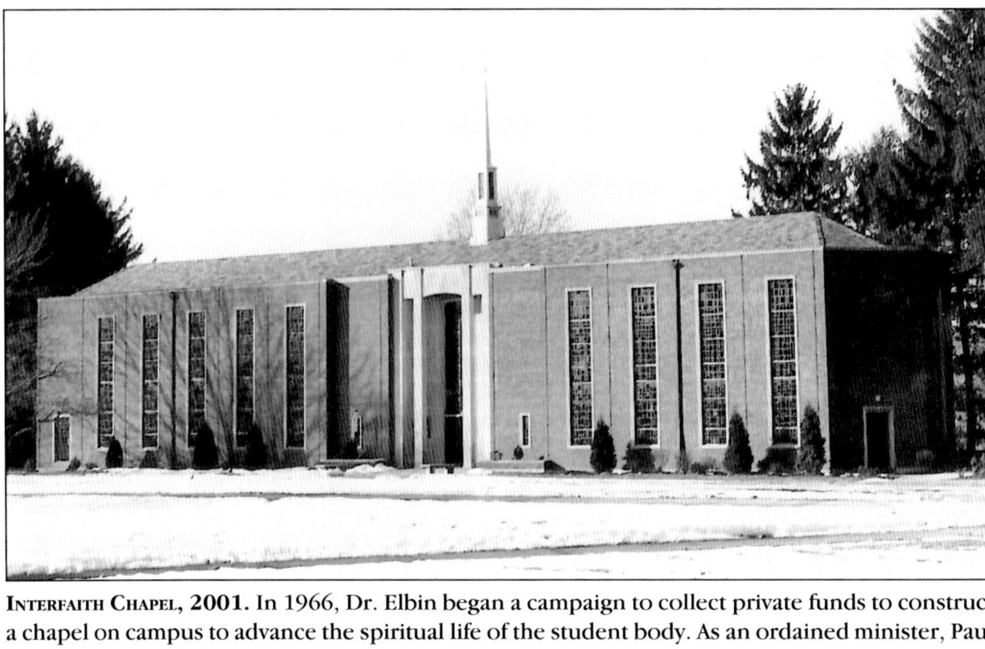

Interfaith Chapel, 2001. In 1966, Dr. Elbin began a campaign to collect private funds to construct a chapel on campus to advance the spiritual life of the student body. As an ordained minister, Paul Elbin had successfully integrated this facet of his personality with his abilities as an administrator. Friends and admirers of Dr. Elbin and members of the Wheeling religious community contributed sufficient funds to complete the building in 1967.

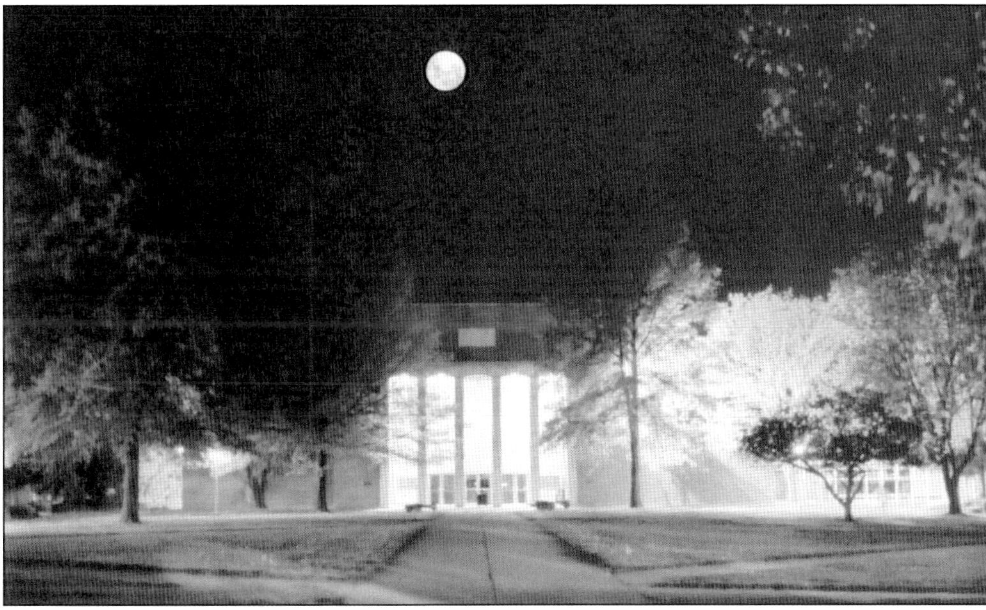

Hall of Fine Arts, 1999. Both Paul and Helen Elbin were accomplished and talented musicians, and the arts were an important part of their life. The construction of a fine arts building, which was completed in 1966, must have been considered by the Elbins as a major achievement of Paul N. Elbin's career. In addition to studios for music and art, the building contained a modern, fully equipped theater in which the Hilltop Players were to perform.

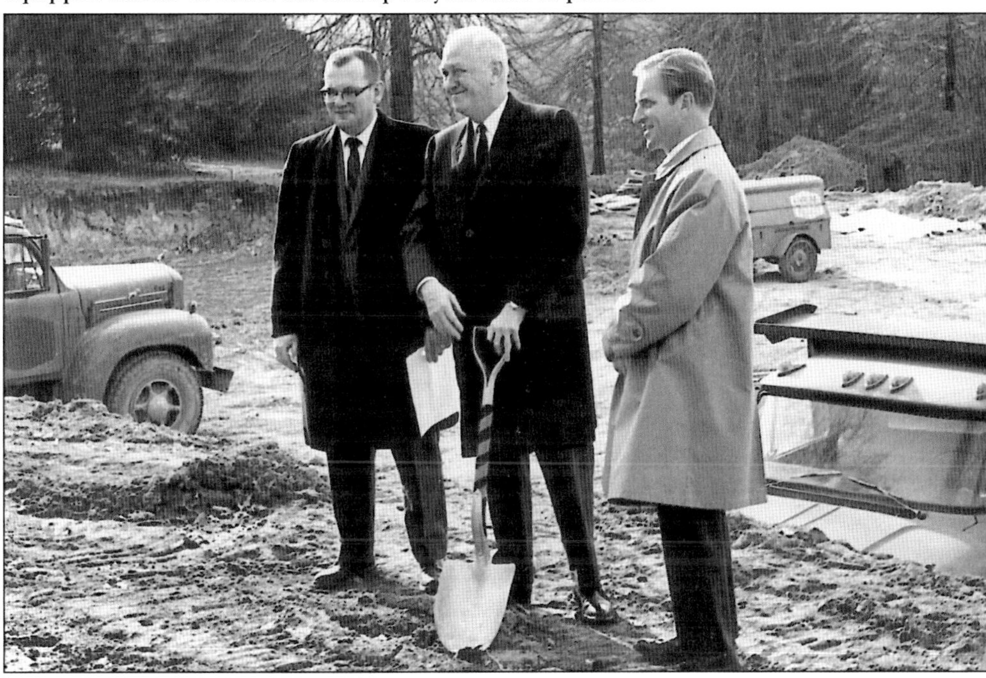

Groundbreaking for the New Library, 1969. During Dr. Elbin's tenure, two more dormitories were constructed in 1968, namely, Bartell Hall (later renamed Beta Hall) and Hughes Hall. Ground was broken in 1969 for a new library, which, in recognition of his services to West Liberty State College, was named the Paul N. Elbin Library.

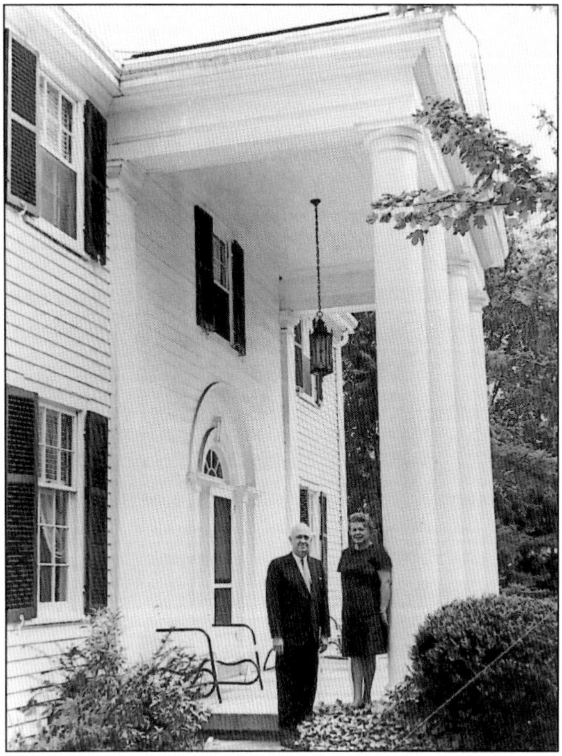

PAUL AND HELEN ELBIN AT HOME, 1968. The Elbins loved to entertain students, faculty, and friends in their home of many years, Colonial Heights.

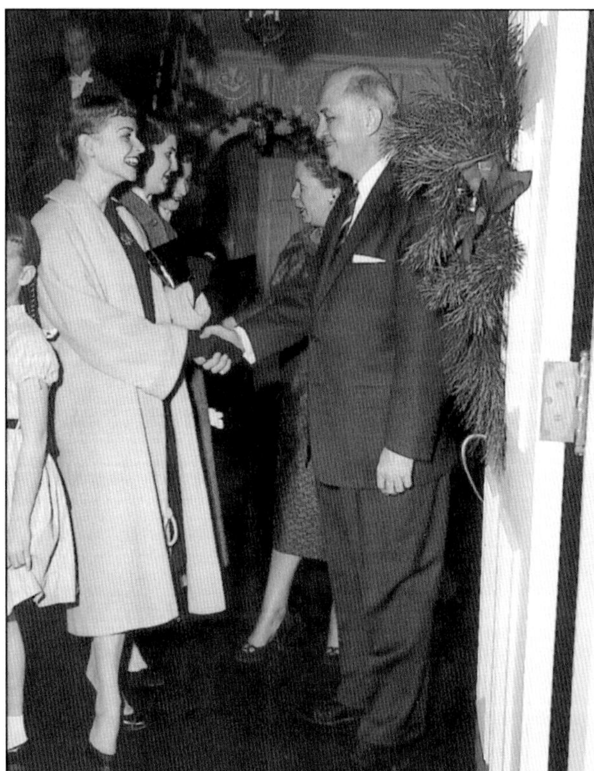

CHRISTMAS GREETINGS, 1957. Christmas at Colonial Heights was always special. Everyone was warmly greeted by both Helen and Paul at the door, and their home was beautifully decorated, inside and out, for the season.

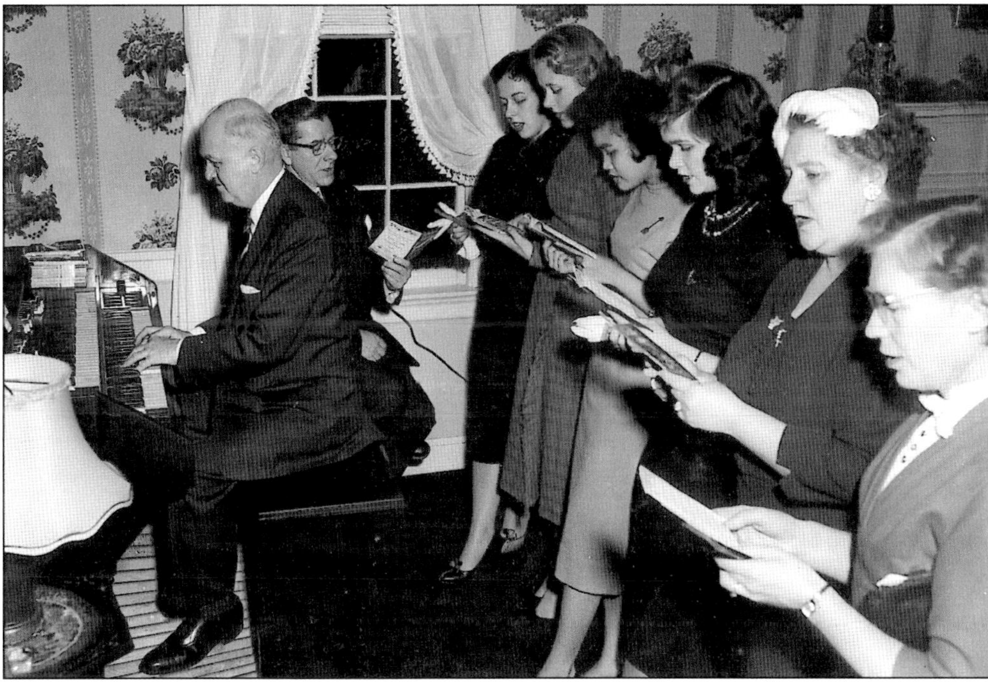

Singing Christmas Carols, c. 1957. A traditional feature of an Elbin Christmas party was the singing of Christmas carols accompanied by Dr. Elbin at the console of the organ. Participation was not voluntary!

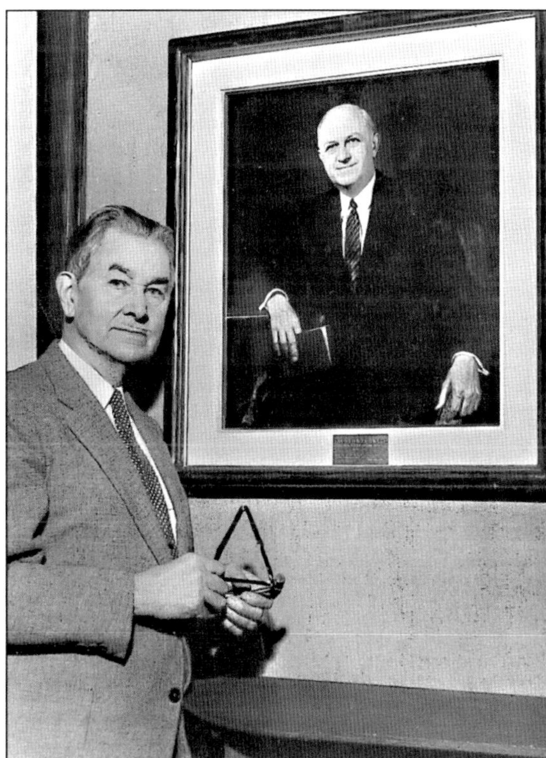

Photographer George Kossuth, 1960. On the occasion of Dr. Elbin's 25th year as president, the alumni association presented the college with a portrait of him made by the nationally known, Wheeling photographer George Kossuth. The portrait hangs in the Paul N. Elbin Library.

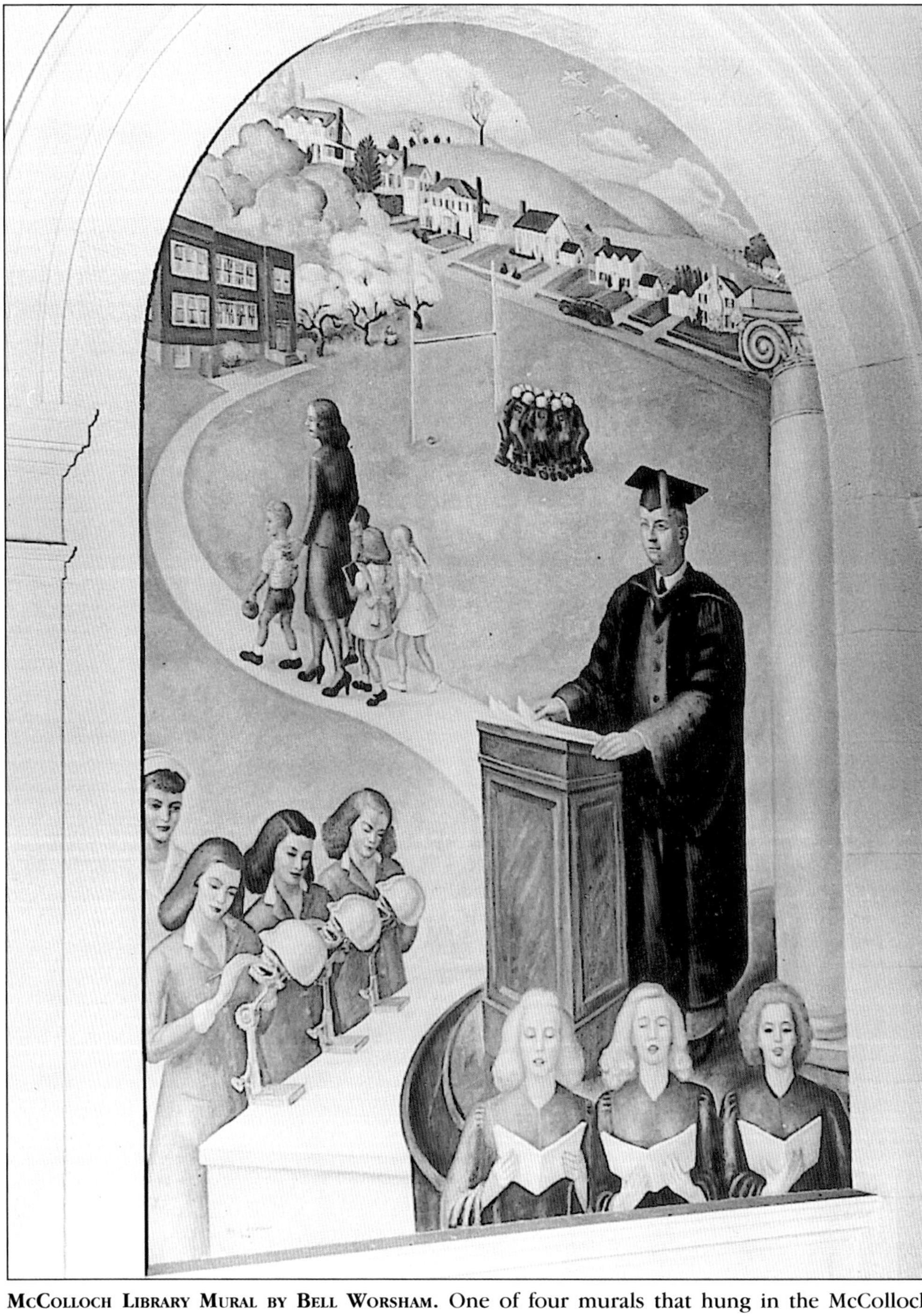

McColloch Library Mural by Bell Worsham. One of four murals that hung in the McColloch Library was this one depicting the "Elbin Era." Education, dental hygiene, music, and athletics are represented by groups around the figure of Paul N. Elbin in academic robes.

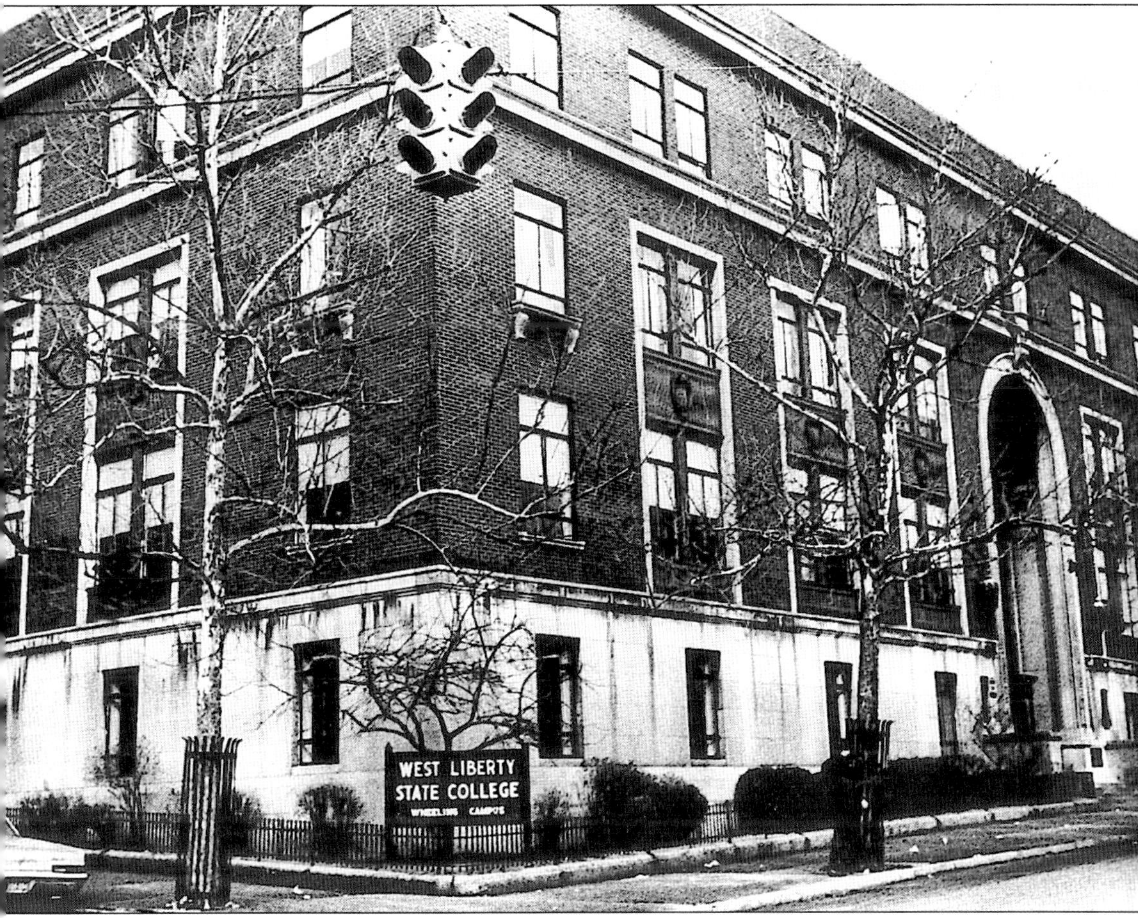

The Hazel-Atlas Building, 1966. In December 1964, the Continental Can Company gave the college its Hazel-Atlas building in east Wheeling for use as a Wheeling campus. By June 1966, the building was completely remodeled. Several new programs in electronics technology, chemical technology, drafting and design technology, and electro-mechanical technology were inaugurated there, in addition to the existing programs in business and nursing. The Wheeling campus also offered freshman and sophomore courses for the four-year programs on the main campus. In October 1971, the governing board of regents decided to take the Wheeling division away from the college in order to create a new, independent community college. The reasons given were cost effectiveness and efficiency. It is difficult to understand how this could be since an entire administrative staff and faculty would be needed to operate as a separate institution what West Liberty State College had been operating with main campus personnel. President James Chapman did not oppose the decision of the board, but retired president Elbin began speaking out against the idea. In his view it would cost more to operate the Wheeling campus as a separate college, and it would ultimately harm both West Liberty State College and the community college program. For his outspoken views, Dr. Elbin was charged with insubordination and fired from his new position as dean of the Interfaith Chapel. West Virginia Northern Community College was created and West Liberty's enrollment fell from over 4,000 students to half that number. Since the College budget was tied to enrollment, it was cut as well.

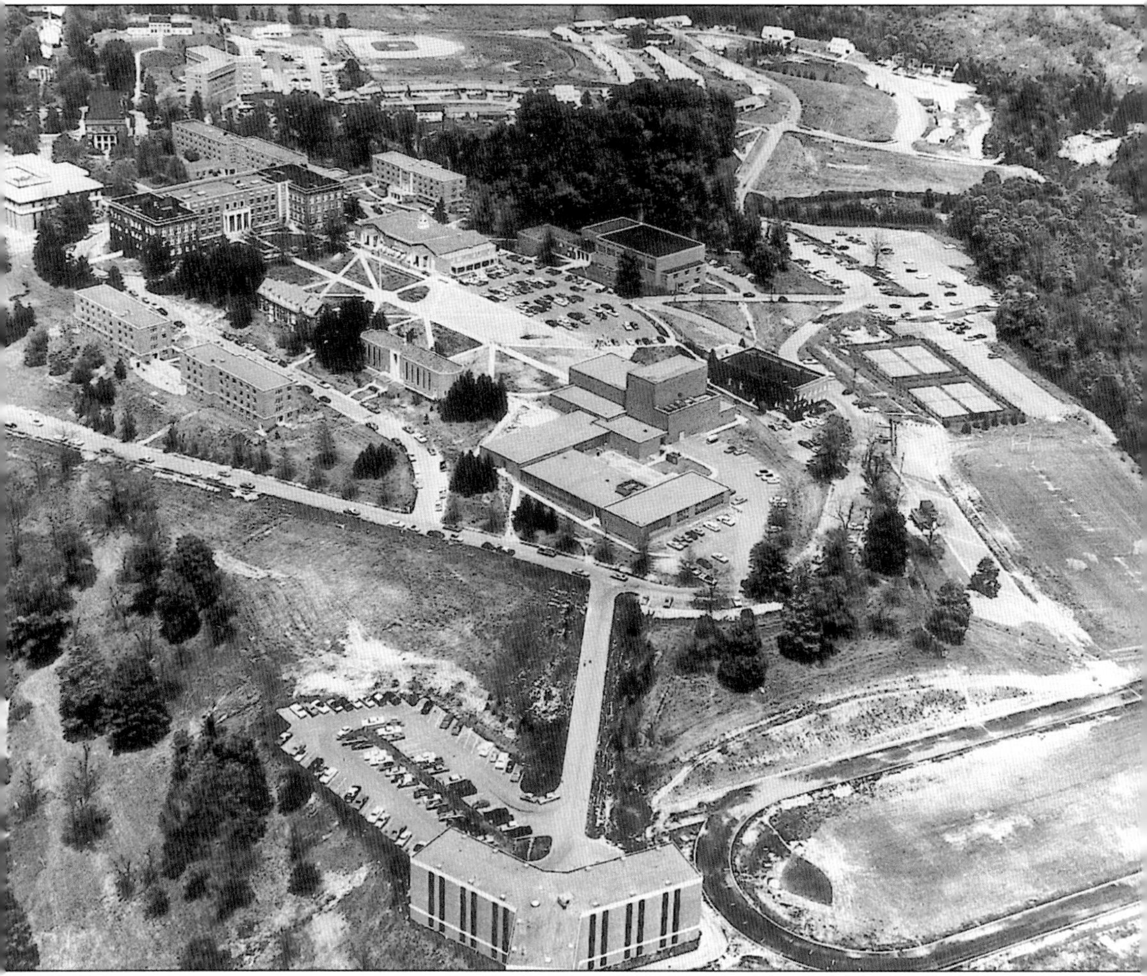

The Campus, 1970. Comparing this photograph with the one on page 34, we see all that Paul N. Elbin contributed to the physical structure of West Liberty State College. What he contributed to the academic and spiritual structure of the institution cannot be so easily visualized but is certainly much greater. More than any other president or principal, his influence shaped the institution we know today as West Liberty State College. Dr. Paul N. Elbin reluctantly retired from office in 1970. He died on May 13, 1985 at the age of 80. Helen P. Elbin lived on in their new home, built on the campus by Dr. Elbin, until her death in 1996.

Four

Transitions

This period in the history of West Liberty State College may be thought of as a time of transition from the old teacher-education, liberal-arts college into an institution that placed greater and greater emphasis on career-training programs. As the college moved into the 1970s, students began to behave more like the conservative students of the 1950s except, of course, in their social life. The college continued to train teachers, but there was increased emphasis and enrollment in business, the health-care professions, journalism, commercial art, and other programs that prepared students for a specific job upon graduation. This trend away from the liberal arts continued throughout the 1980s and 1990s and beyond. Gradually, the college relaxed or did away with many of its rules for student conduct. This increasingly liberal attitude with regard to student behavior resulted in many changes in the way students dressed, talked, and interacted with each other.

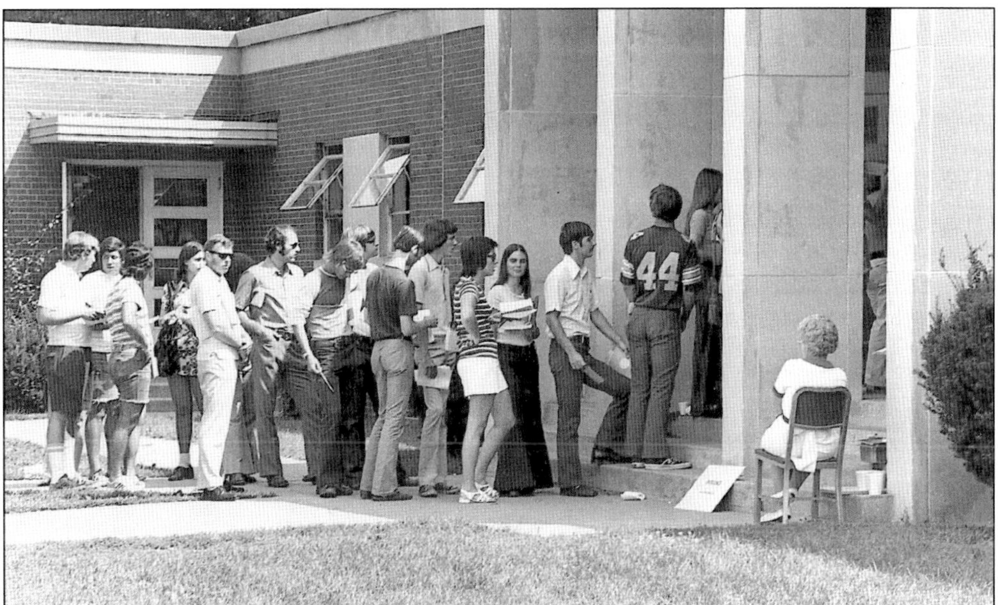

Waiting to Get into Registration, 1972. Enrollment was at an all-time high in the early 1970s before the separation of the Wheeling and West Liberty campuses. This meant long lines at registration. Students were given time cards that required them to register during a certain period. Classes filled rapidly and closed early so that the biggest problem was working out a schedule.

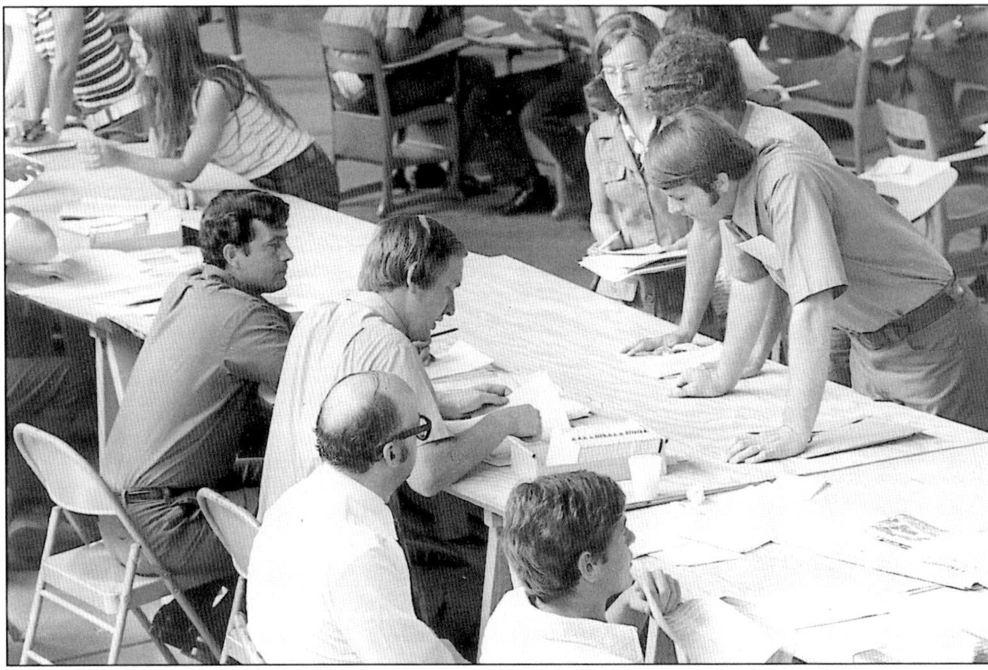

TRYING TO GET INTO CLASSES, 1972. Students met with their advisors in the gym to put together their class schedules. Each student had to ask department representatives for a class card for every class in his or her trial schedule. Often, classes filled quickly so that it took numerous revisions before class schedules could be finalized. Needless to say, registration wasn't much fun for either the students or the faculty.

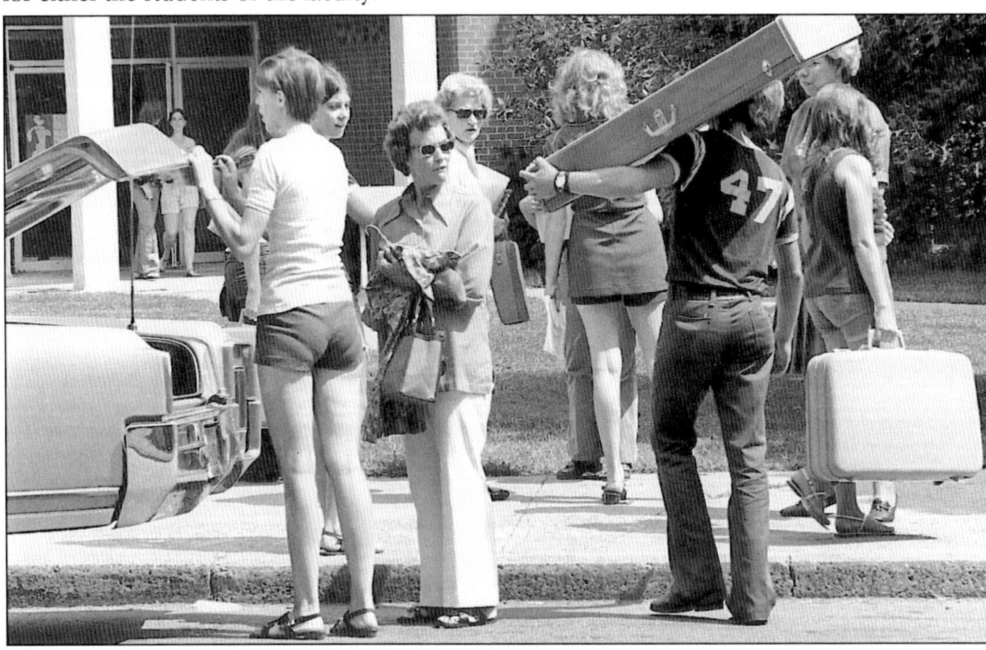

MOVING-IN DAY, 1972. Getting all of your stuff into your dorm room was also not fun but there were always some frat guys around who were eager to help carry the luggage of the freshman coeds. Usually Mom and Dad were there to help as well.

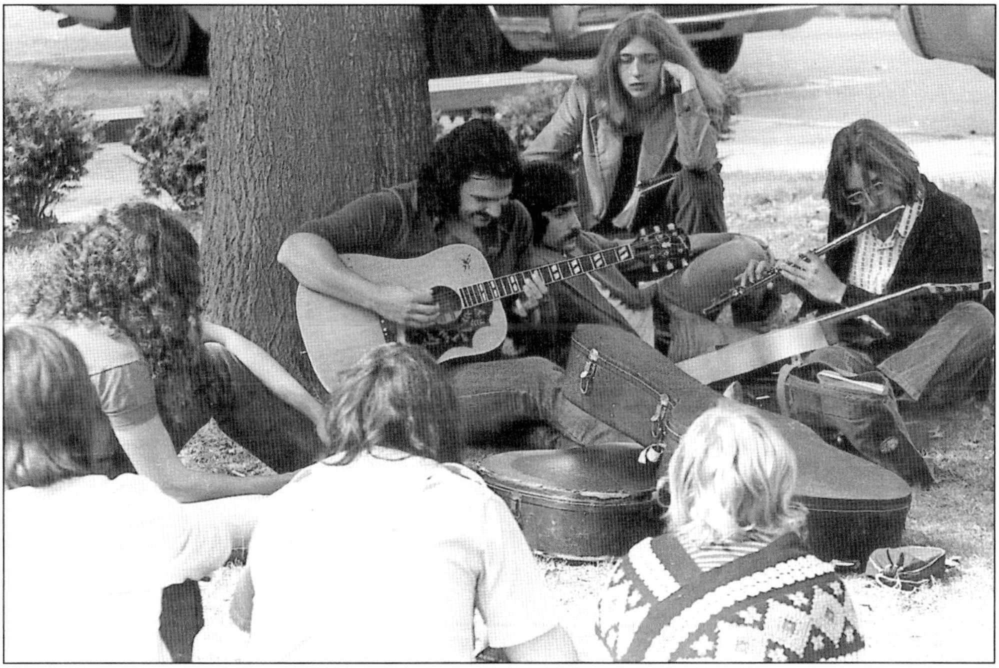

A GATHERING OF STUDENTS ON THE QUAD, 1972. Music was an important part of student life, and impromptu concerts were common. Here we see the rather unusual combination of acoustic guitar and flute.

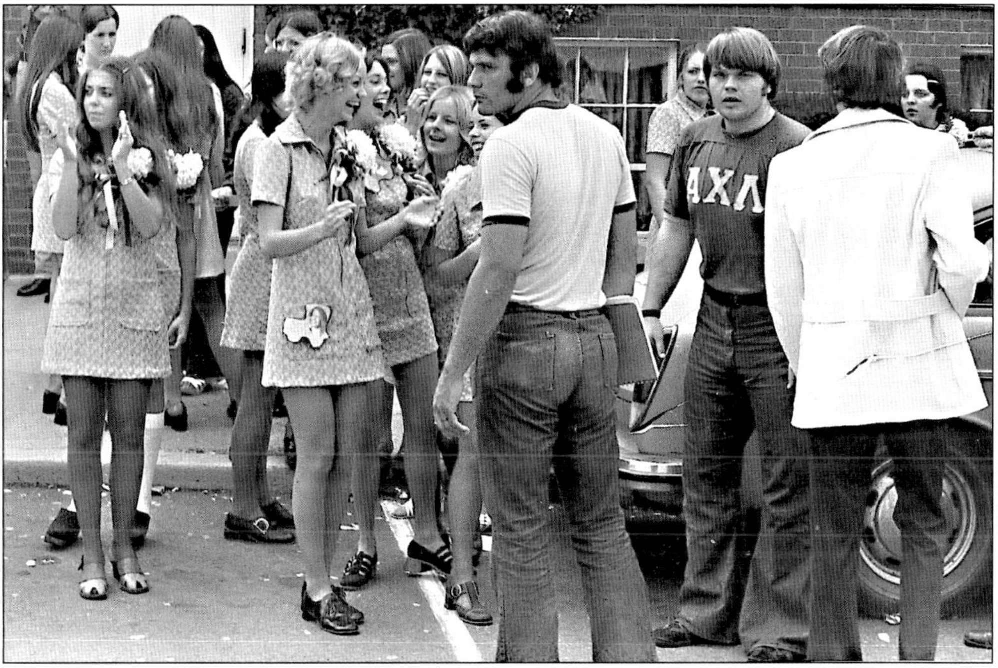

HOMECOMING QUEEN CAMPAIGNING, 1972. In the words of Bob Dylan, "the times they are a' changin." And so they were, but some traditions remained the same. Handing out candy and campaigning for your homecoming queen candidate has been a tradition for many years, and it continues today.

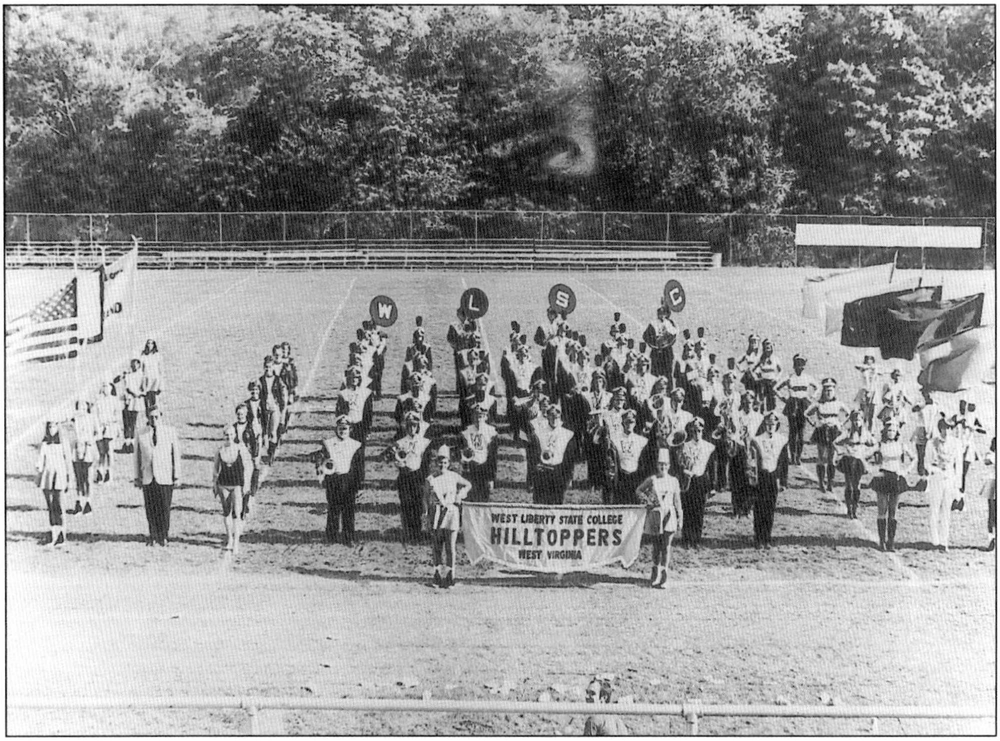

MARCHING BAND, 1973. At a time when students were questioning the relevance of many things, the college band was still of importance, as were drum majorettes and the flag corps.

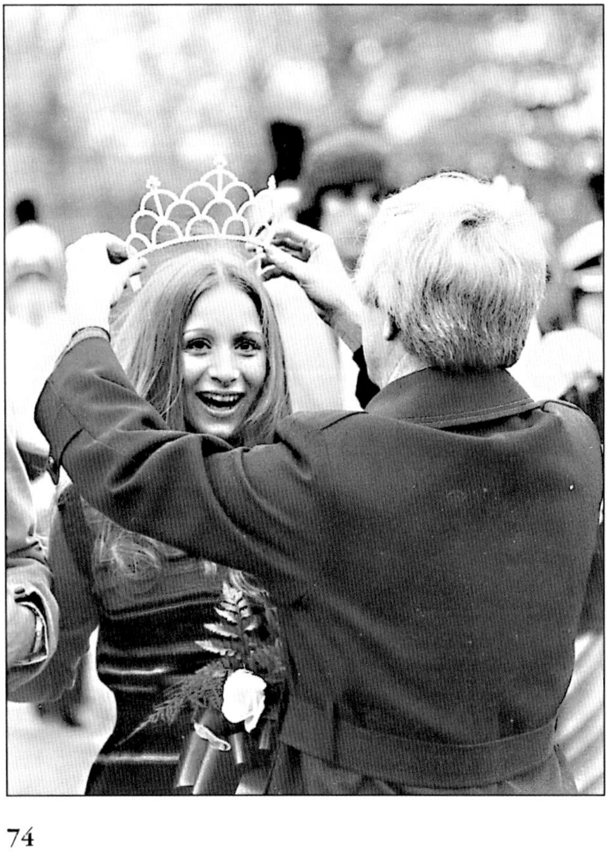

CROWNING THE HOMECOMING QUEEN, 1976. Some traditions seem to defy social change. Crowning the homecoming queen at halftime is a tradition that extends to today.

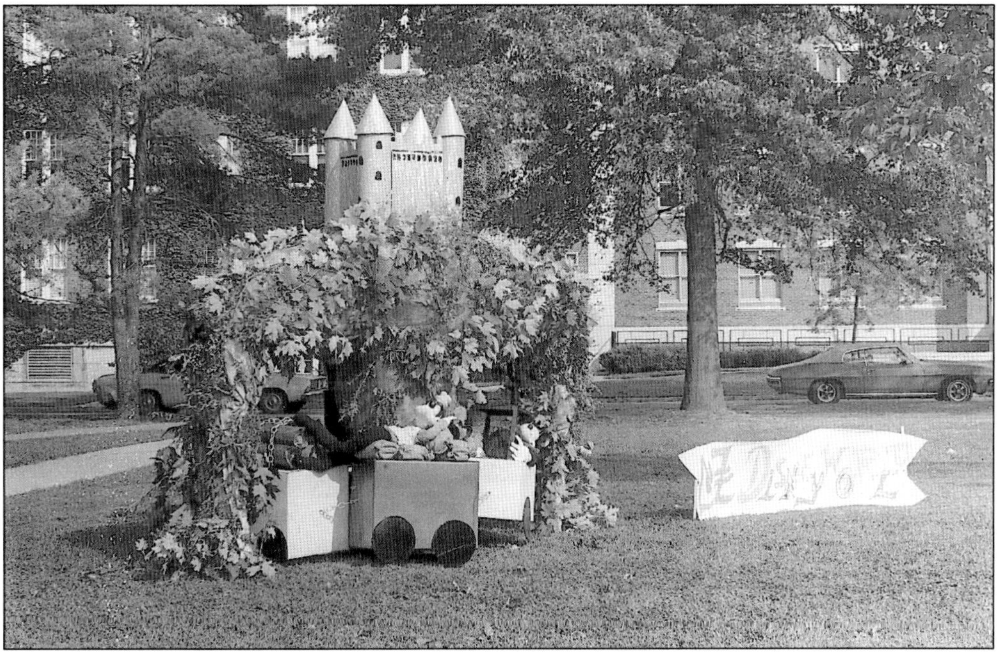

Delta Zeta Homecoming Display, 1973. In the 1970s, the homecoming parade and the floats were replaced by displays on campus. This Delta Zeta display, with a Disney World theme, is typical.

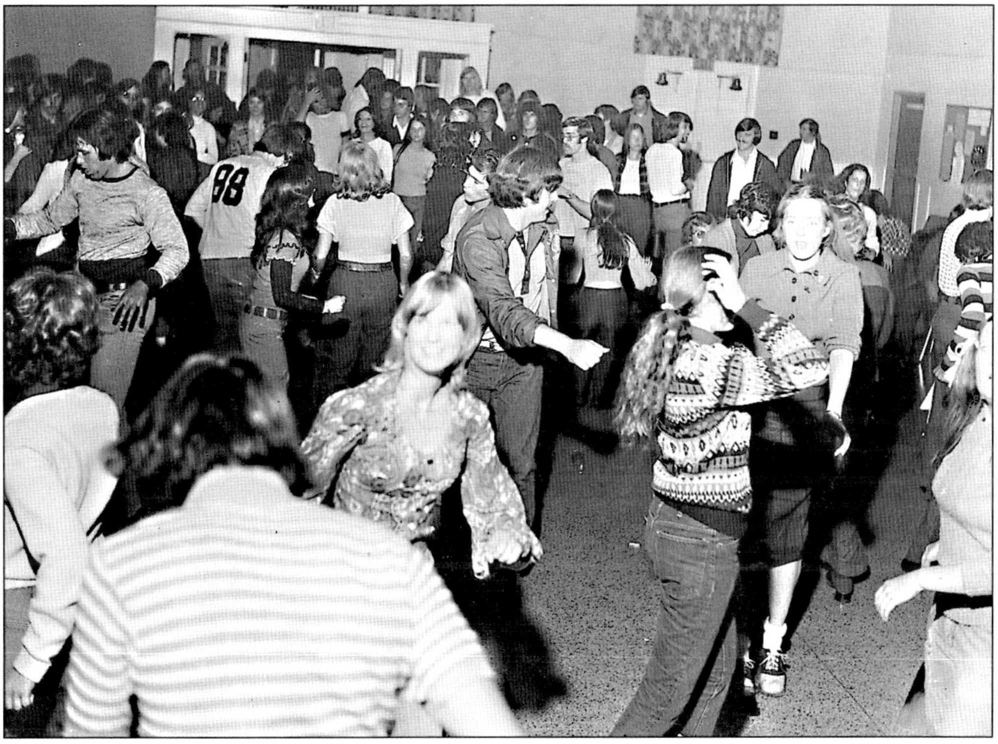

Dance in the Center, 1973. This "Greaser" dance was considerably less formal than in previous decades. Dress styles were different but the important thing was that everyone had fun.

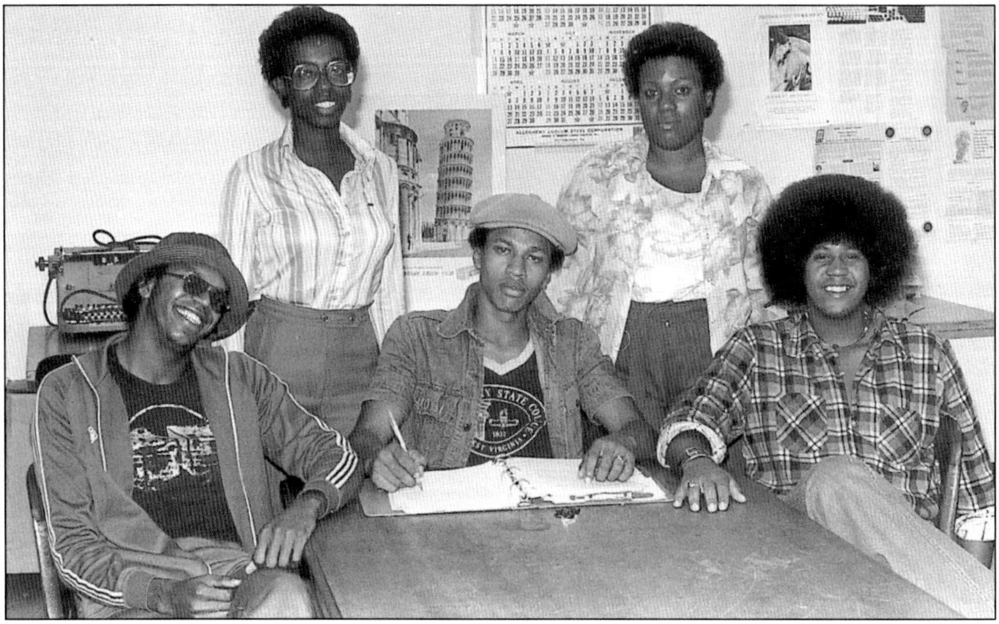

Progressive Young Blacks Officers, 1976. Pictured, from left to right, are (front row) Davey Carter; Gary Williams, president; and Warren Price; (back row) Ruth Royal and Sarah Wilson. Political activism was the "in thing" at this time. Students supported any organization that was opposed to racism, prejudice, and war. The PYB was organized so that African-American students could experience pride in their racial heritage.

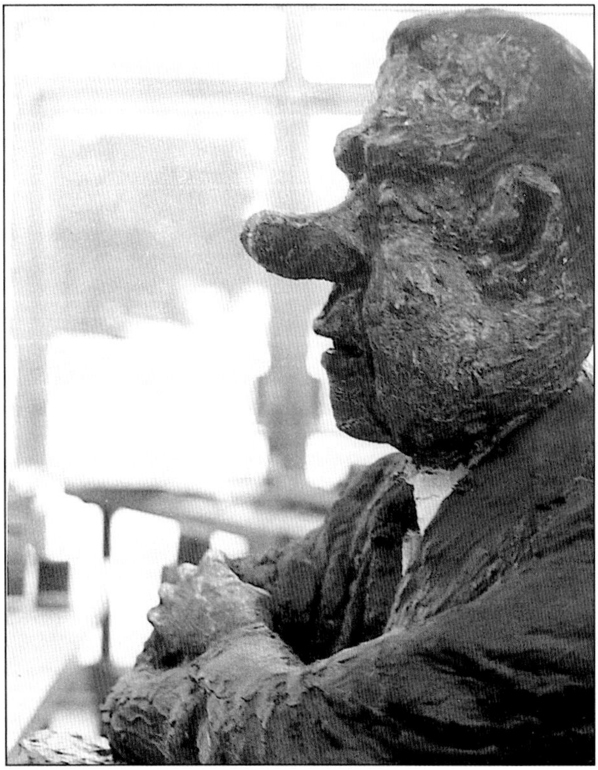

Nixon Sculpture, 1974. Political views often spilled over into the arts. Typical of the times was this student sculpture of "Tricky Dick," U.S. President Richard M. Nixon, who would resign in disgrace during this year.

Professor Ted Spickler's Class, 1974. The rather laid-back and casual attitude of the period often extended to the classroom. This young physics professor has moved his class to the more pleasant environment of the sunny steps of Main Hall.

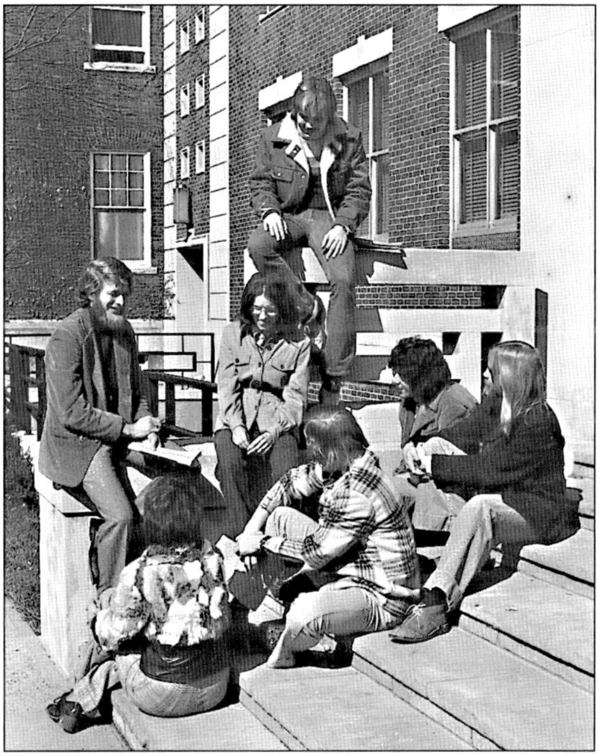

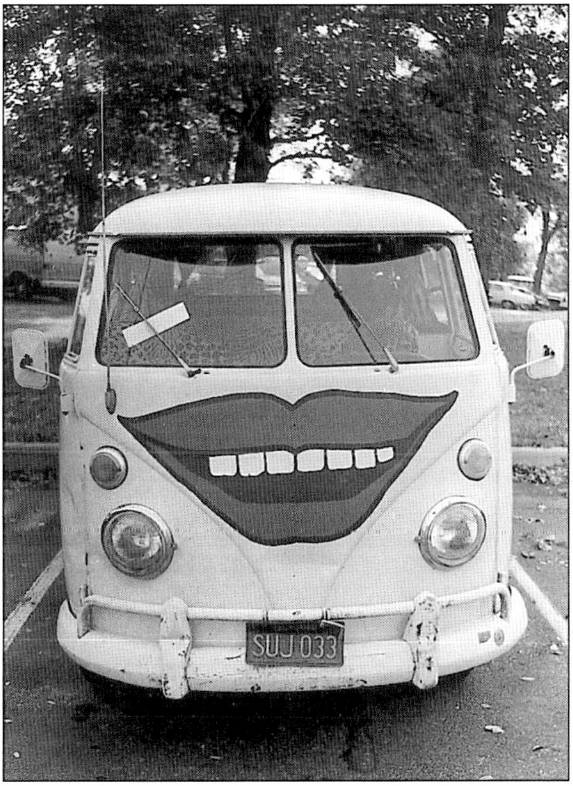

VW Bus with Warning Ticket, 1973. One major concern of the students of the 1970s was parking. There was just barely enough space for all the cars, and the large commuter population wanted to park near the classroom buildings. Every student who wanted to keep a car on the campus had to buy a parking sticker and put it on the bumper.

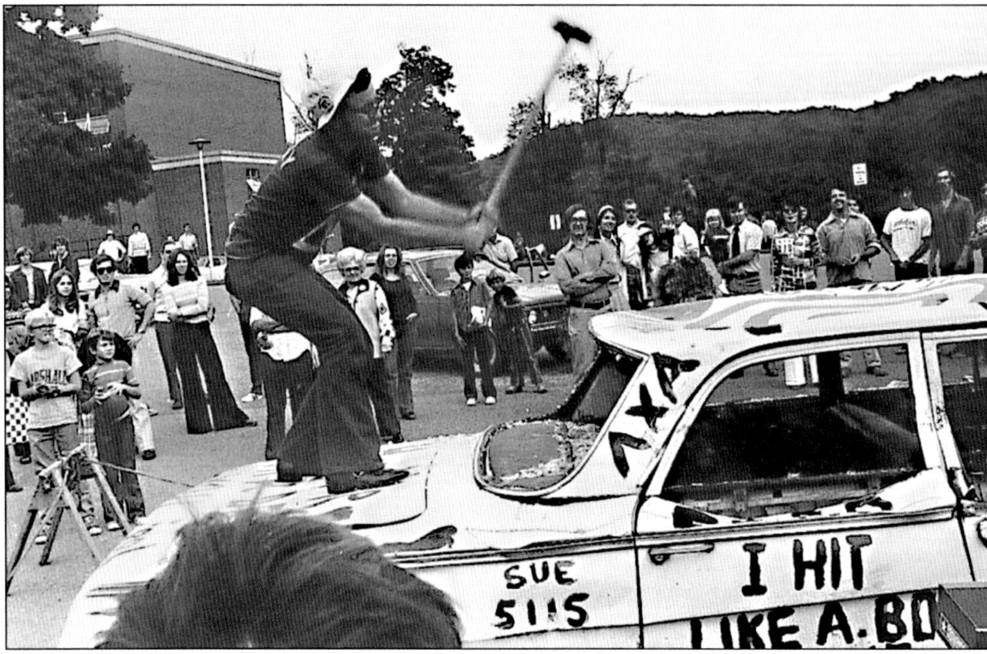

Car Smash, 1972. As a money-raising event, Delta Chi fraternity sponsored this "car smash." For a small fee you got to smash a car with a sledgehammer. Frustrated commuters who had received tickets for illegal parking or towing bills could relieve their tension via this event. Students became very upset when cars were towed. Even though only cars with 10 or more unpaid tickets were towed, students still considered this practice overkill.

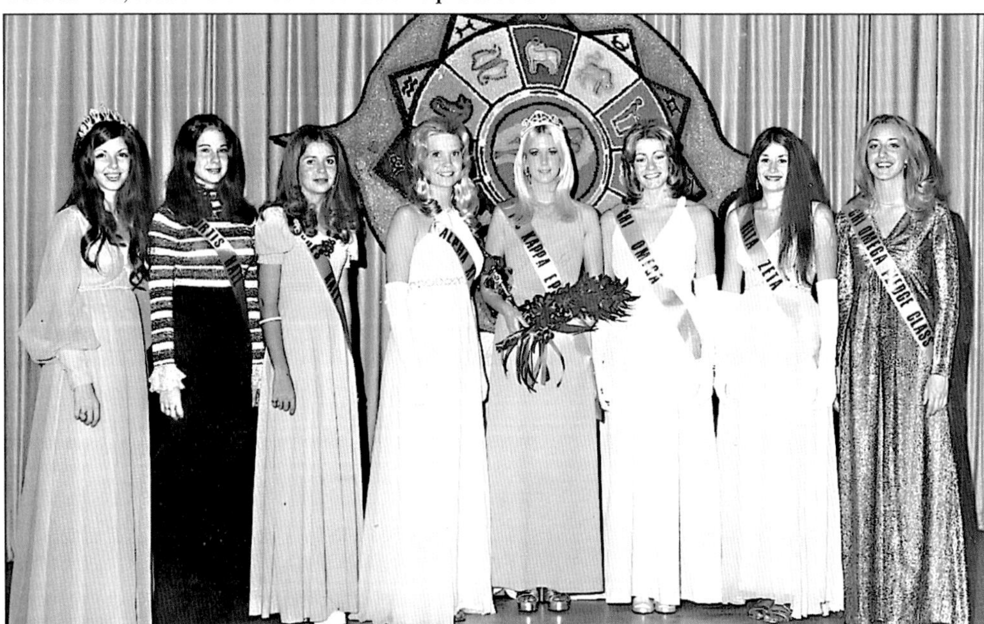

Miss West Liberty Contest, 1973. During the 1970s, students amused themselves with a number of pageants. The winner of the Miss West Liberty Contest was named a candidate in the Miss West Virginia Pageant.

MISS WEST LIBERTY, 1973. The swimsuit competition was a popular part of the contest. Many similar events were held in the 1970s including the best-dressed coed contest, the Water Follies, which consisted of swimming competitions and a beauty contest to select Miss Water Follies, the Sweetheart Couple contest, the Mr. and Miss Hilltopper Contest, and the traditional Homecoming Queen Contest.

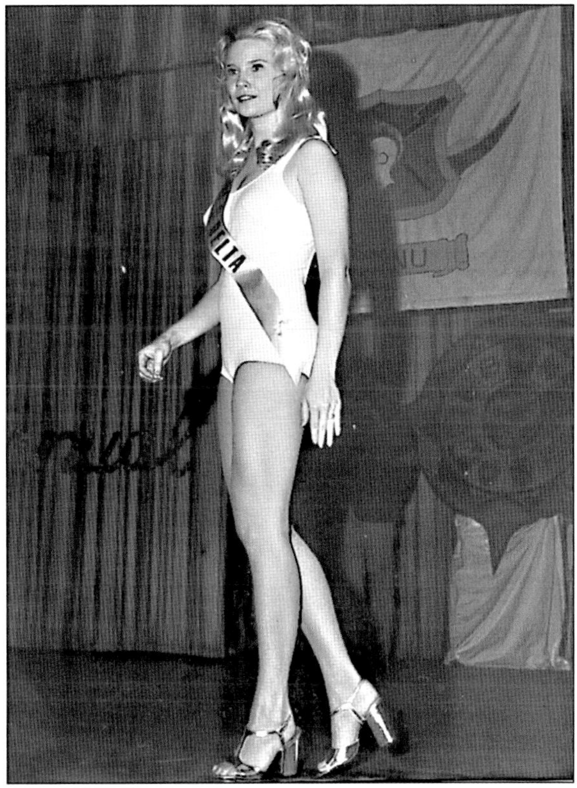

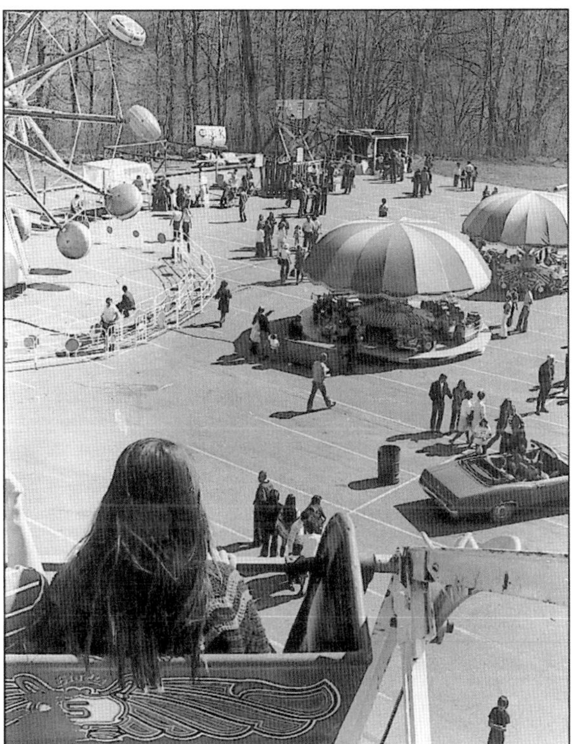

SPRING CARNIVAL, APRIL 1973. Another highly popular event was the annual spring carnival. In 1973, the carnival featured real carnival rides and booths sponsored by fraternities, sororities, and other organizations.

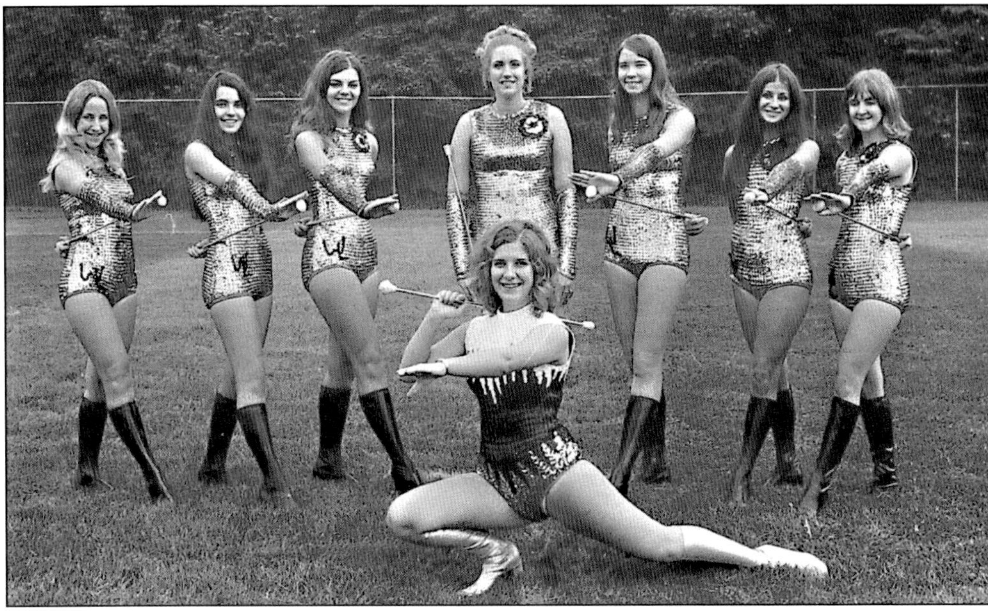

TOPPERETTES, **1972.** Students continued to participate in traditional activities. These majorettes are, from left to right, (front row) Gail Horner; (back row) Autumn Lilly, Bonnie Mallace, Mary Ann Turek, Shelly Burge, Leigh Fisher, Joyce Messimino, and Debbie Doll.

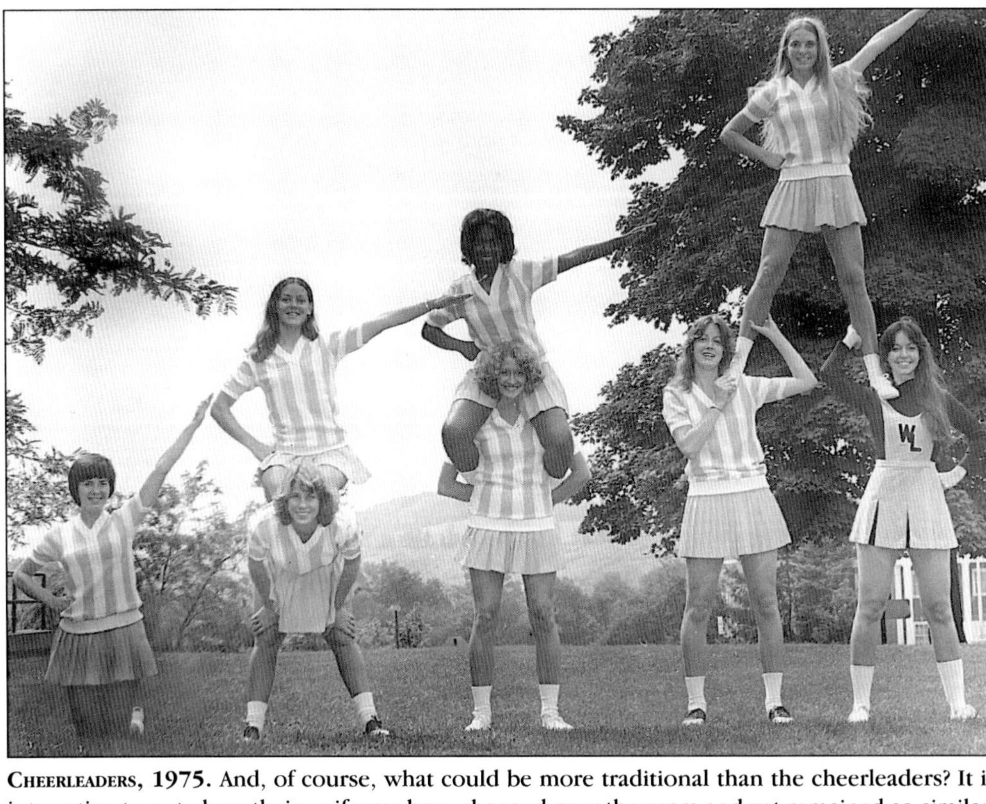

CHEERLEADERS, **1975.** And, of course, what could be more traditional than the cheerleaders? It is interesting to note how their uniforms have changed over the years and yet remained so similar. See the photos on pages 41 and 52.

COACH BOB ROE AND COACH LEO MILLER, 1972. Certainly, in the 20th century, football games have been major events. Here we see Coaches Roe (left) and Miller (right) reviewing team strategy during a home game.

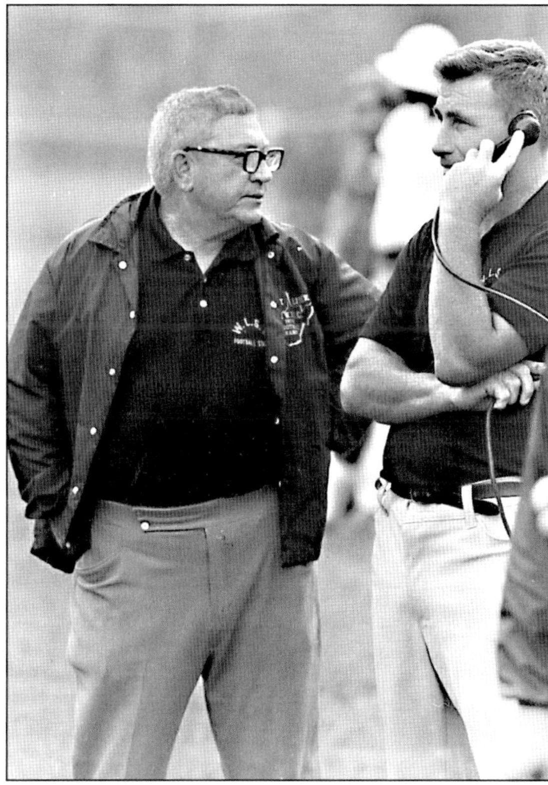

THE HILLTOPPER FOOTBALL TEAM, 1972. What could be more pleasant than a crisp fall day in the stands, rooting for your team, enjoying the antics of the cheerleaders, watching the band's halftime display, and consuming peanuts, popcorn, and hotdogs?

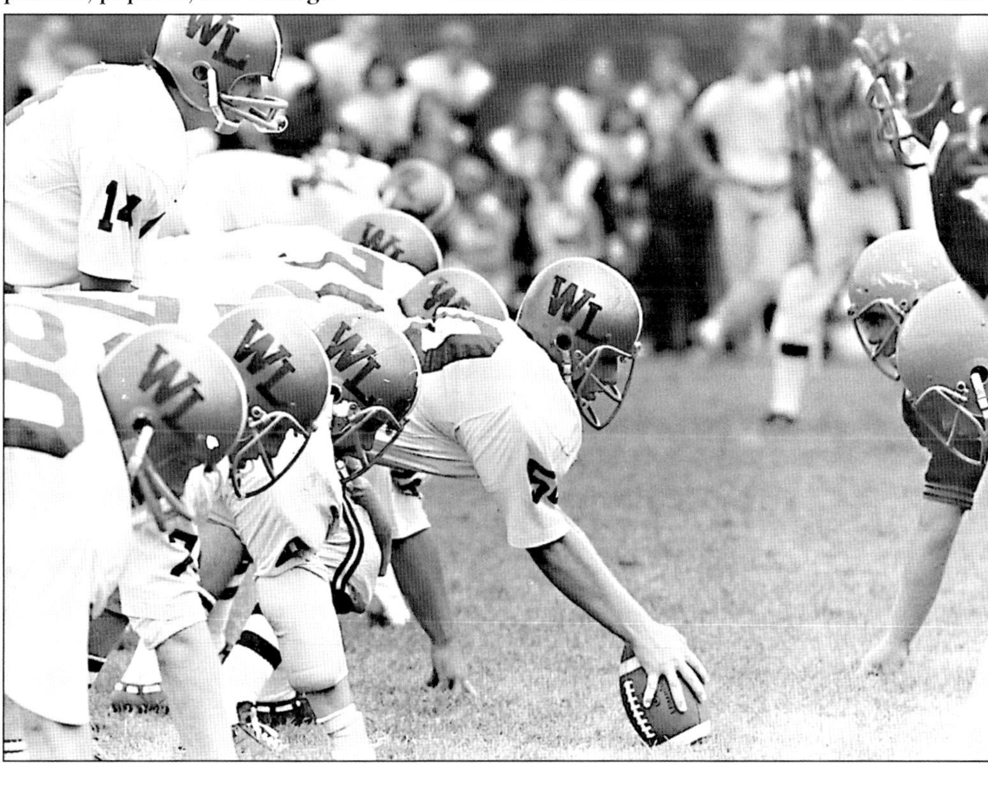

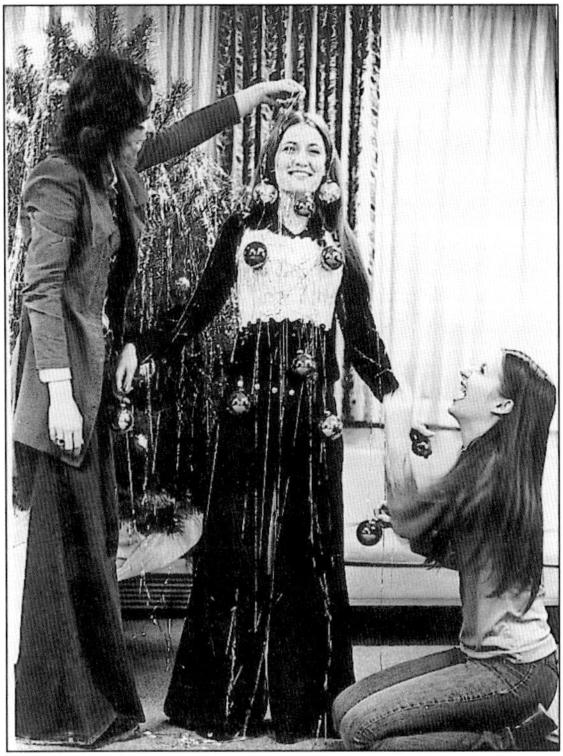

Goofing Around in the Dorm Lounge, December 1972. In 1972, students protested the education department's dress code for student teachers. For women, the code banned skirts above the knees and excessive eye shadow and required the wearing of a bra and girdle. Men were not permitted to sport sideburns below the ear or mustaches. They were also told to wear jockey shorts rather than boxer shorts. It appears that the coed in this photo would not be in violation of the dress code in spite of her unusual costume.

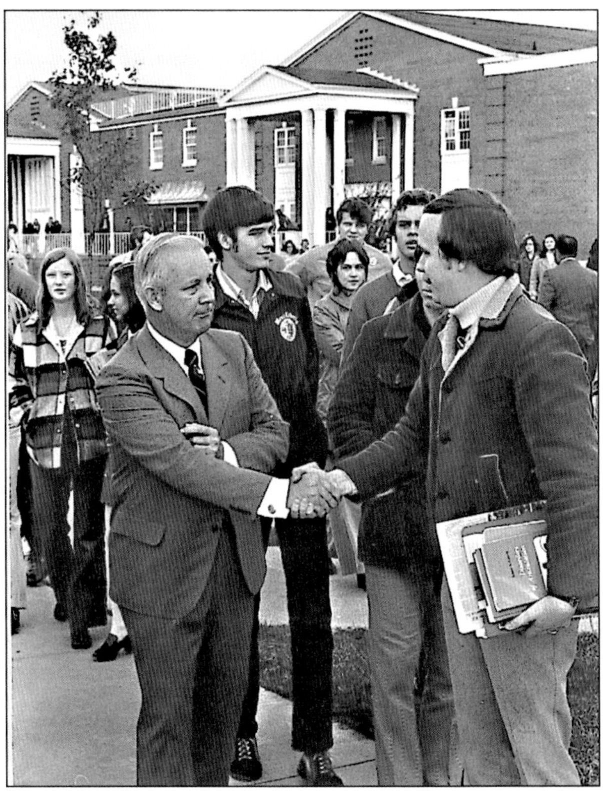

Gov. Arch Moore with Students on the Quad, 1972. In October 1972, Governor Moore landed via helicopter on the quad and proceeded to greet and talk with students as part of his campaign. He lost the election to John D. Rockefeller IV; Rockefeller later became a U.S. senator. The center can be seen in the background.

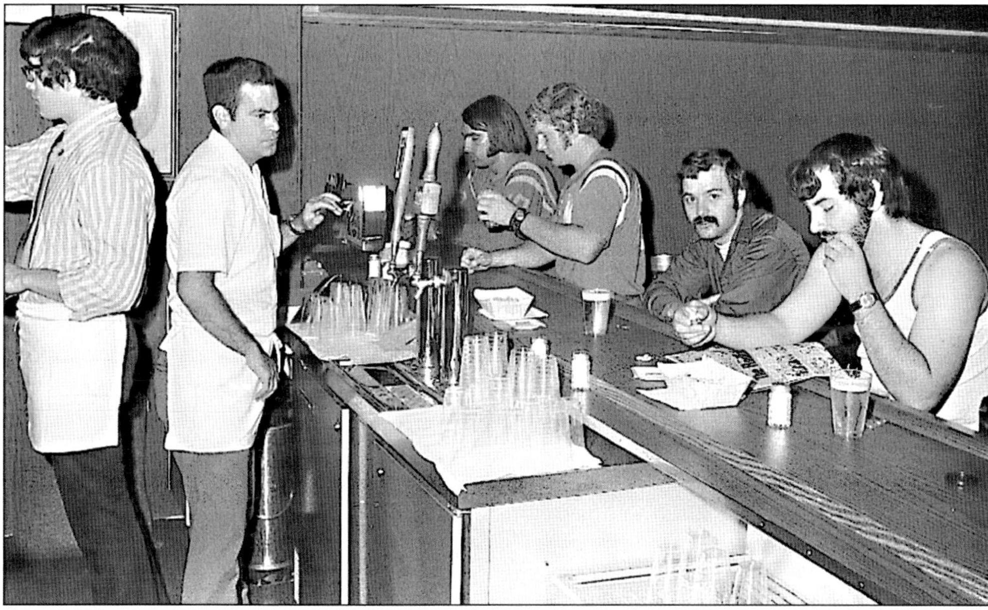

The Pub, 1972. Perhaps the most incredible transition of this era was the opening of "The Pub" in the basement of the Student Center on September 5, 1972. For the first time in the history of the college, alcoholic beverages were permitted on campus. Draft beer was on tap and students could purchase canned beer to go. A lot of small refrigerators appeared in dorm rooms. The Pub was open Monday through Thursday from 6 p.m. to midnight and on Friday and Saturday from 1 p.m. to 1 a.m.

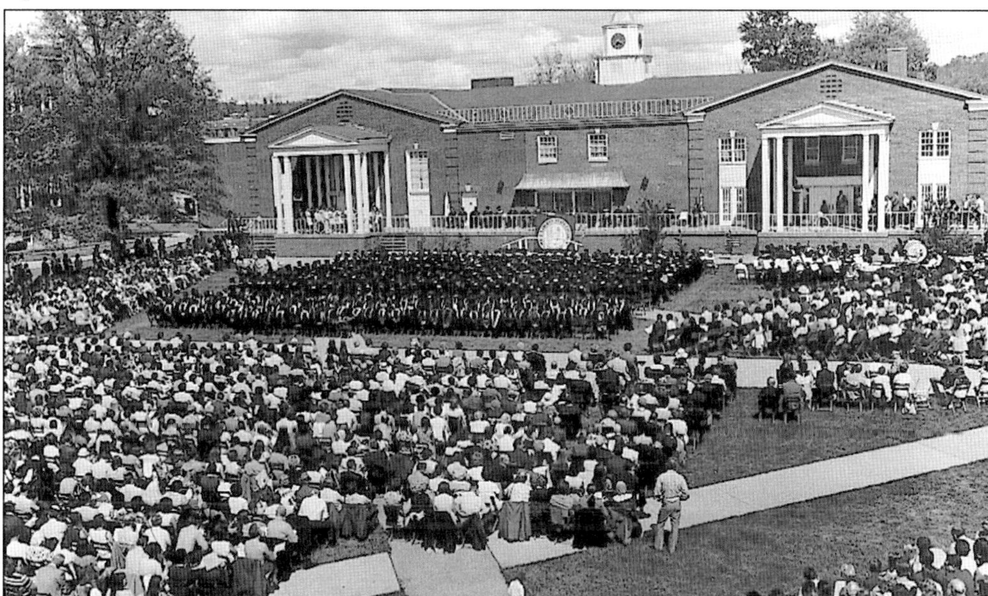

Spring Graduation on the Quad, 1972. Graduation was first held in Academy Hall, then College Hall, and as attendance increased, it was moved to the football field and then to the quad in 1972. The porch of the Student Center was used as a speaker's platform. The prospective graduates sit in front, the faculty is behind them, and the college concert band can be seen on the right.

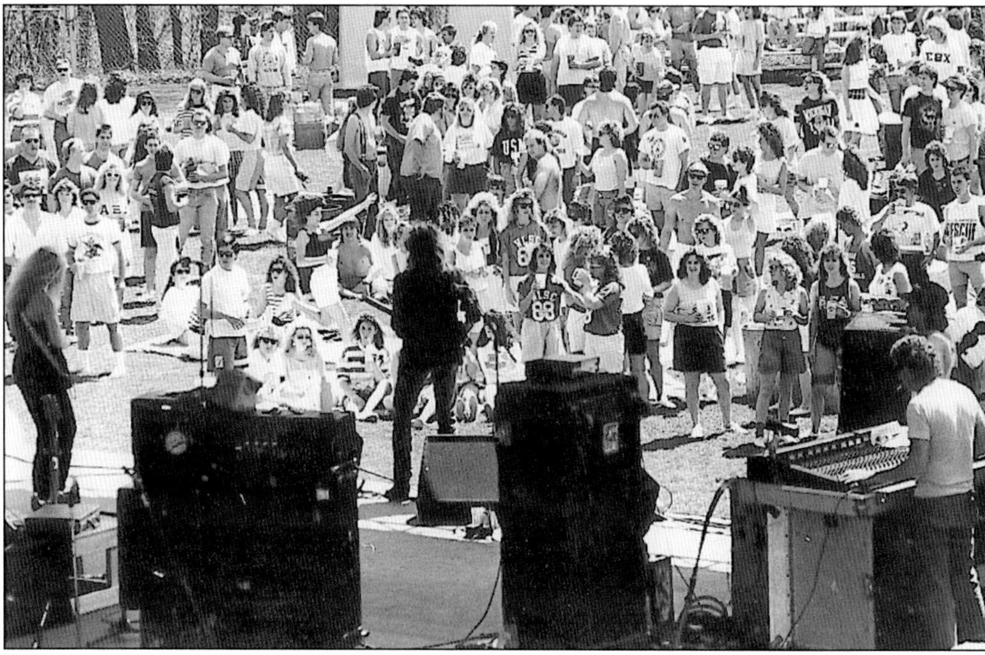

Joan Jett and the Blackhearts Entertaining Students at Band Blast, 1988. The 1970s was the era of another phenomenon, namely, the "Band Blast." Student programming brought well-known rock bands to campus to perform on the football field. Kegs of beer were permitted and Porta-Potties® were a necessity. Excessive drinking by a small percentage of the students resulted in the college putting an end to the presence of alcohol at the Band Blasts and to the closing of The Pub.

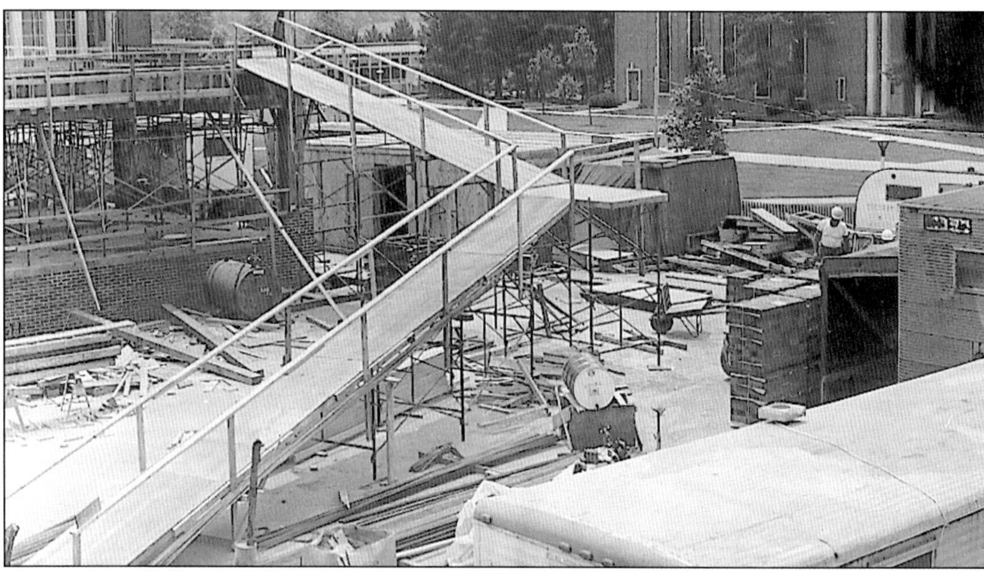

Science Building Construction, 1974. The college had outgrown the biology and chemistry laboratories in Main Hall and the maintenance building was woefully inadequate. Funds were obtained from the state to begin construction of a new science building and a new maintenance building in 1974. The Arnett Hall of Science and the Myers Maintenance Building were both completed the following year.

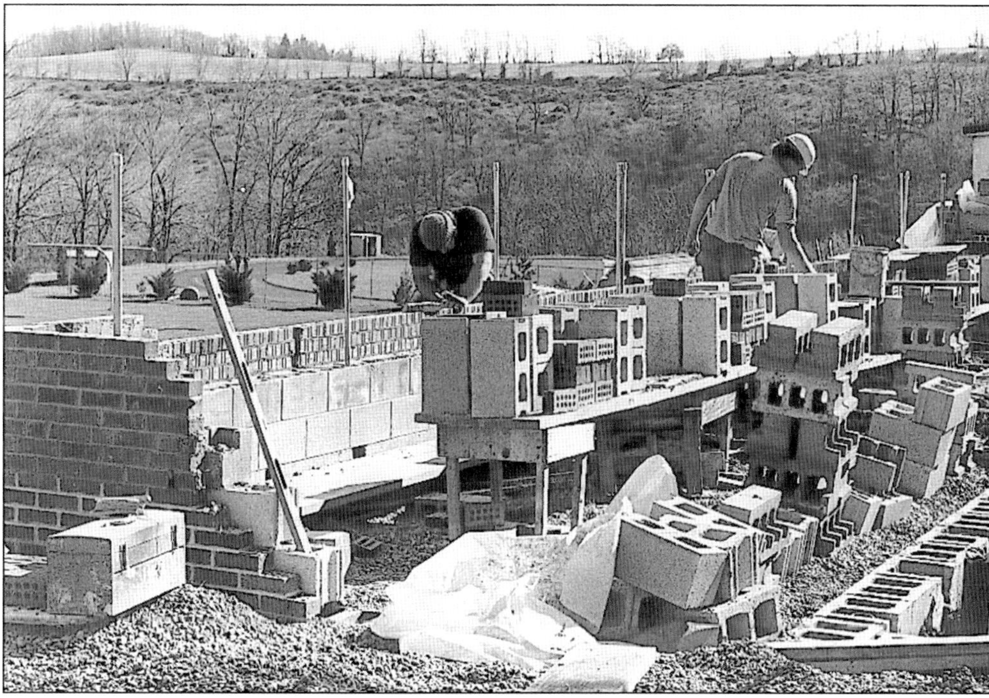

PRESS BOX CONSTRUCTION, 1976. Construction also began on a long-needed press box/concession stand for the football field in 1976. The old wood-frame press box was replaced by a modern brick structure that also contained restrooms.

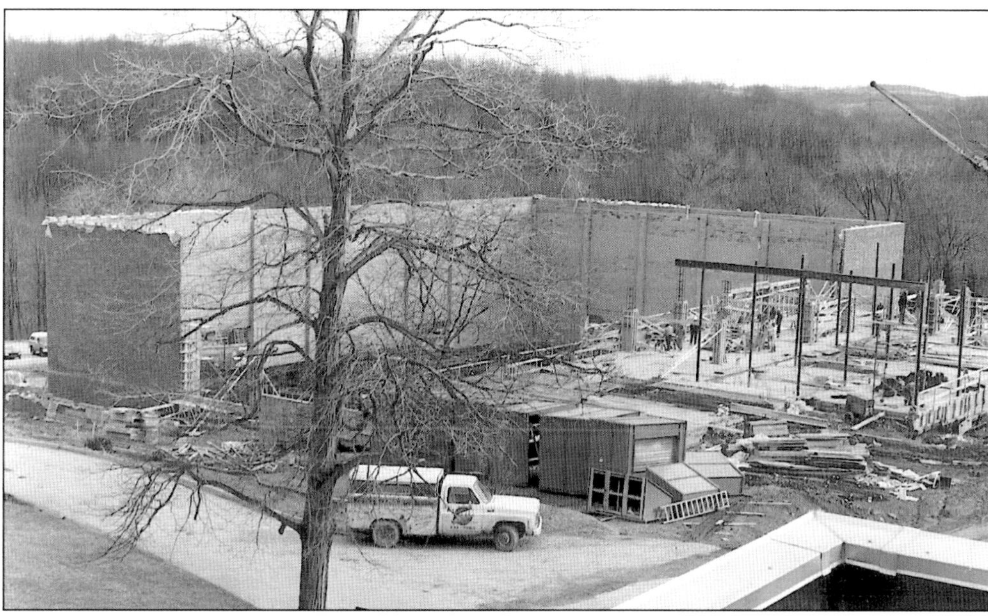

FIELD HOUSE CONSTRUCTION, 1980. During the administration of President James L. Chapman, construction began on the most controversial building ever erected on the campus. In spite of protests by the faculty of the Department of Physical Education, this poorly engineered building was completed in 1981. Almost immediately it began showing signs of structural defects. In 1994, the college was ordered to close the building because it was in danger of collapsing.

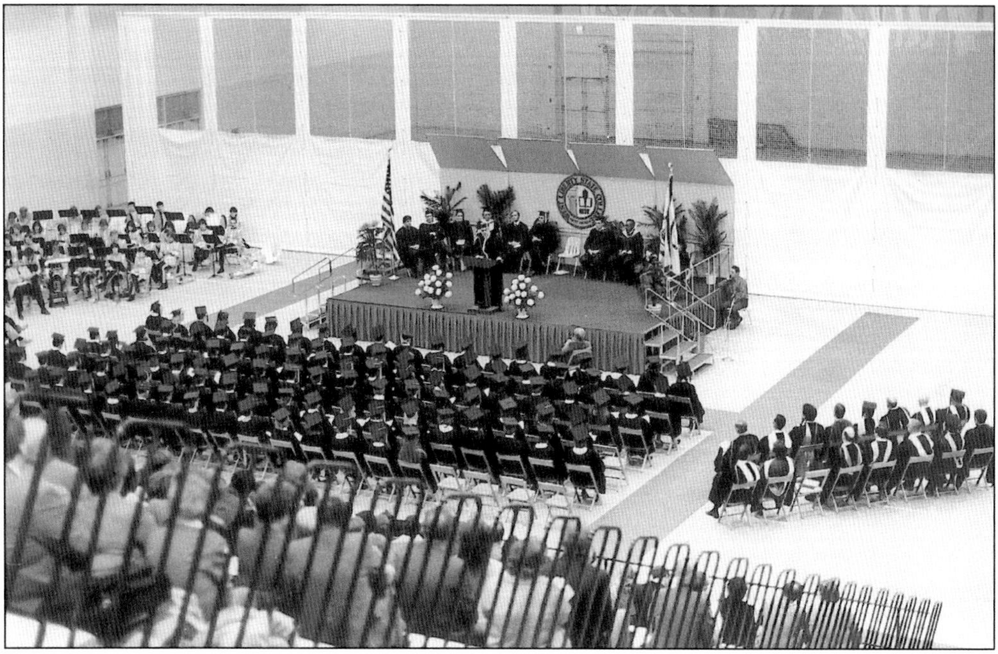

WINTER COMMENCEMENT IN THE FIELD HOUSE, **1993.** The college held winter commencement in the field house each year since its completion. However, a Charleston engineering firm determined that the arena portion of the building was unsafe and should be demolished; it was torn down in 1995.

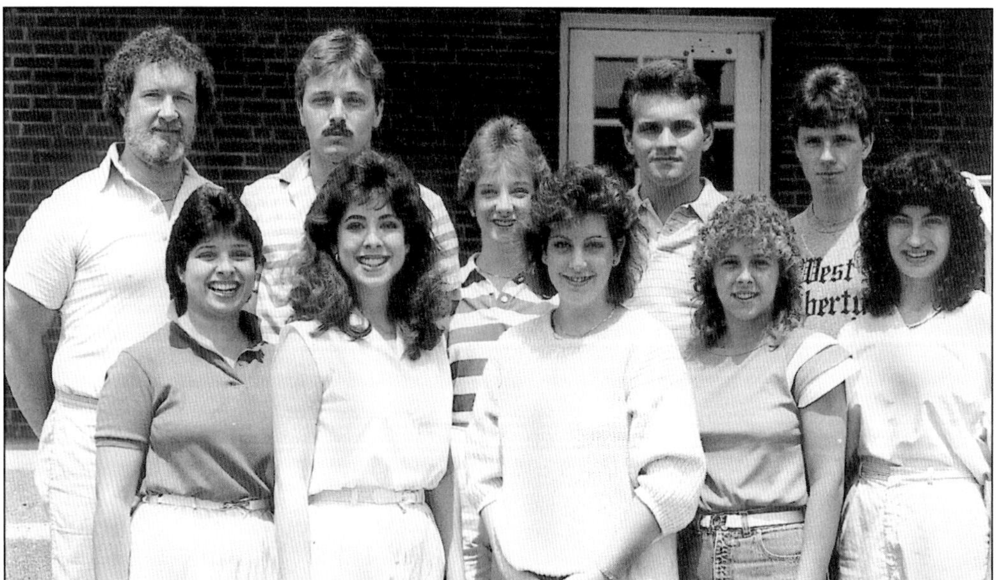

THE TRUMPET STAFF, **1985.** Possibly because of lack of interest, the last college yearbook was published in 1969. Fortunately, *The Trumpet* filled in the gap. It not only increased the number of photographs per issue but also began publishing photos of graduation, candids of campus life, photos of graduating seniors, as well as photos of special events such as Greek Week, sorority rush parties, homecoming, and other social events. Staff members are pictured here with their advisor, Professor William Hanna (back row, left).

Gary Smith, 1974. In January 1974, Gary Smith, an art major, constructed a mosaic of the college seal and presented it to the college. It appeared at every commencement program and at every major college function until its retirement in 2001.

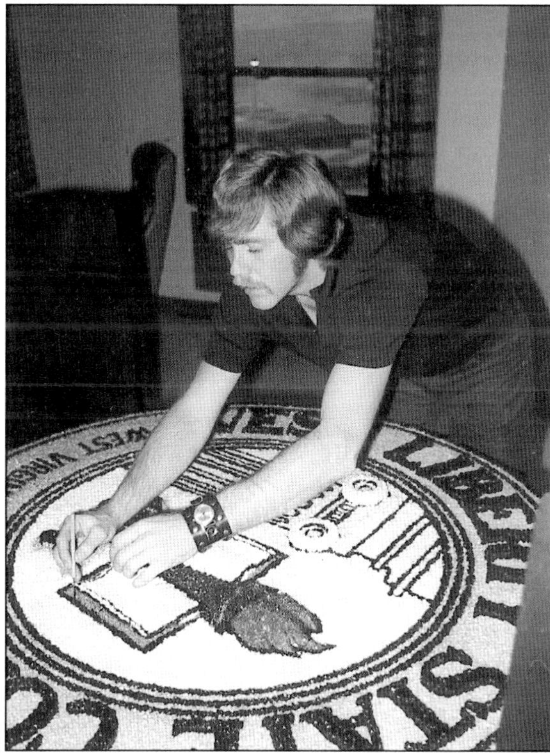

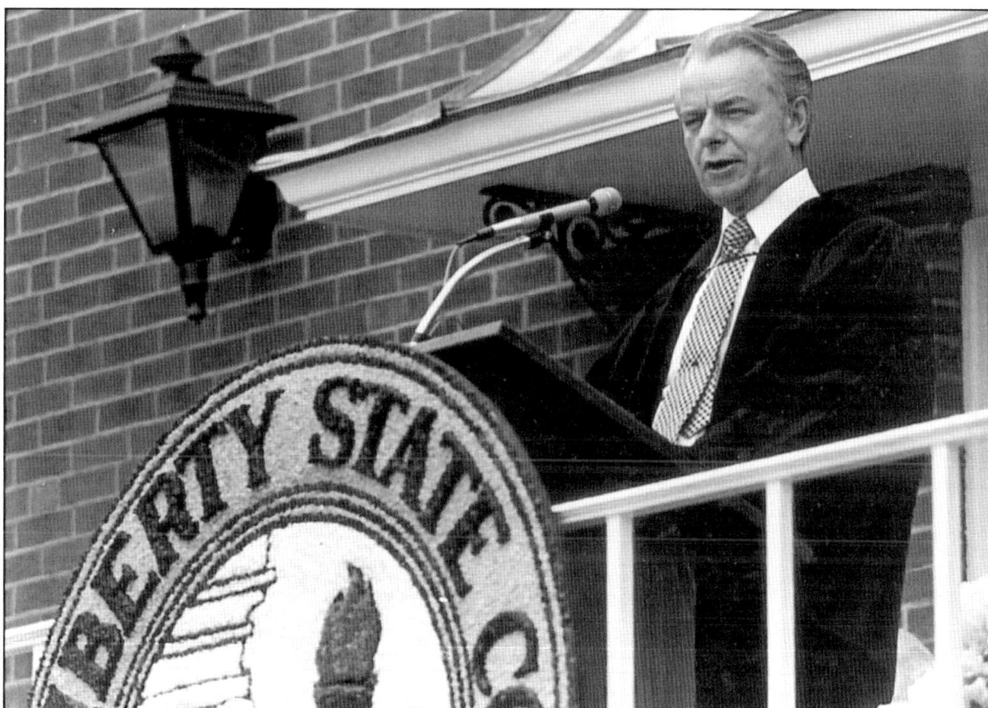

Sen. Robert C. Byrd, 1976. Senator Byrd visited the West Liberty campus as a graduation speaker in September 1976. Notice the mosaic of the college seal in the foreground.

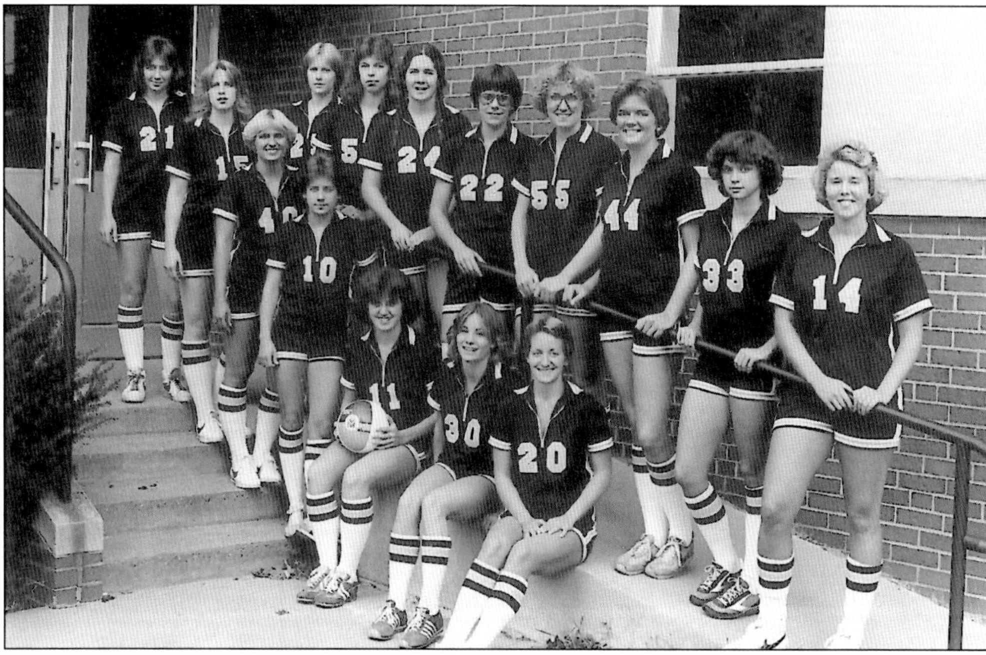

Women's Volleyball Team, 1978. In the 1970s, a "new" sport, volleyball, became popular. This women's volleyball squad looks "sharp" in their uniforms. Soccer and volleyball had long been popular in European countries but not in this country. Probably interest in these two sports was the result of the influence of foreign exchange students.

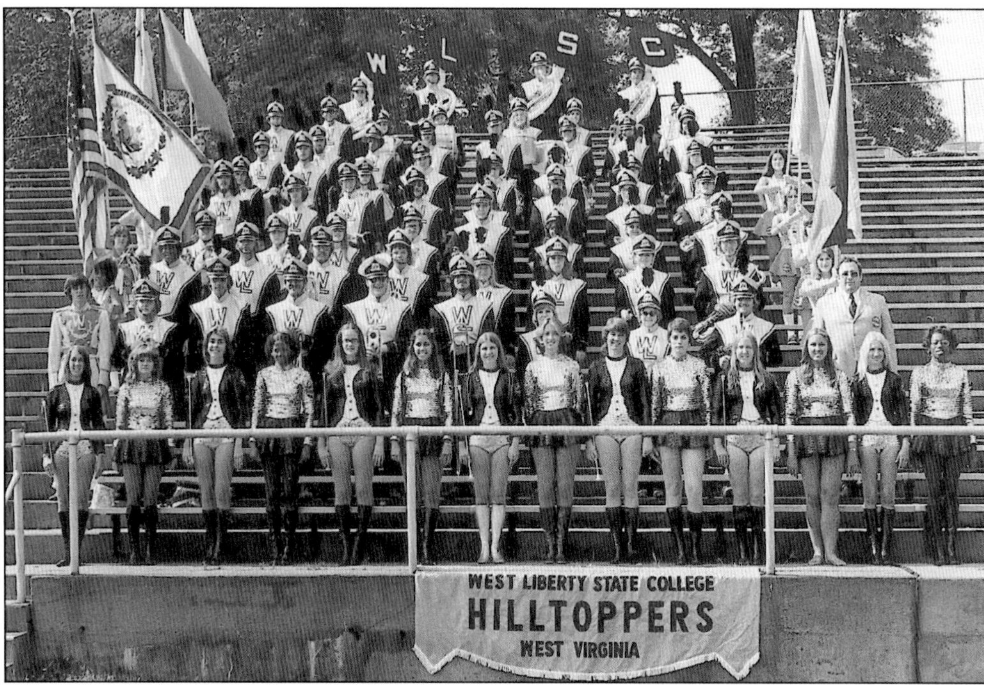

Marching Band, 1974. The 1974 Hilltoppers Marching Band, complete with the "Topperettes" and the Flag Corps, also look very "sharp" in this photo. Note the " W L S C" covers on the sousaphones. Compare this photo with the one on page 41.

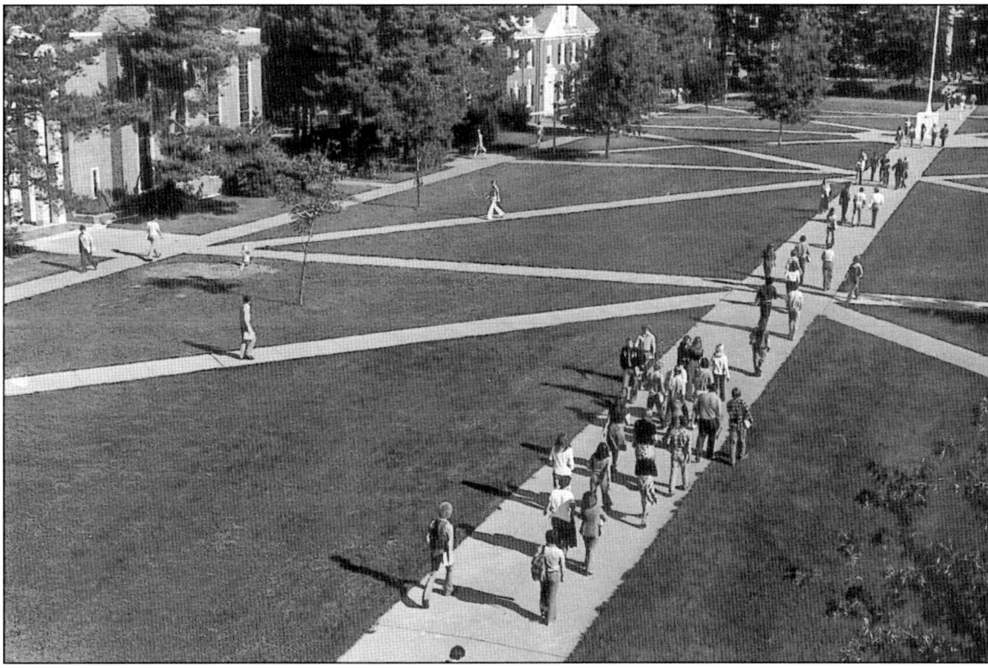

THE QUAD, 1977. Another change was the formation of the faculty senate in 1973. The senate effectively replaced monthly faculty meetings but its purpose was not the same. It was "devoted to the concept of faculty participation in academic governance" and its first officers were Dr. Jack Hattman, chairman; Dr. Lawerence Talley, vice chairman; Professor Karen Rychlewski, recording secretary; and Dr. Wallace Cayard, corresponding secretary. Senators were elected by every academic department.

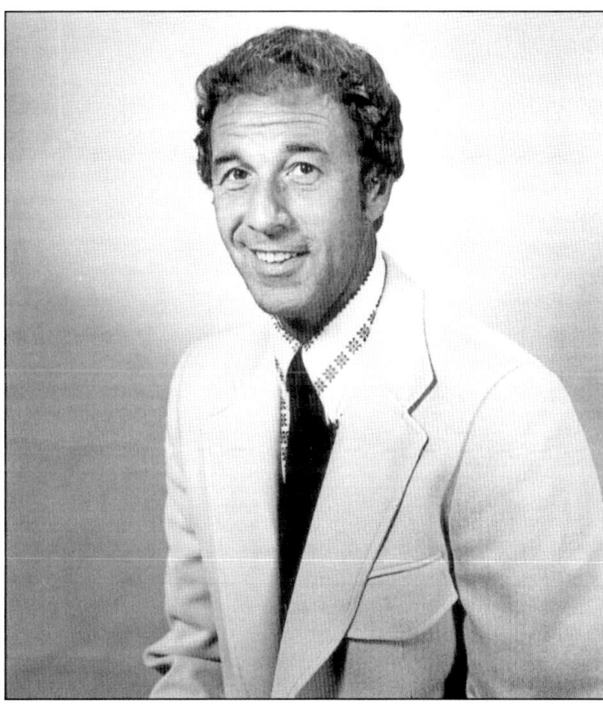

DR. CLYDE D. CAMPBELL, 1977. In February 1984, President Chapman resigned. In October of that same year, Dr. Clyde D. Campbell, a graduate of West Liberty State College and former member of the faculty and administration, became the college's president. Dr. Campbell foresaw the growing need for external fund-raising and created the college's first development office. He also revitalized the alumni association, that, under his guidance, grew from a small group in the Wheeling area to a national organization with chapters in several states, including Florida and California.

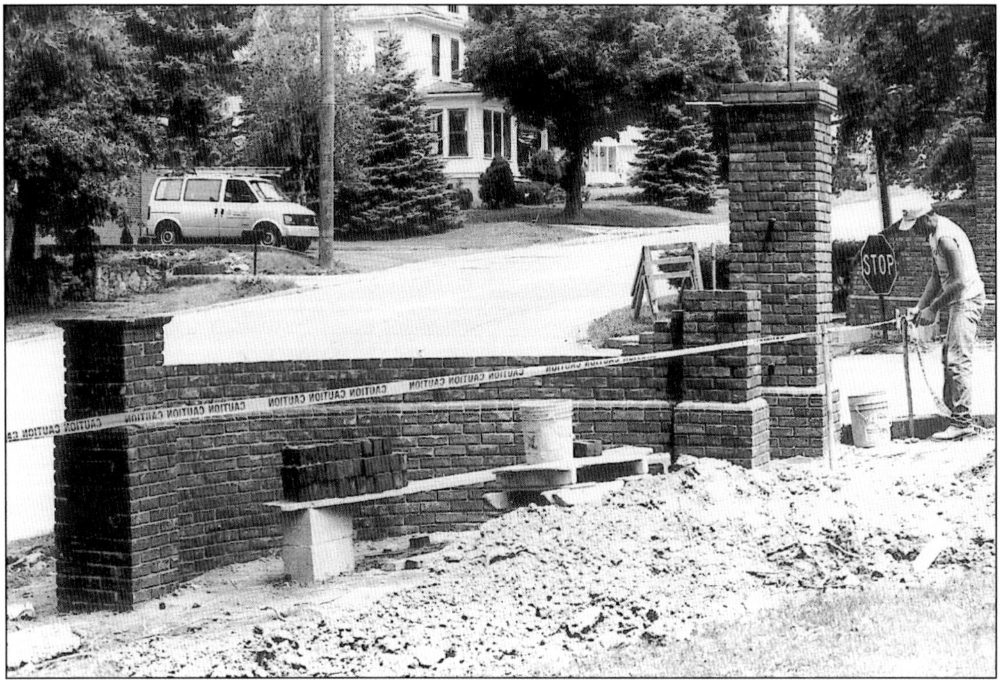

Alumni Gate Construction, 1987. President Campbell established an alumni office on campus and hired the first alumni director. The Alumni Association Board of Directors was formed and the organization grew. During the college's sesquicentennial celebration in 1987, the alumni made their first major gift to the college in the form of a new front gate and a scholarship fund.

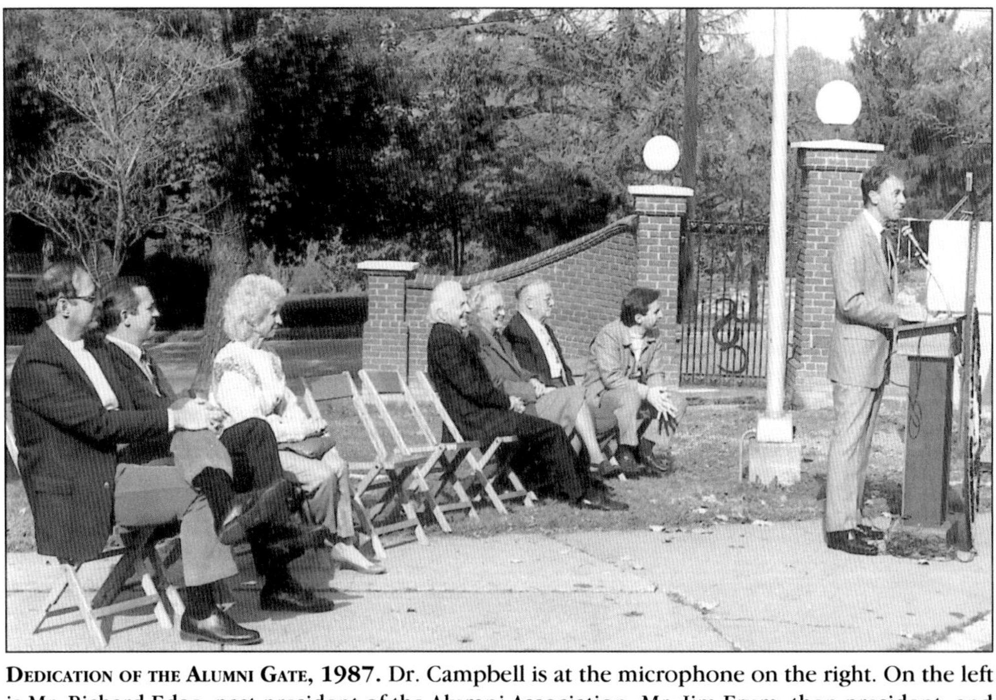

Dedication of the Alumni Gate, 1987. Dr. Campbell is at the microphone on the right. On the left is Mr. Richard Edge, past president of the Alumni Association; Mr. Jim Frum, then president; and Joan Campbell.

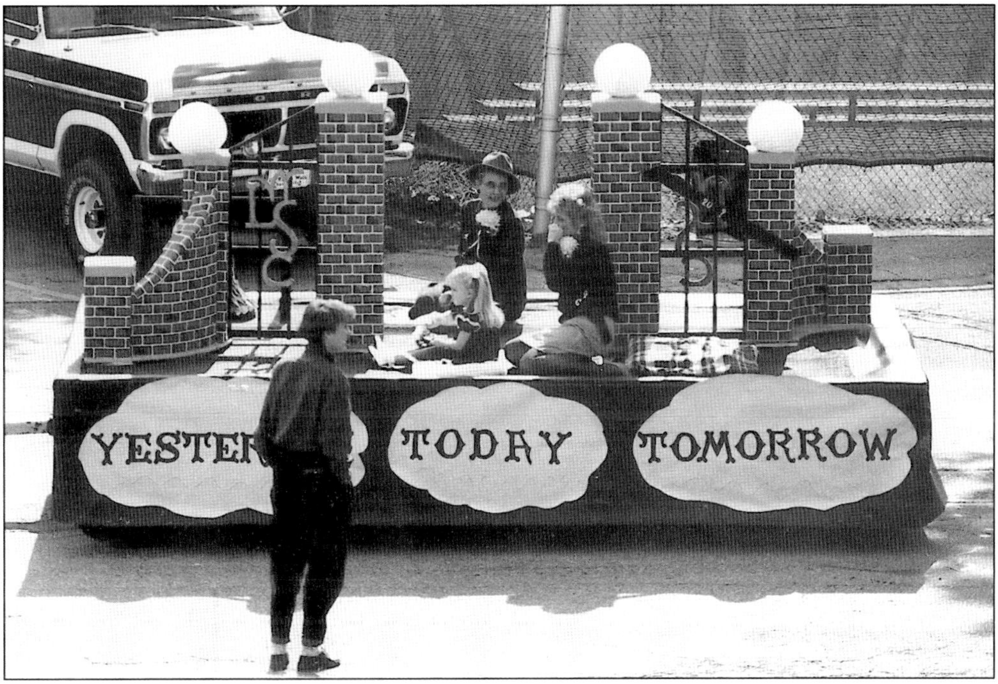

Alumni Float, 1987. The Alumni Association revived the homecoming parade, moved it from Wheeling to the town of West Liberty, and built a sample float as an example for the students. After homecoming, the float was redesigned by Professor Robert Schramm, wired for lights and sound, and entered in the first Festival of Lights parade in Wheeling, where it won an award.

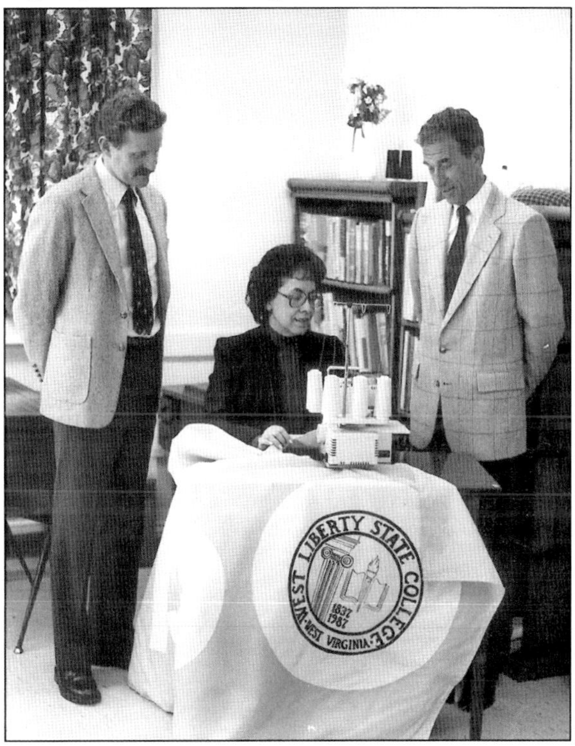

Sesquicentennial Flag, 1987. A flag, designed by Professor Paul Padgett (left) and created by Professor Julie Groux (center), flew over the campus all year. President Campbell (right) formed a committee to plan the sesquicentennial celebration. Professors David Javersak and Robert Schramm created a 150th-anniversary photo exhibit that went on display at the Custom House in Wheeling, the first capital of West Virginia.

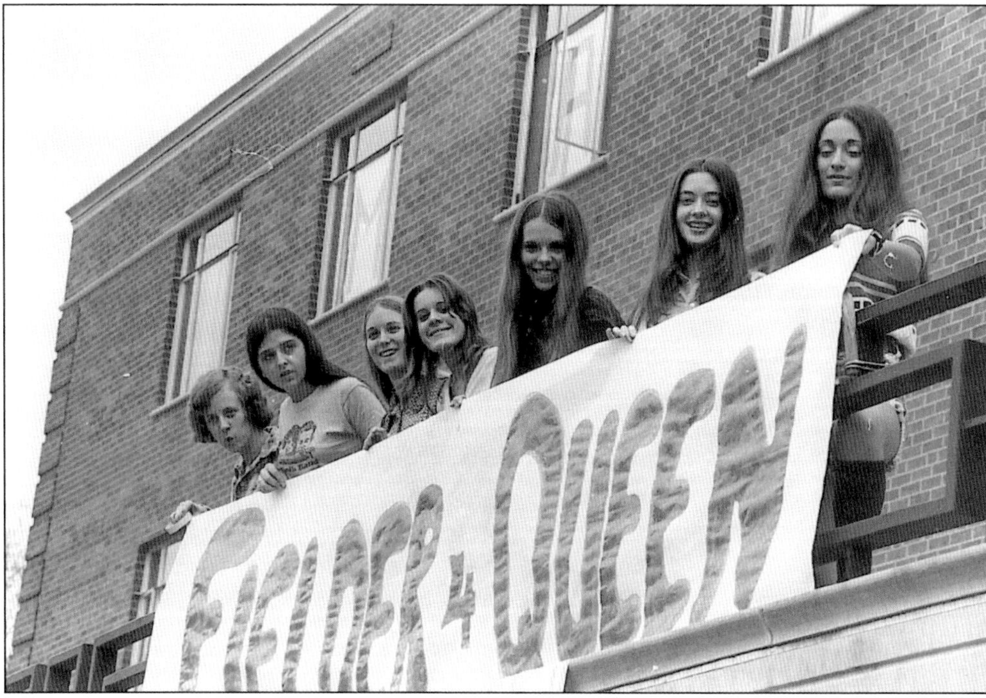

HANGING A BANNER FOR A QUEEN CANDIDATE, 1988. Traditional student activities continued in the 1980s and 1990s. In October, the buildings on campus sprouted a multitude of colorful signs urging students to vote for various candidates for homecoming queen.

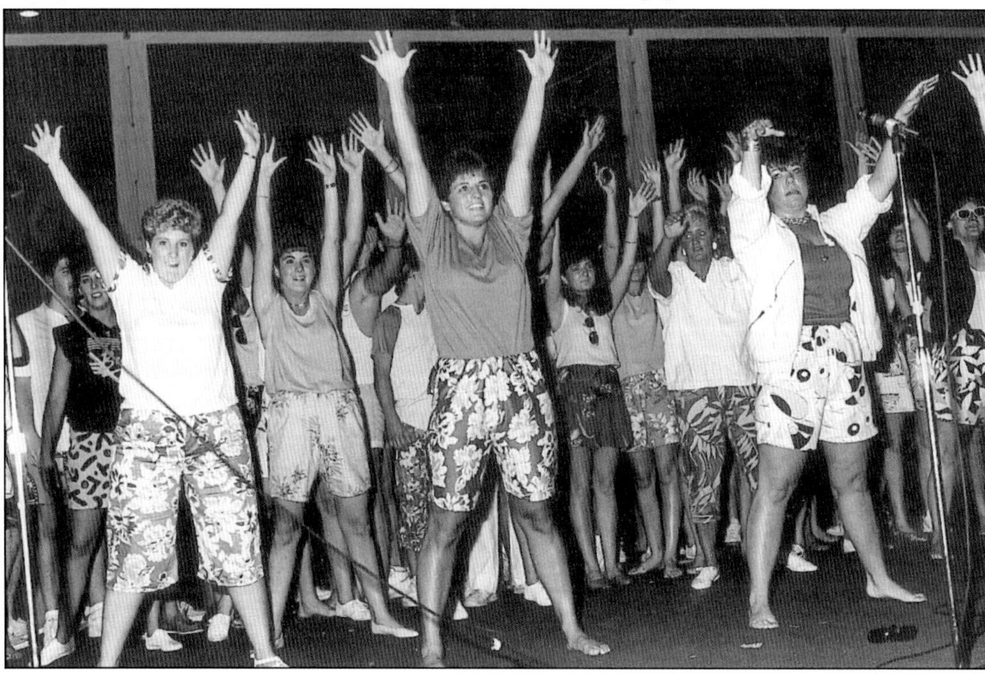

SERENADES, 1986. By the late 1980s, serenades had grown into major musical presentations featuring clever costumes, lively dancing, and a lot of screaming. Aside from the decibel level, these productions were great fun.

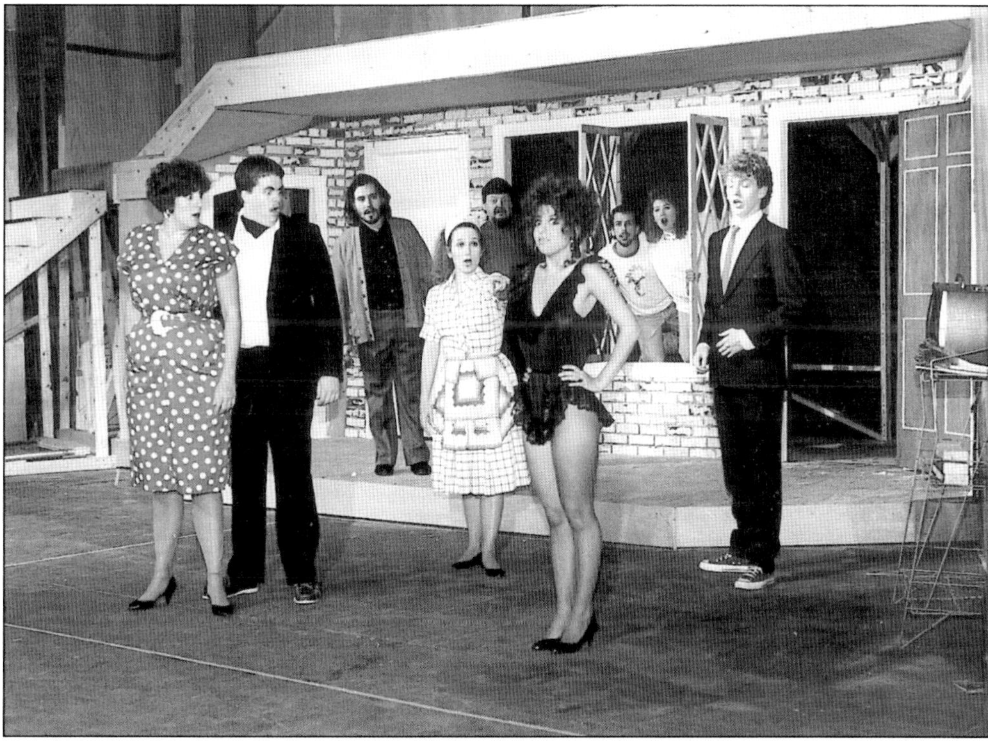

Hilltop Players, 1988. The Hilltop Players had been in existence for 62 years when this photo was made. The subject matter and the costumes were certainly a lot different from that of 1926, when the theatrical company was first organized. The Hilltop Players celebrated its 75th anniversary in 2001.

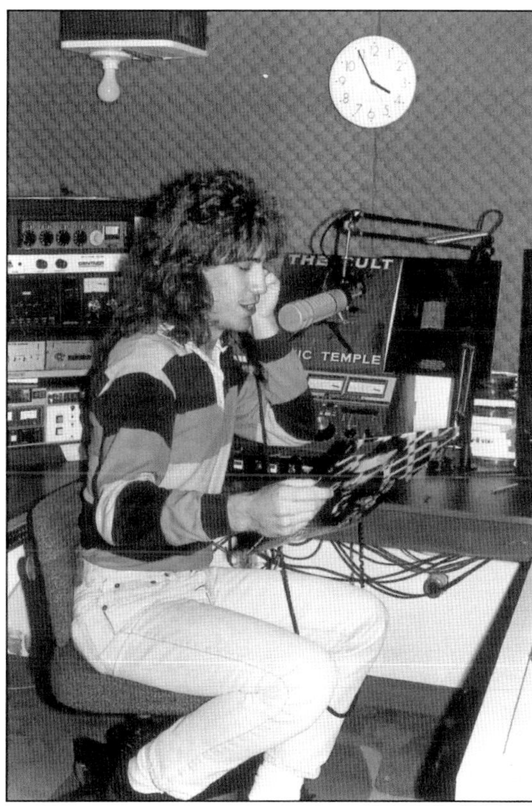

College Radio Station, 1990. On March 6, 1990, the college's first student-operated radio station began broadcasting. WGLZ's signal (91.5 FM) was strong enough to cover the campus and the town of West Liberty.

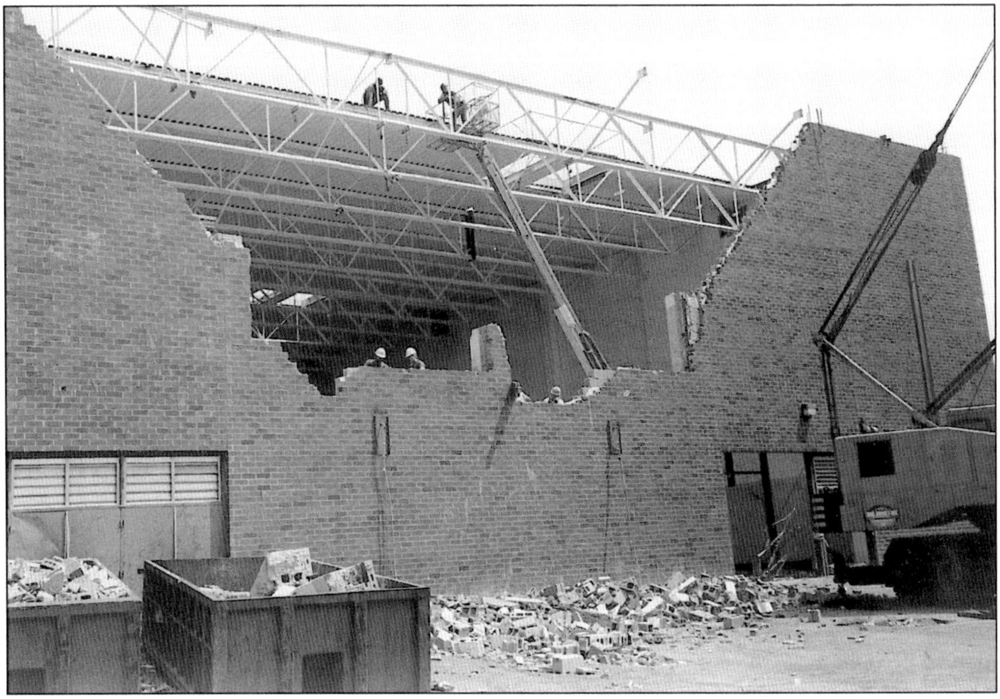

Demolition of the Bartell Field House, 1995. The field house named after Joe Bartell, a coach and the dean of men, was closed in 1994 after it was declared unsafe. It was razed in 1995.

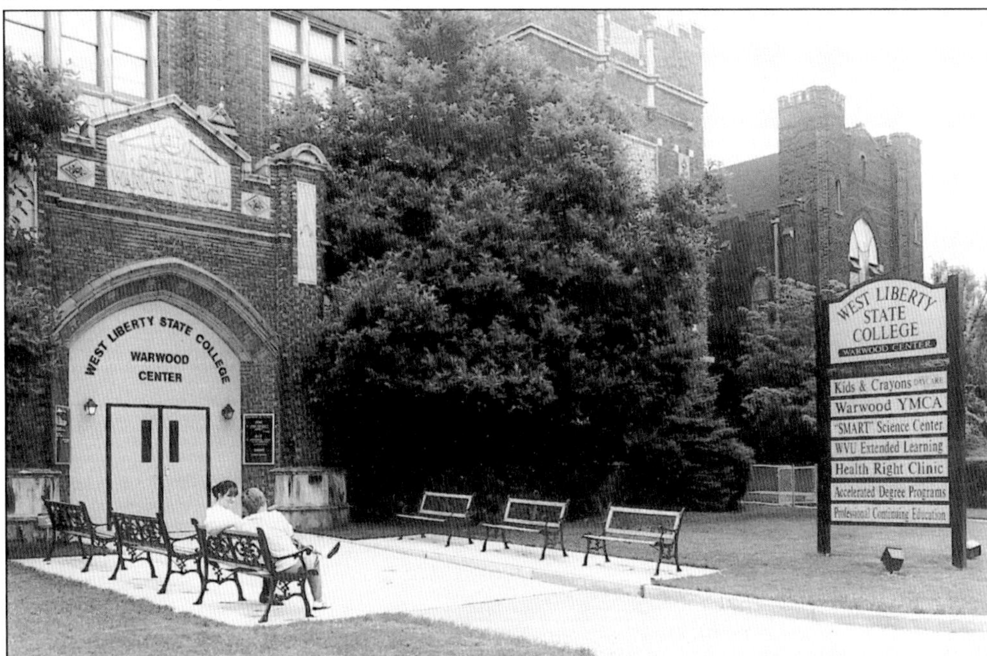

The Warwood Center, 1998. In 1995, the old Warwood High School building was purchased by the college for use as an extended learning center in Wheeling. Several other programs were located in this building later on. The Warwood Center opened on January 2, 1996. Dr. Campbell ended his term as president the following August.

Five

Into the New Millennium

On July 1, 1996, Dr. Ronald M. Zaccari became president of West Liberty State College. One of his first acts as president was to develop a ten-year plan (an on-going project) and a strategic plan that would be updated at a yearly retreat. In many ways this is reminiscent of Paul N. Elbin, who, upon becoming president of West Liberty State Teachers College, began by developing a plan for converting a teachers' college into an accredited, four-year, degree-granting state college with the necessary physical facilities. Similarly, President Zaccari began converting the college into an institution that could better meet the needs of the students of the late 1990s. This meant changing the academic programs, restructuring the administration, and modifying and enlarging the physical plant. All of this would require increased funds that could only come from the state by increasing enrollment or obtaining special appropriations or from private donations to the foundation.

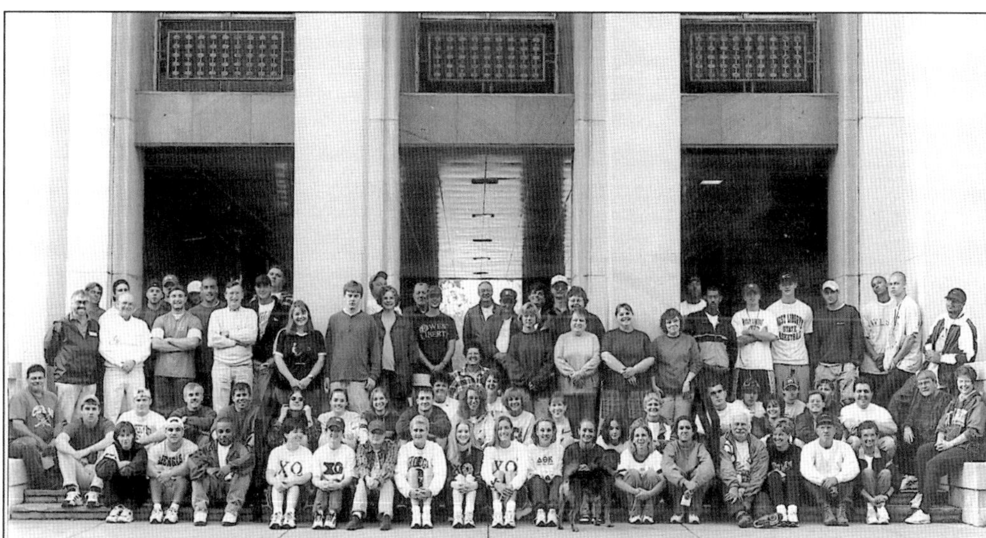

The First Campus Clean-up Volunteers, 1996. President Zaccari called for volunteers from the student body, faculty, and staff to donate a day of their time in order to clean up the campus. Zaccari can be seen in the very center of the back row.

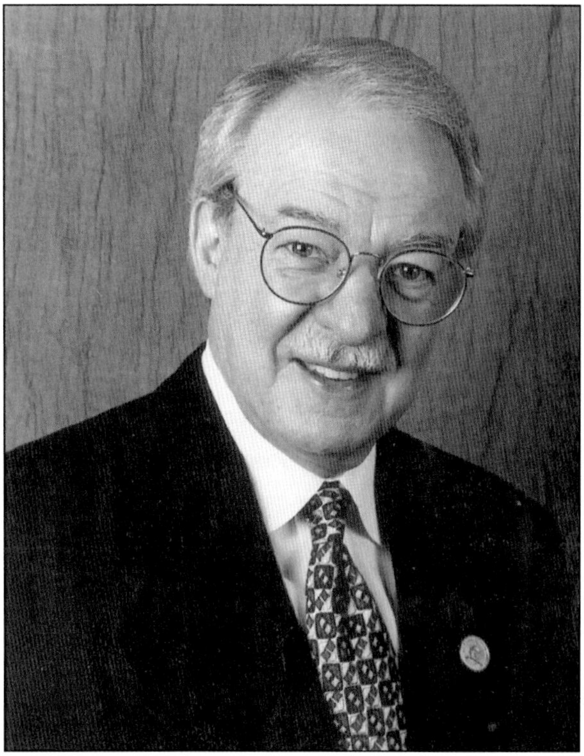

Dr. Ronald M. Zaccari, 1999. While at one time 100 percent of the college's budget was supplied by the state, this was no longer the case. Each year a smaller percentage of the budget came from state funds. President Zaccari strengthened both the development office and the alumni office by adding full-time staff members in hopes of increasing contributions to the college.

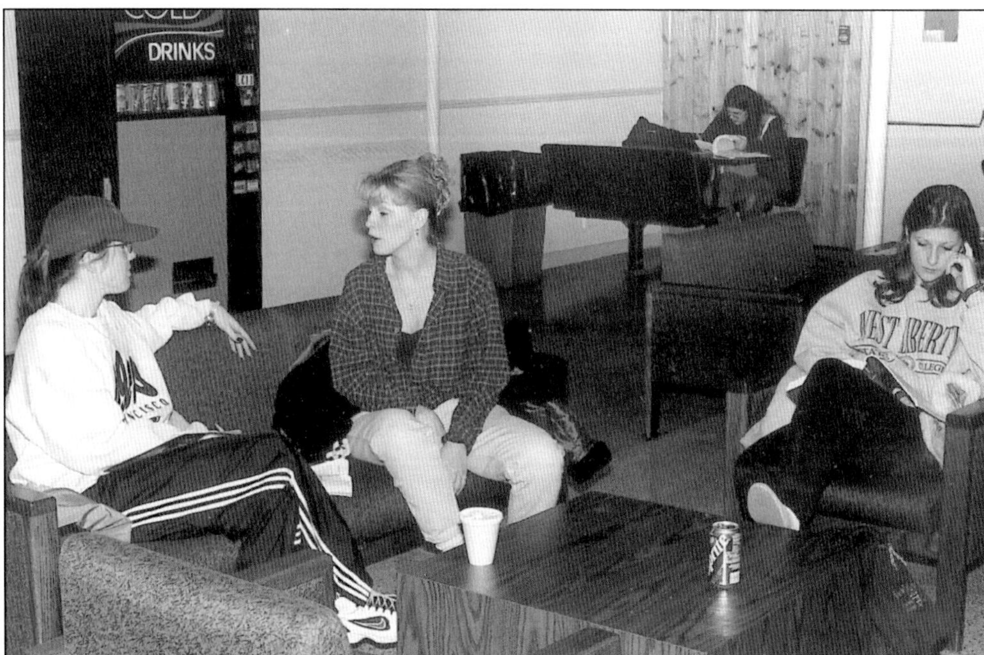

Commuter Lounge, Student Center, 1998. Since state funds were tied to enrollment, ways to make the college more attractive needed to be found. In 1997, a commuter lounge, "Bear Necessities" (a packaged food and sundries store), and a computer room were all added to the Student Center.

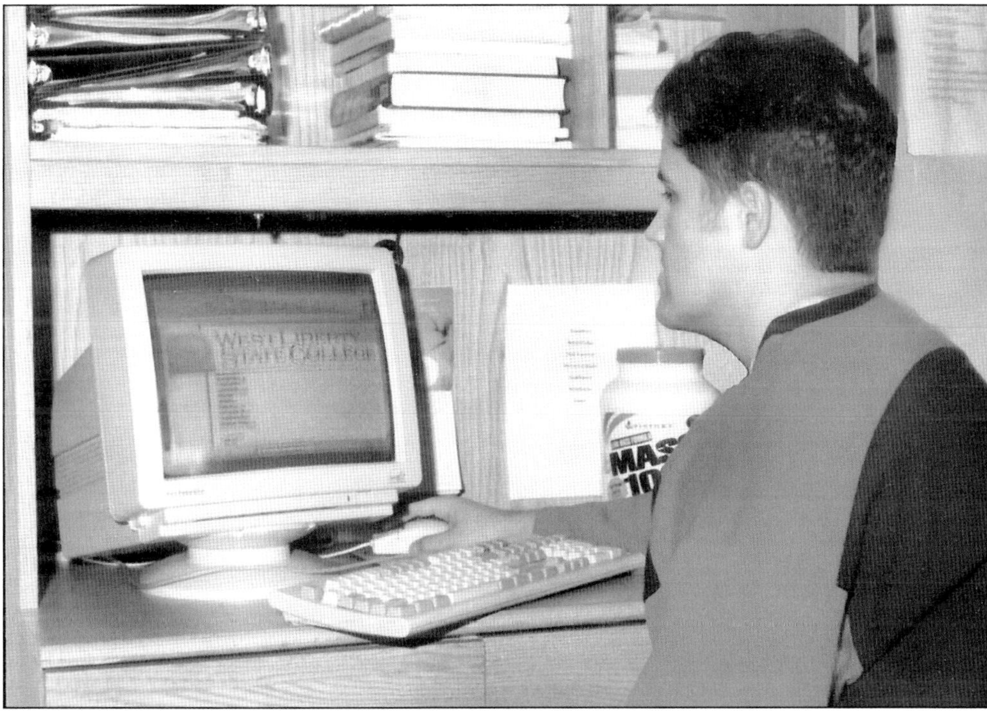

Honors Student in Bonar Hall, 1998. One of the men's dormitories, Bonar Hall, was completely renovated in 1997, so that it could be used as a coed honors dorm. The hall featured fiber optics connections in every room.

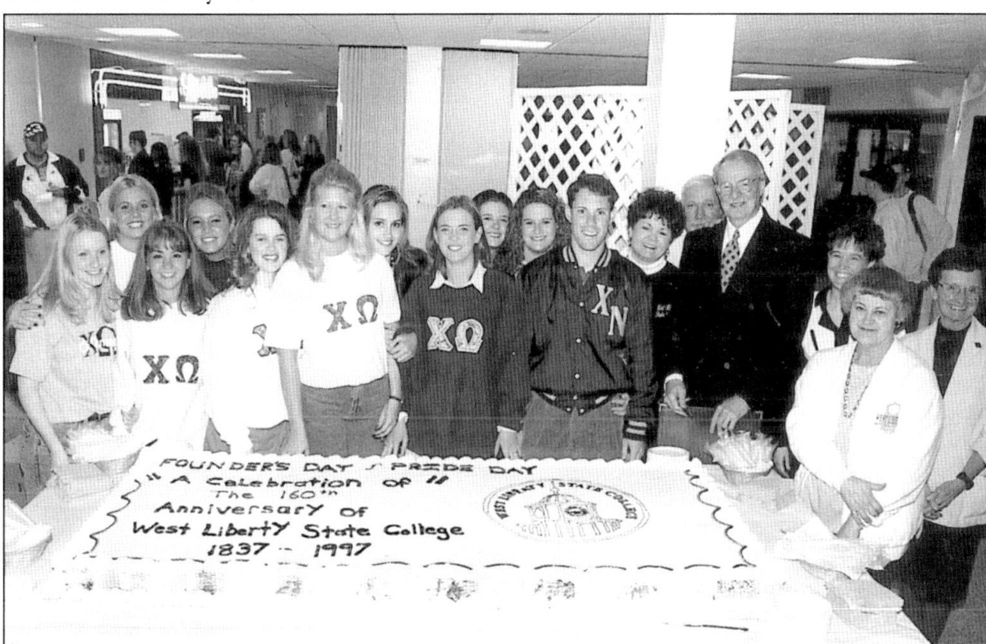

Founders' Day Celebration, 1997. A new tradition, Founders' Day, began in 1996. Students, faculty, administrators, and staff members are gathered around this giant cake in celebration of the 160th birthday of West Liberty State College.

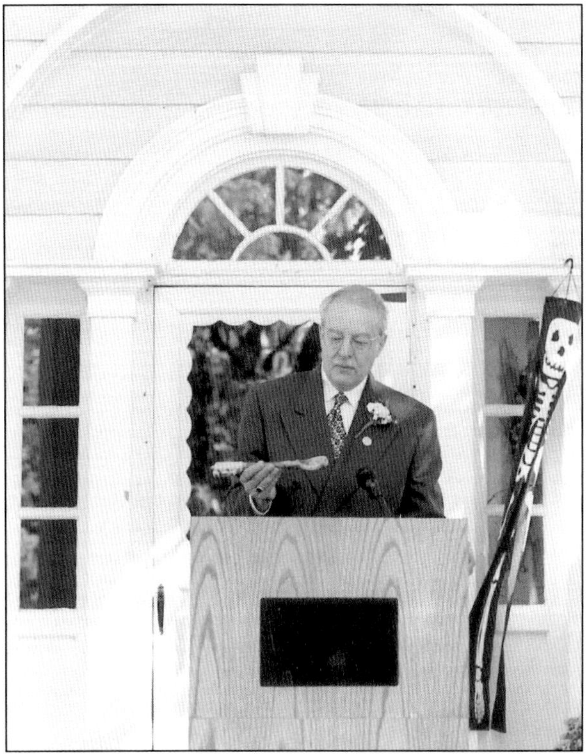

Opening of the Alumni House, 1997. In October 1997, the old president's home, "Liberty Oaks," was converted into an alumni house and bed-and-breakfast. President Zaccari holds the ceremonial key during this official opening.

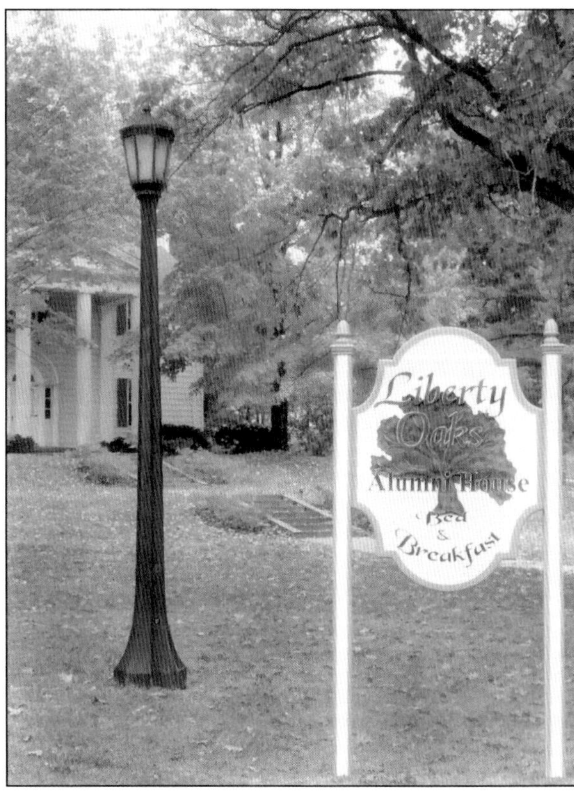

Liberty Oaks, 2001. The purpose of the alumni house was to provide a home for visiting alumni and also to be a laboratory for students in the hotel management program. Extensive remodeling, resulting from generous gifts from alumni and friends, is already underway at the time of this photo.

Cheerleaders, 1997. Cheerleaders' routines were considerably more complex in the 1990s. Often cheerleading squads engaged in competitions on the state and regional level. Cover the bottom of the photo with your hand to see the illusion of the "floating cheerleader."

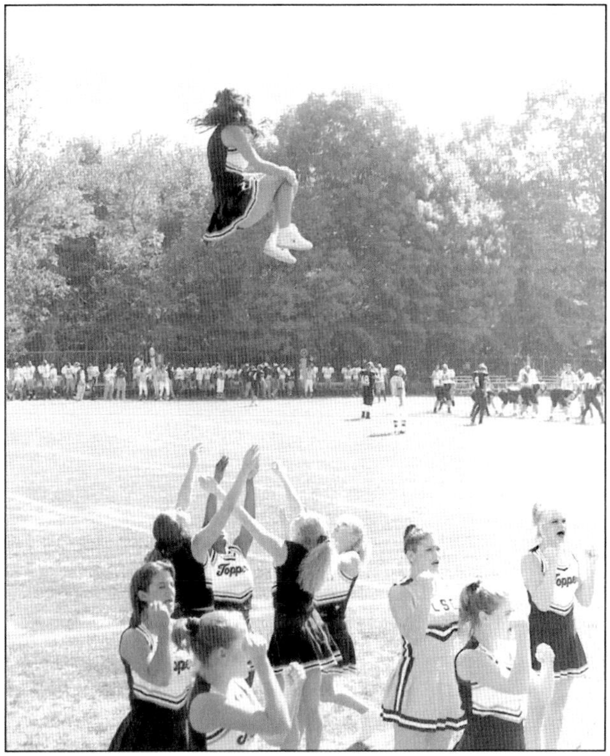

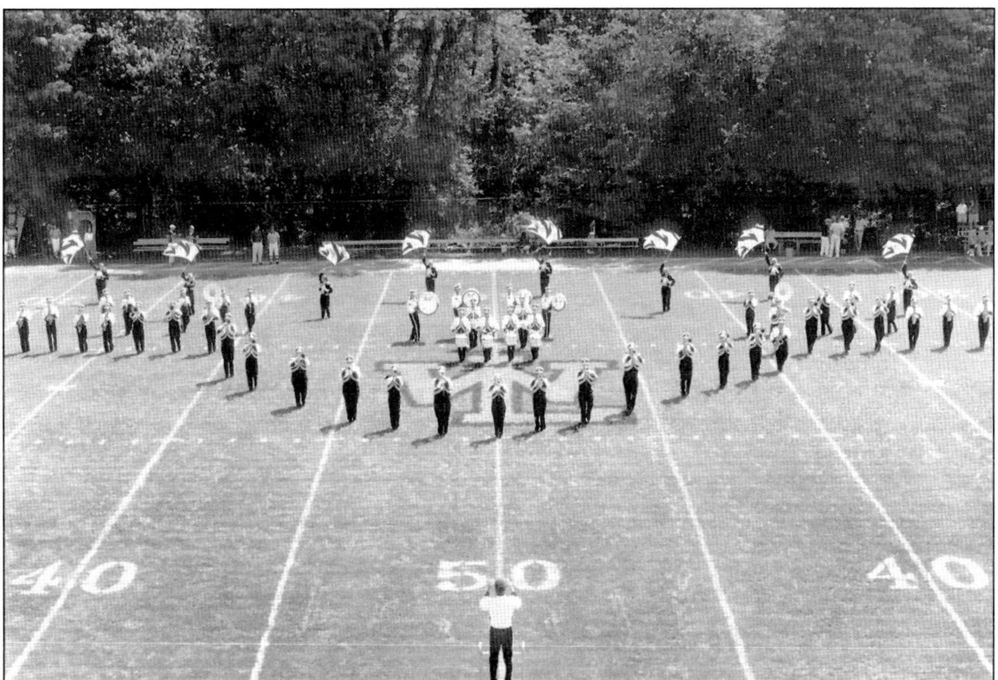

Hilltopper Marching Band, 1998. After a lapse of several years, when lack of interest resulted in the college having no marching band, it was revitalized under the leadership of Professor David Dayton. Also under his leadership, a jazz band and a pep band were established.

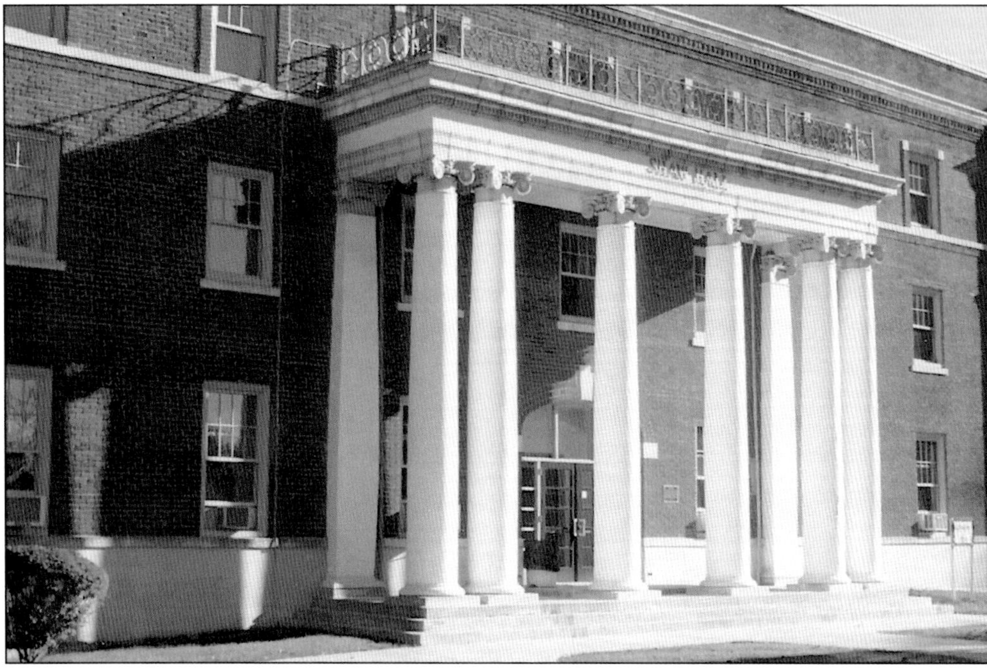

SHAW HALL, 1999. In 1997, the ground floor wings of Shaw Hall were remodeled to provide offices for Campus Safety, Student Services, Development, Alumni, and Publicity and Publications. The following year the center section of the ground floor underwent extensive remodeling to house offices and reception areas for Admissions and Recruitment.

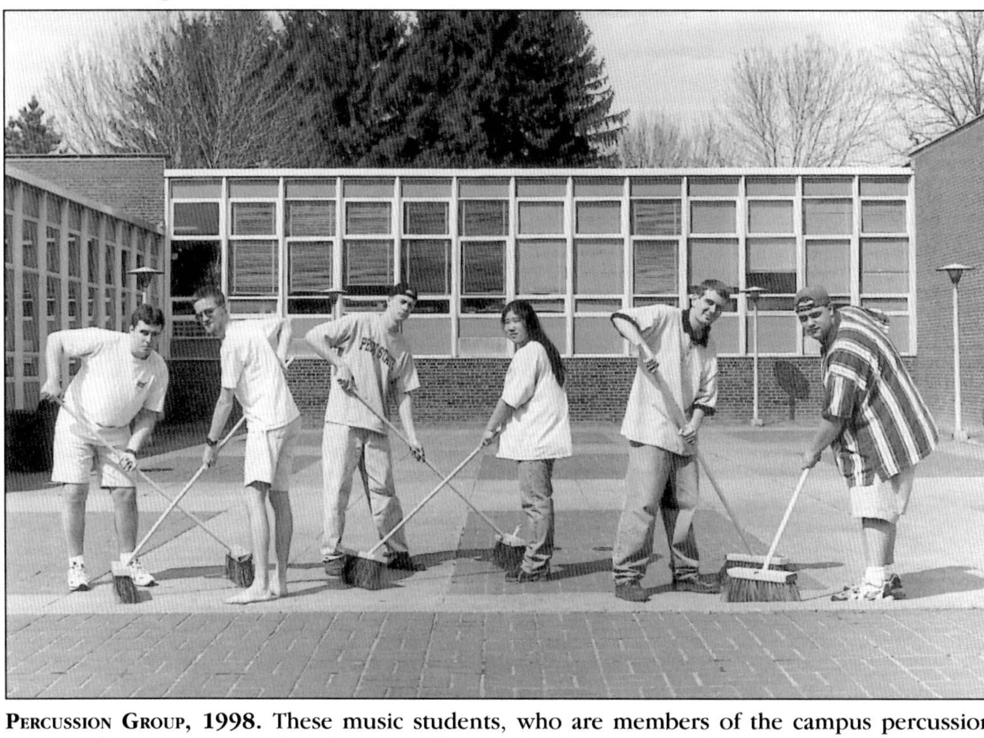

PERCUSSION GROUP, 1998. These music students, who are members of the campus percussion group, rehearse an unusual performance during which brooms are the instruments.

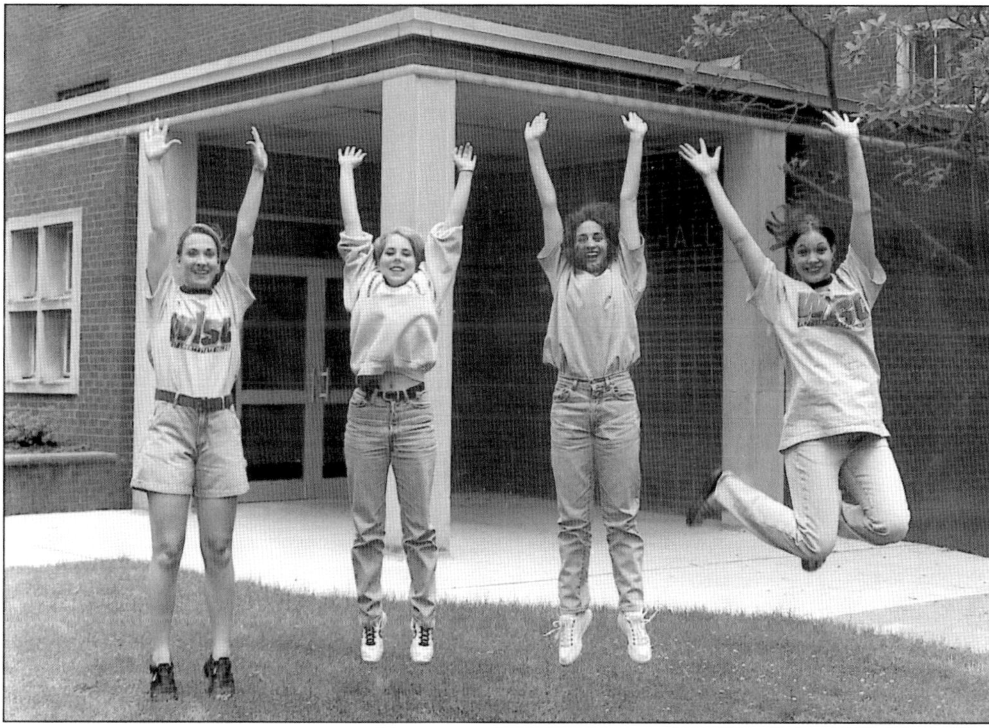

ROGERS HALL RESIDENT ASSISTANTS, 1998. These Rogers Hall resident assistants are jumping for joy at the news of the return of the students to the campus in the fall of 1998.

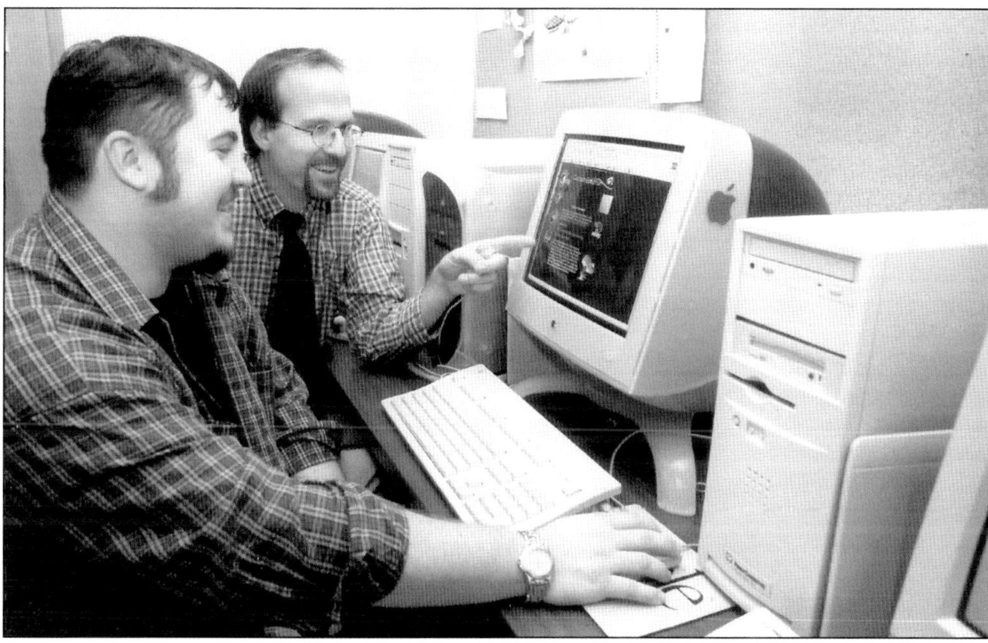

PROFESSOR JAMES HAIZLETT AND A GRAPHIC DESIGN STUDENT, 1999. The existing computer laboratory in the Hall of Fine Arts was expanded and updated in 2001 to meet the needs of students majoring in graphic design. West Liberty's excellent program provides all of the modern tools and training necessary for today's graphic design graduates.

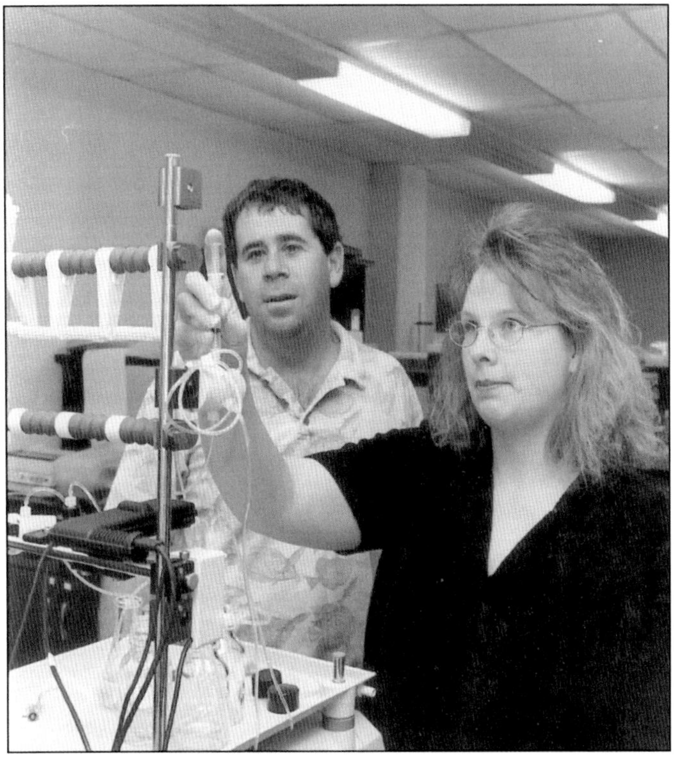

Professor Robert Kreisberg and the First Biotechnology Student, 1999. The biotechnology program is another outstanding example of the many career-oriented programs offered by the college in the 21st century. West Liberty's laboratories contain the up-to-date equipment essential in the growing field of biotechnology research.

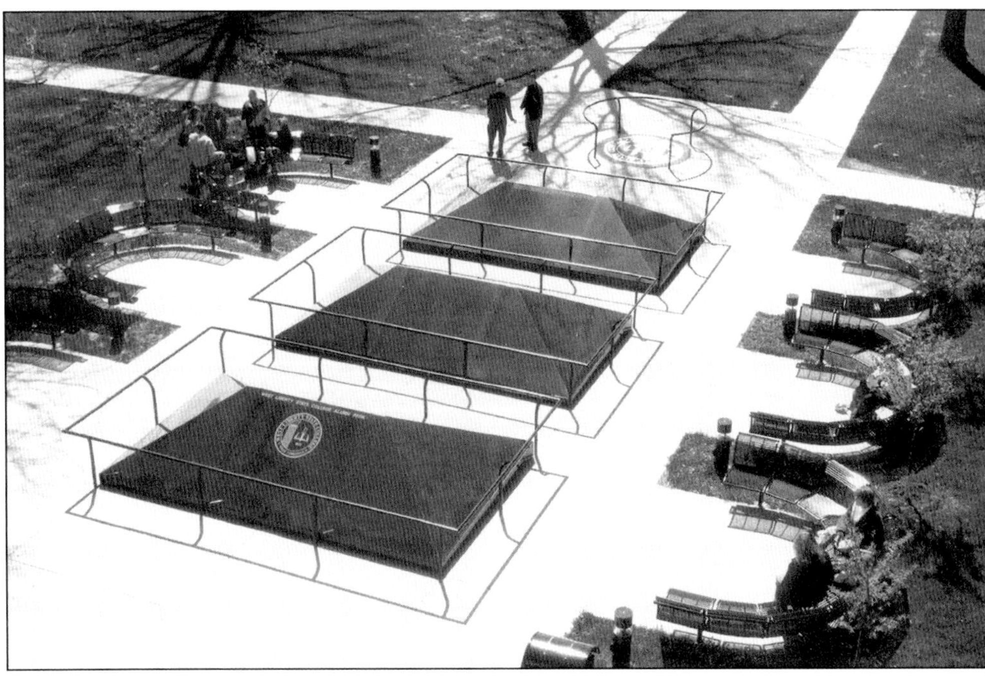

Alumni Park, 1999. Gary Inclan, an active alumnus from the Florida chapter, originated the idea of an alumni park. The original plan called for a brick wall and paving with the names of alumni engraved on the bricks. President Zaccari created a more original pyramid design that was adopted by the Alumni Association. Ground was broken for the park in June 1997.

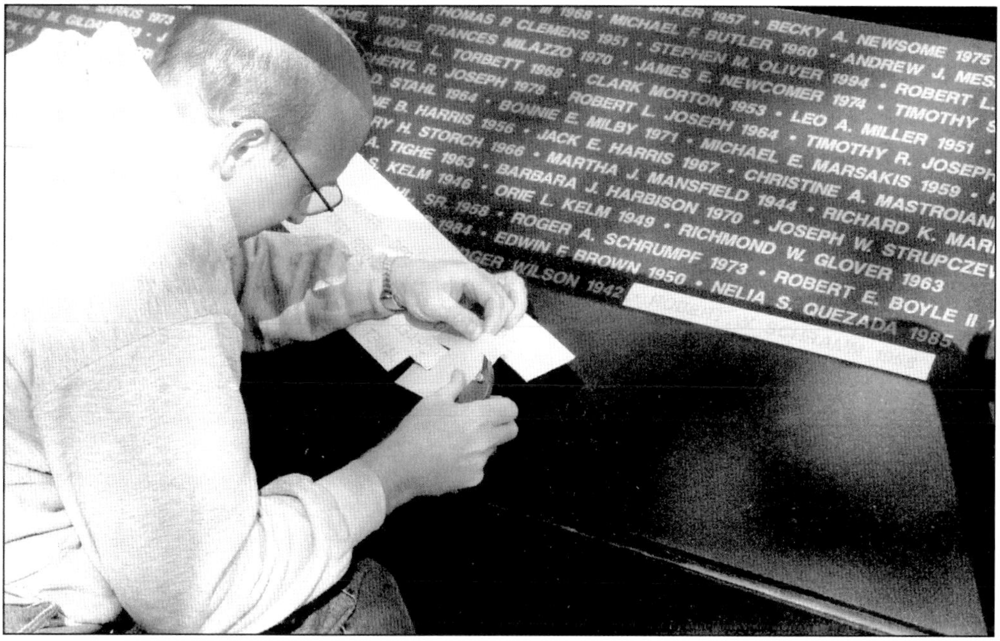

Etching Names on the Pyramids in Alumni Park, 1998. Alumni and friends of the college who contributed to the Alumni Scholarship Fund had their names etched on one of the pyramids. When the park was completed in 1999, it became an attractive gathering place for students, as intended.

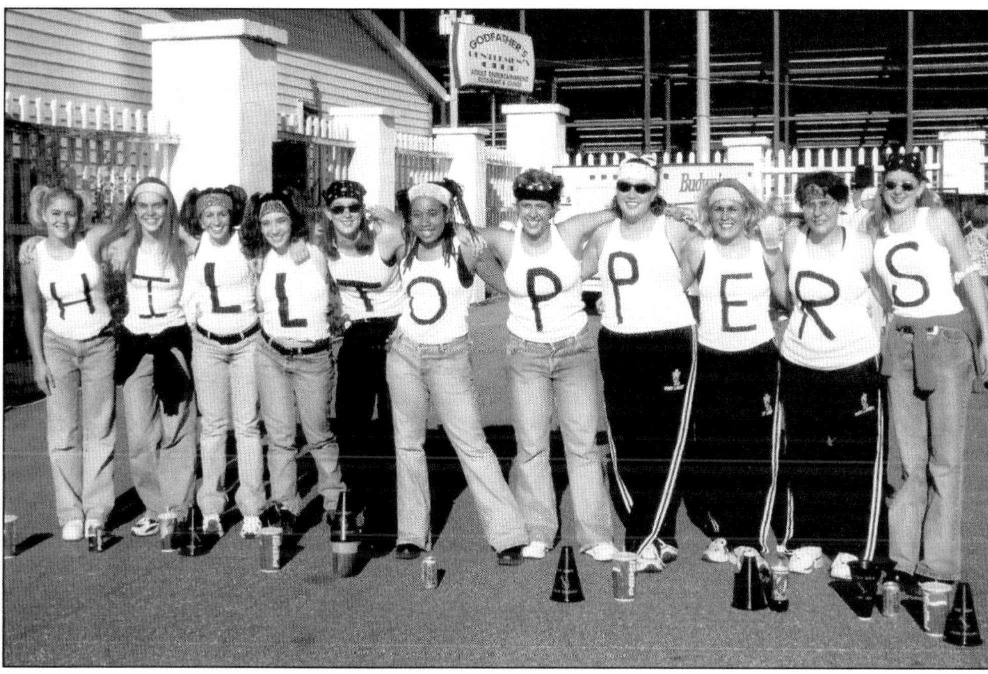

Coeds at the Alumni Bowl, 1999. John Westenhaver, president of the Ohio Valley Chapter of the Alumni Association, developed a plan to bring college football to the Wheeling area in the form of a bowl-type atmosphere. The annual Alumni Bowl has proven to be very popular and raises money for the athletic and alumni scholarship funds.

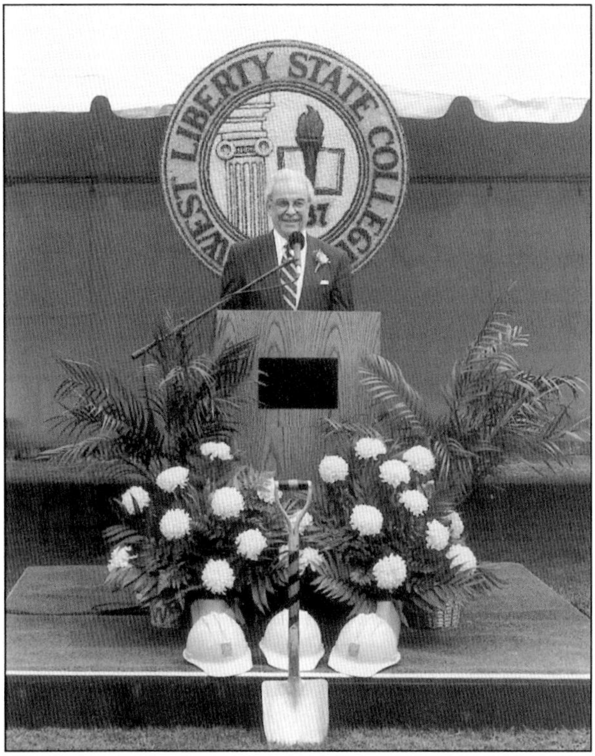

Gov. Cecil Underwood at the Groundbreaking of the ASRC, 1998. Funds were obtained from the state to construct a replacement for the Bartell Field House. A multipurpose building was designed and named the Academic, Sports, and Recreation Complex (ASRC). The building would connect Blatnik Hall and what remained of Bartell Hall.

ASRC Groundbreaking, 1998. From left to right are Chancellor Clifford Trump, Governor Underwood, President Zaccari, and Director of Athletics James Watson. These groundbreakers are trying to catch up to Governor Underwood who is making the dirt fly in an effort to get the new building underway.

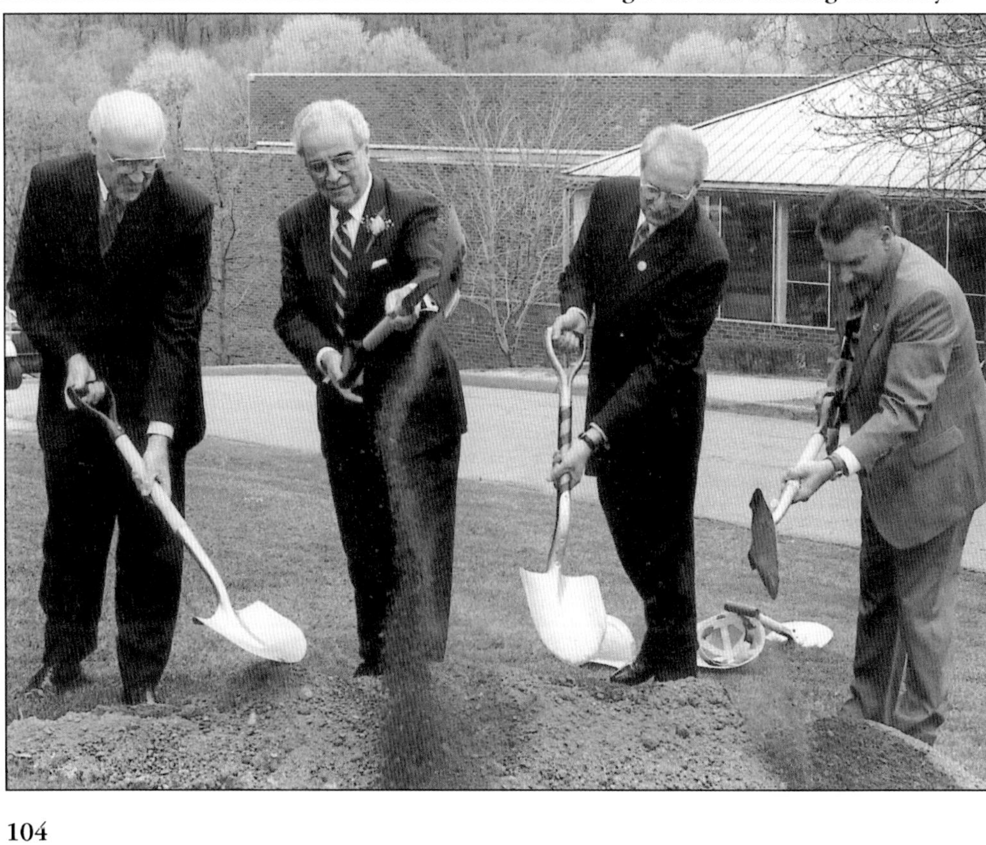

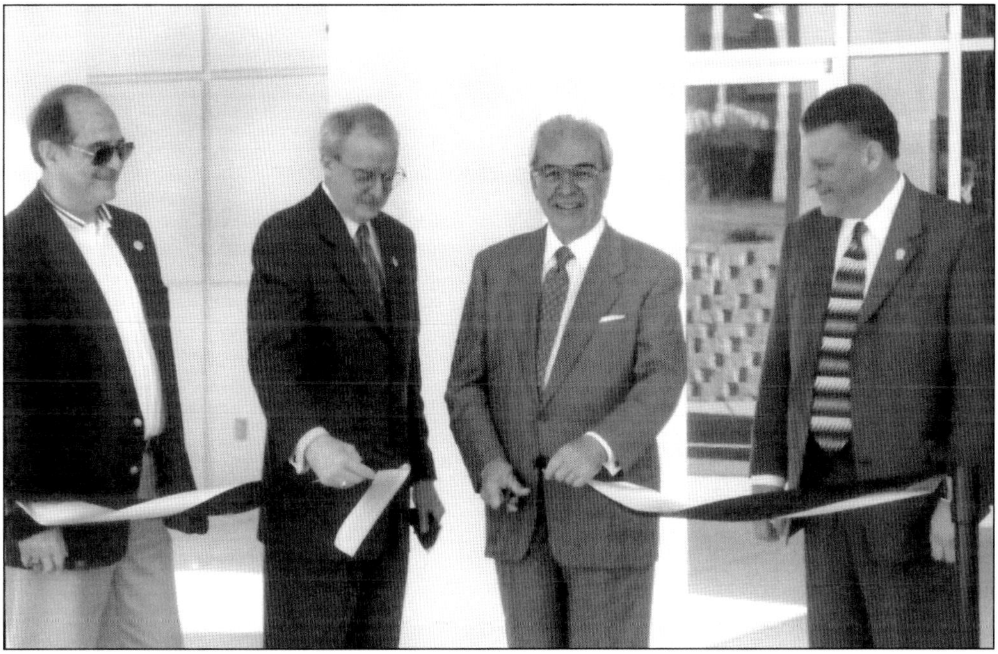

Ribbon Cutting for the ASRC, 2000. Governor Underwood returned to the campus in October 2000 for a ribbon-cutting ceremony for the opening of the new building. Pictured, from left to right, are Mr. Richard Edge, president of the Alumni Association; President Zaccari; Governor Underwood; and Professor James Watson, director of athletics.

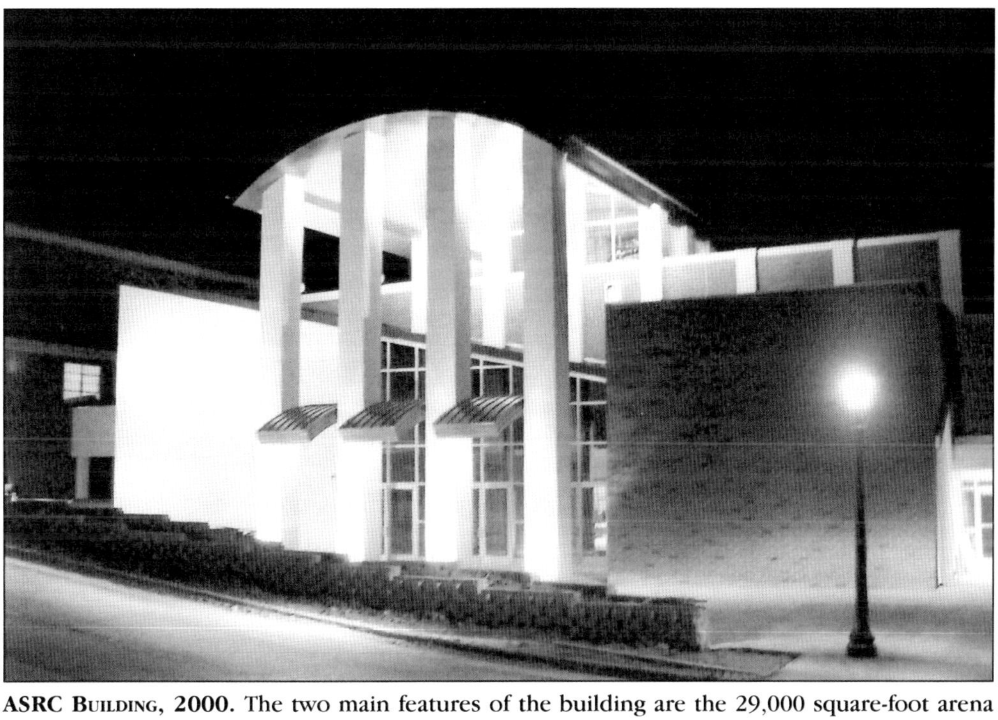

ASRC Building, 2000. The two main features of the building are the 29,000 square-foot arena and the R. Emmett Boyle conference room, which contains an original sculpture by Colorado artist Roy Blackwood.

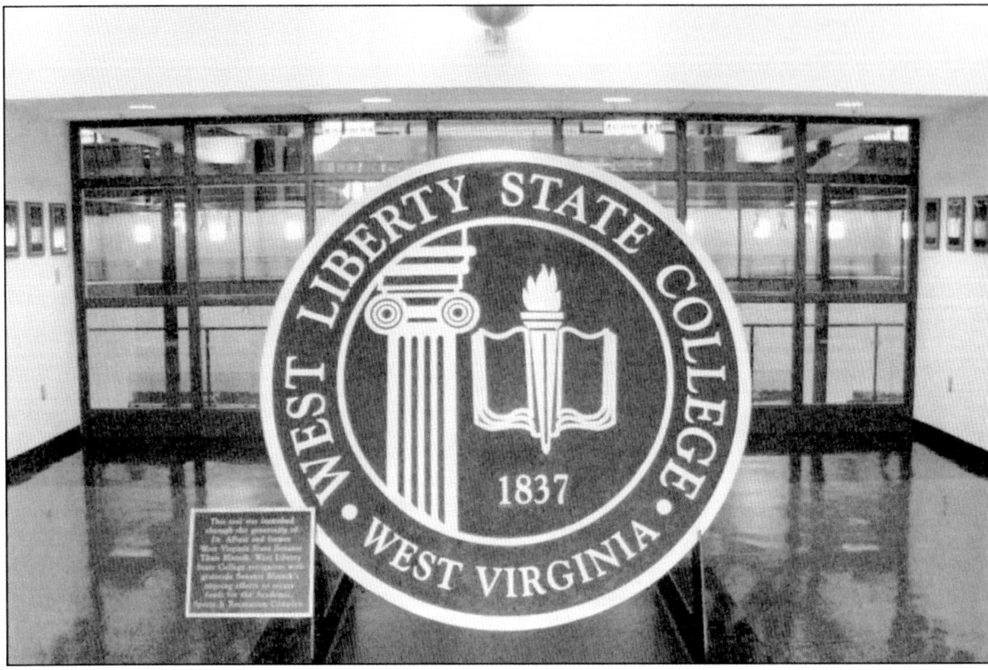

BRONZE SEAL, 2000. Former West Virginia senator Thais Blatnik and her husband, Professor Emeritus Albert Blatnik, donated this 1,200-pound bronze college seal as a centerpiece for the ASRC lobby. Senator Blatnik was instrumental in obtaining state funds for the construction of the ASRC building. Dr. and Mrs. Blatnik are both graduates of West Liberty State College.

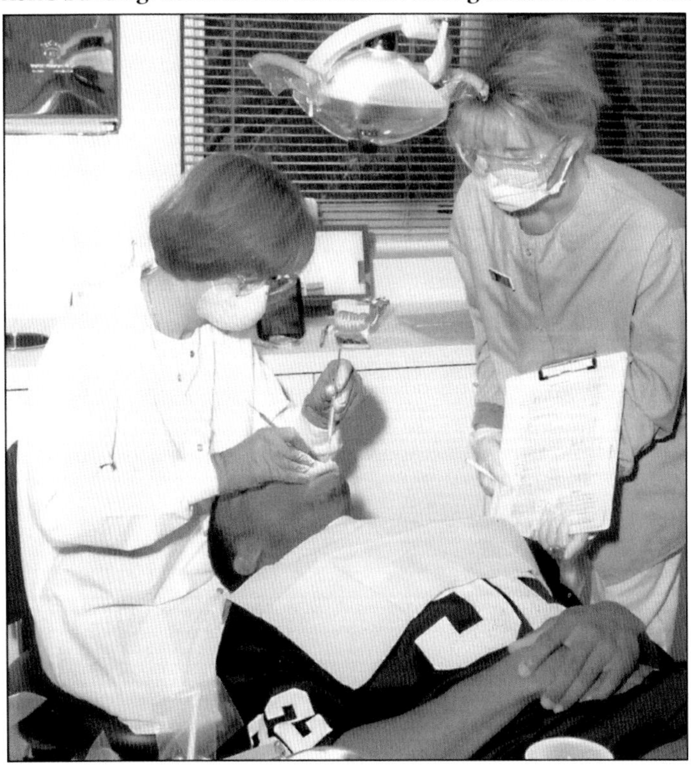

DENTAL HYGIENE CLINIC, 2000. In August 2000, the third major remodeling and upgrade of the Dental Hygiene Clinic was completed. Its purpose was to provide current technology for instruction and improved patient care. Previous remodelings had occurred in 1956 and 1980.

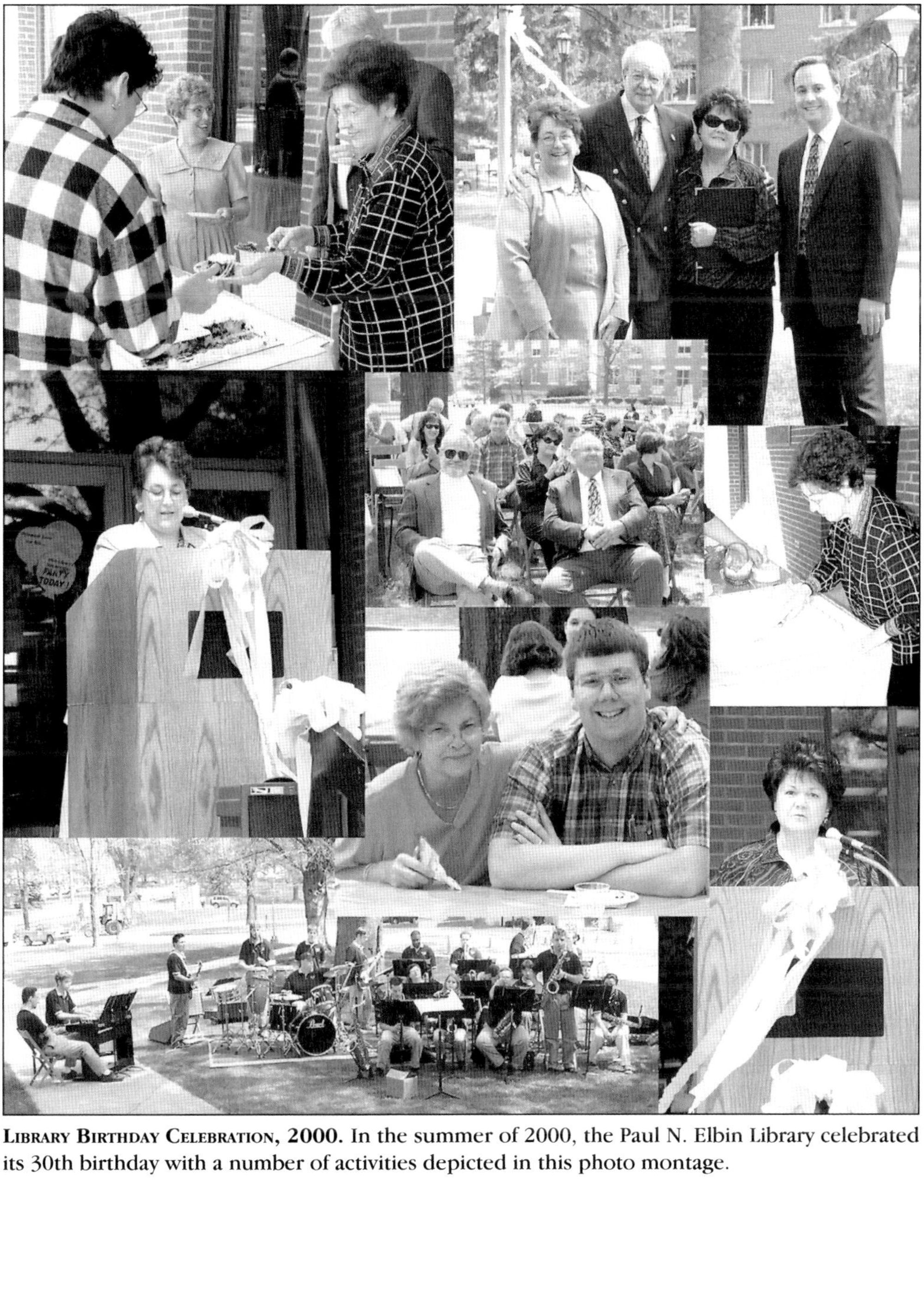

Library Birthday Celebration, 2000. In the summer of 2000, the Paul N. Elbin Library celebrated its 30th birthday with a number of activities depicted in this photo montage.

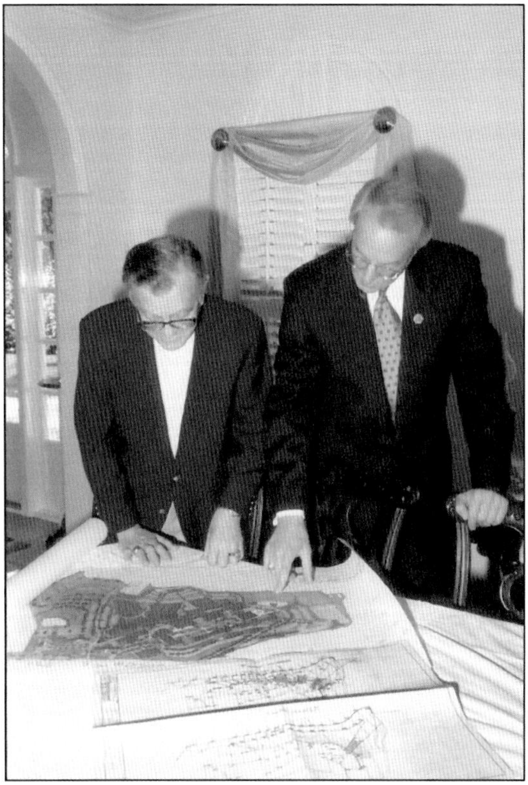

RUDY MUMLEY AND PRESIDENT ZACCARI, 1999. In 1999, Mr. Rudy Mumley, a 1950 graduate of West Liberty State College, donated funds that were used to construct a park and outdoor performance area across from the new ASRC building. Mr. Mumley and President Zaccari are seen here conferring over plans for this facility.

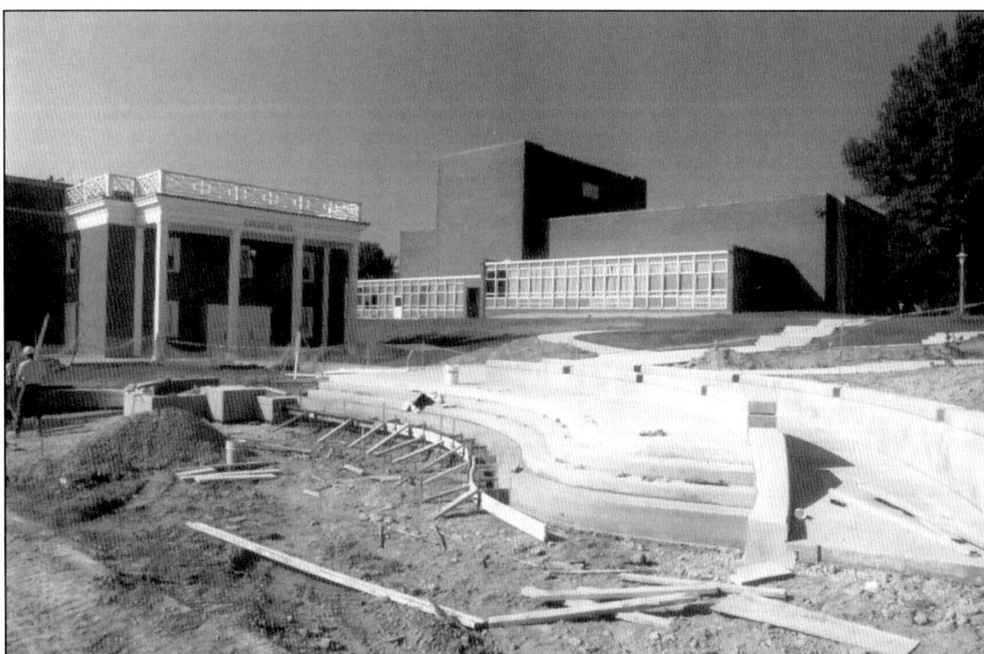

MUMLEY PARK UNDER CONSTRUCTION, 2000. Rudy Mumley was the founder and first president of the West Liberty State College "Hilltopper Club." He was inducted into the college Athletic Hall of Fame in 1985. The park, which bears his name, was dedicated on October 14, 2000.

Six

TRADITIONS

Every school has its traditions, and a college as old as West Liberty has acquired many traditions over the years. The origins of some of these are lost in time. For example, we know from the ribbons on diplomas from the 19th century that the school colors were gold and black but we do not know how these colors were chosen. However, during World War II, gold-colored materials could not be obtained so the college began using orange and black. This continued for about 25 years until the mid-1960s when President Elbin brought the matter to the attention of the students and alumni. Upon their recommendation the college reverted to the original gold and black colors that are used today. Many of West Liberty's traditions are relatively new, as traditions go. One such example follows below.

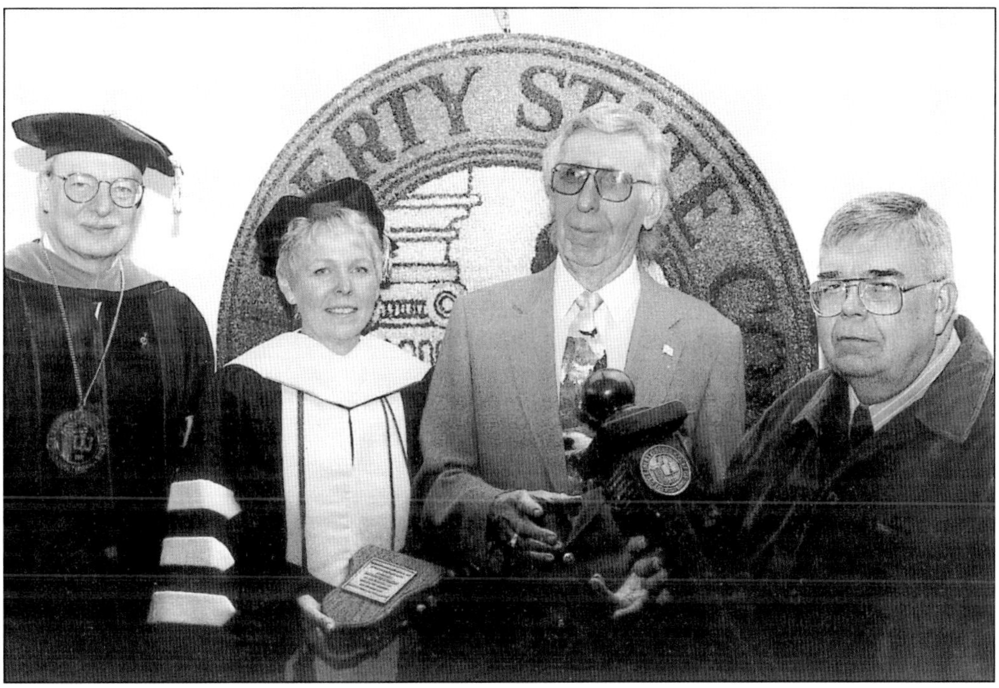

THE MACE. In 1996, the Faculty Senate wished to obtain an official mace for the college to be used at graduation ceremonies. Professor McCorkle agreed to donate the funds necessary to have a mace constructed. It was presented to the college in honor of Dr. Talley, a former academic dean and longtime friend of Professor McCorkle. Pictured here, from left to right, are President Zaccari, Professor Kay Clawson, Dr. Lawerence H. Talley, and Professor William E. McCorkle Jr.

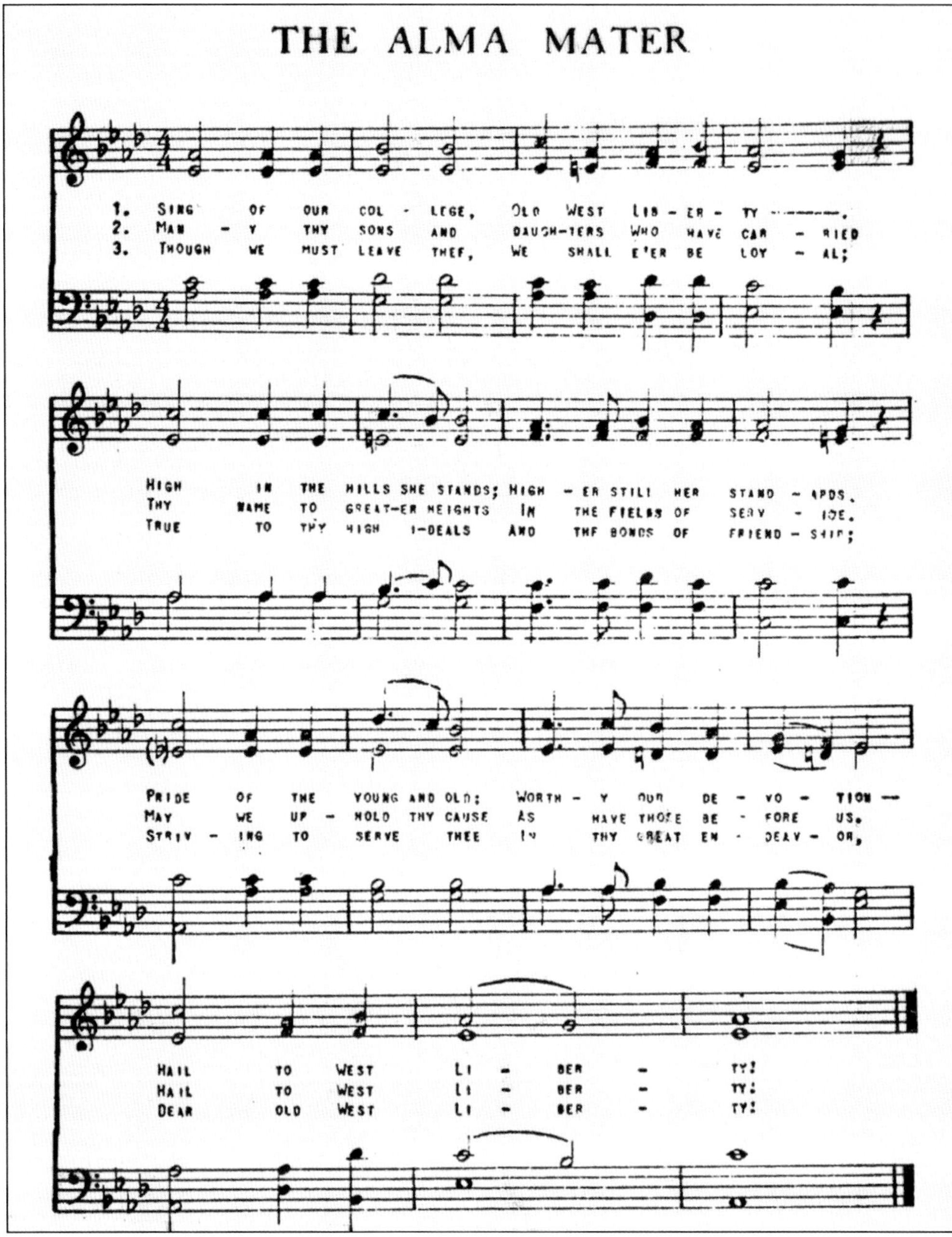

The Alma Mater. The college's alma mater was created by Dr. and Mrs. Paul N. Elbin. They took a European hymn entitled "Father in Heaven," written by Friedrich Flemming, and wrote lyrics for it that expressed their feelings for the college and, hopefully, those of the students. The song was officially accepted in 1935. Prior to that time there was no known alma mater.

Hilltopper's Fight Song

Words and music by Robert W. Schramm '5

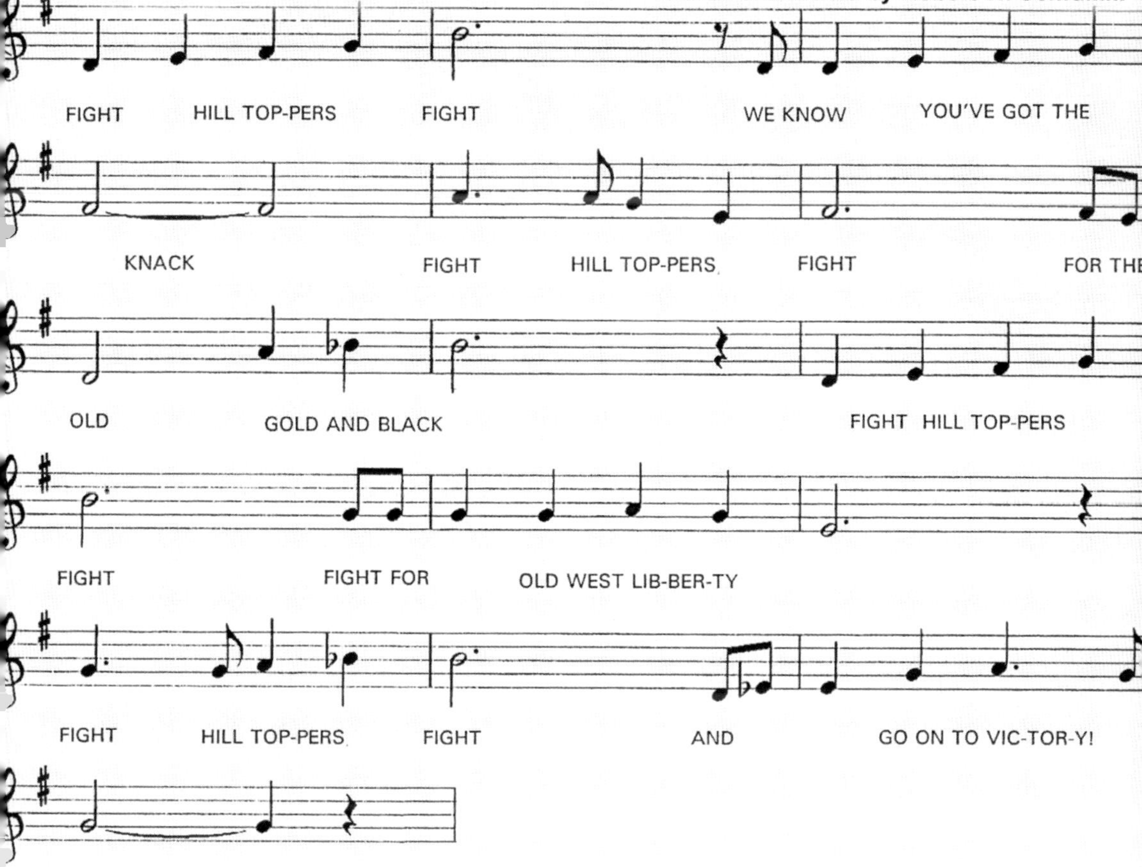

The Hilltoppers Fight Song. The words and music to the fight song were written by Professor Robert W. Schramm, WLSC Class of 1957. An original melody, it was presented to the students and alumni in 1994 and given official approval by the student government and alumni association in the same year. Prior to that time there was no official fight song. Professor Schramm has said he was tired of hearing the college band play "On Wisconsin" and thought it was time for the college to have its own unique fight song.

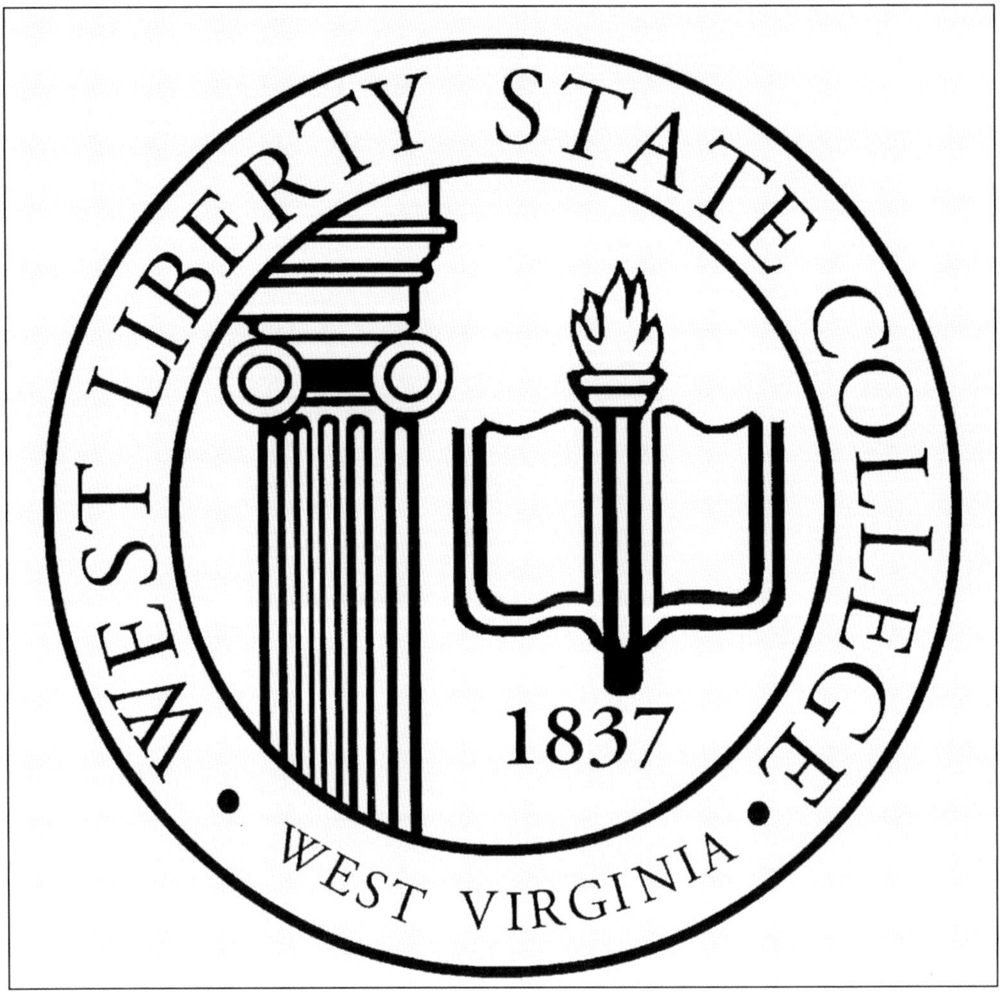

The College Seal. The college seal was designed in 1965 by Roy Everson, an art and speech major, for an assignment in a class taught by Professor William T. Martin. The previous seal was that of the State of West Virginia with "State of West Virginia" replaced by "West Liberty State College." The new seal was officially approved for use that same year. The ionic column symbolizes classic civilization, and the book is a symbol of knowledge. The torch is a symbol of the quest for learning, and 1837 is the year the college was founded.

The Logo. In the last 20 years the college has had several logos. The current logo was created by Patty Byrd, the college graphic designer, and was based on designs suggested by Dr. Zaccari. The logo is a depiction of the clock/carillon tower on the Student Center.

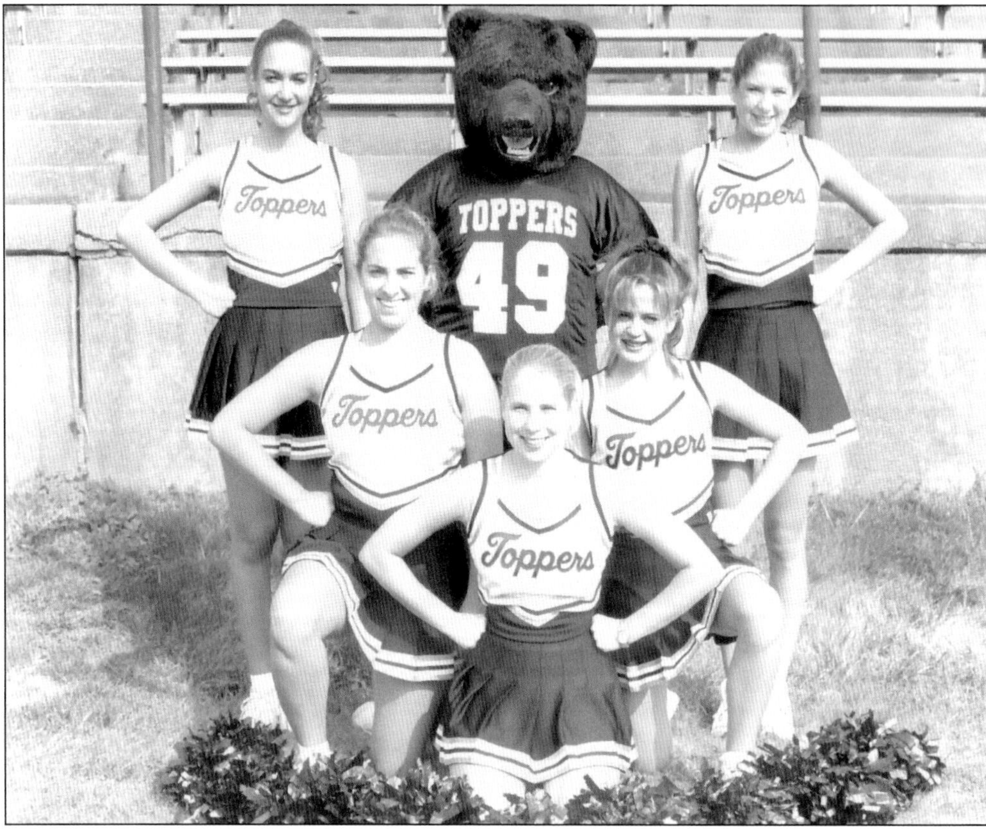

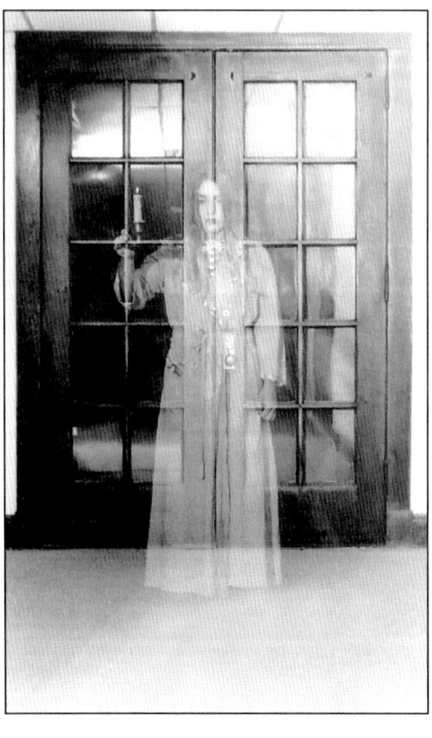

The Mascot. The college mascot was chosen by popular vote of the student body from a list of proposed mascots in a 1963 *Trumpet* poll. A black bear, the official animal of West Virginia, won and was named "Topper" after, of course, the "Hilltoppers." The very first appearance of Topper at a football game was as a real bear cub. Topper's image is embossed into the cover of the 1963 yearbook, *The Winding Road.*

The Ghosts. Beginning in the 1930s and recurring at intervals as long as Shaw Hall was a women's dorm there were reports of a ghost who haunted the third-floor hallway and played harmless tricks on the students. The spirit, named "Helen" (origin unknown), was described as having long hair, dressed in a white nightgown, and carrying a candle. This photograph was made by the author with the assistance of his daughter Adriane. Once the theater in the Hall of Fine Arts was completed, rumors of a ghost who inhabited the catwalk were reported also. There is no evidence that anyone died in Shaw Hall or the Kelly Theater.

CAMPAIGNING FOR HOMECOMING QUEEN. For the last 50 years, at least, campaigning for homecoming queen has begun with decorating the dormitories with signs and handing out candy outside the polling places on election day.

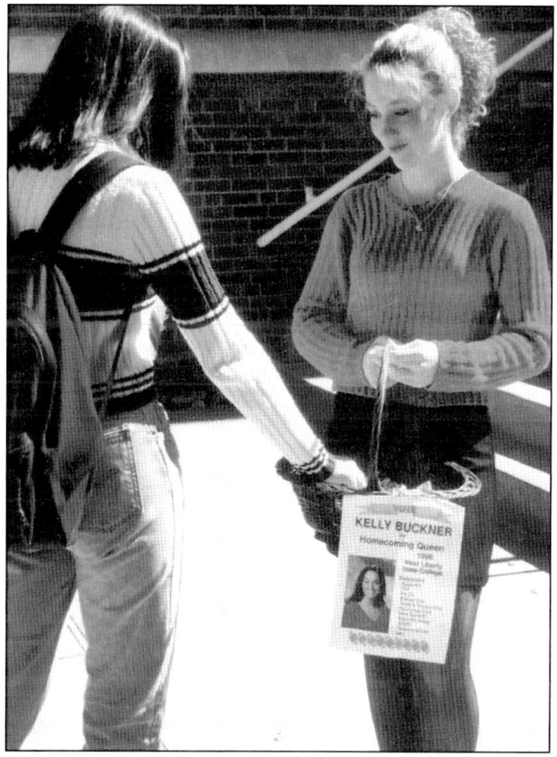

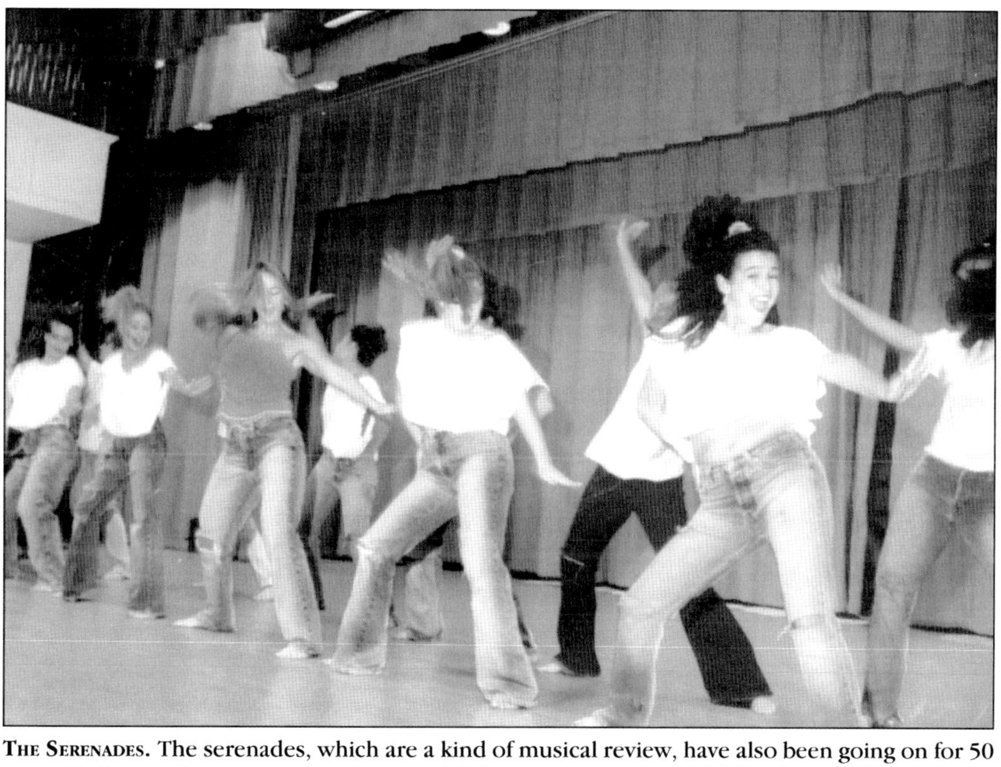

THE SERENADES. The serenades, which are a kind of musical review, have also been going on for 50 years. Each year they seem to grow more elaborate, more exciting, and louder.

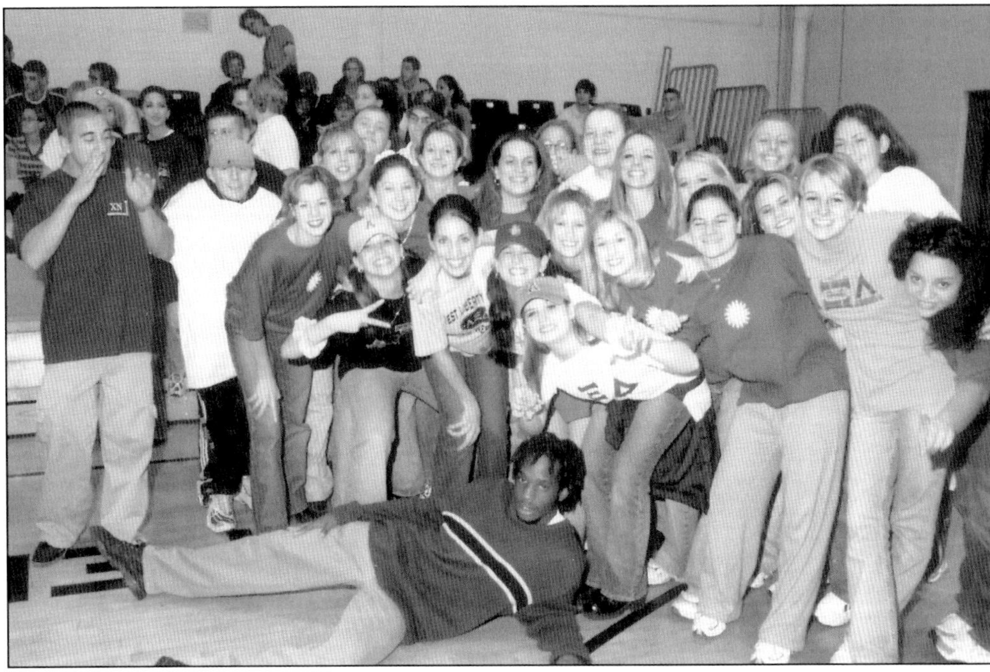

The Pep Rally. The pep rally is a relative newcomer to homecoming, but it is even louder, if that's possible, than the serenades. The important thing is that everyone has a great time as can be seen in this photo.

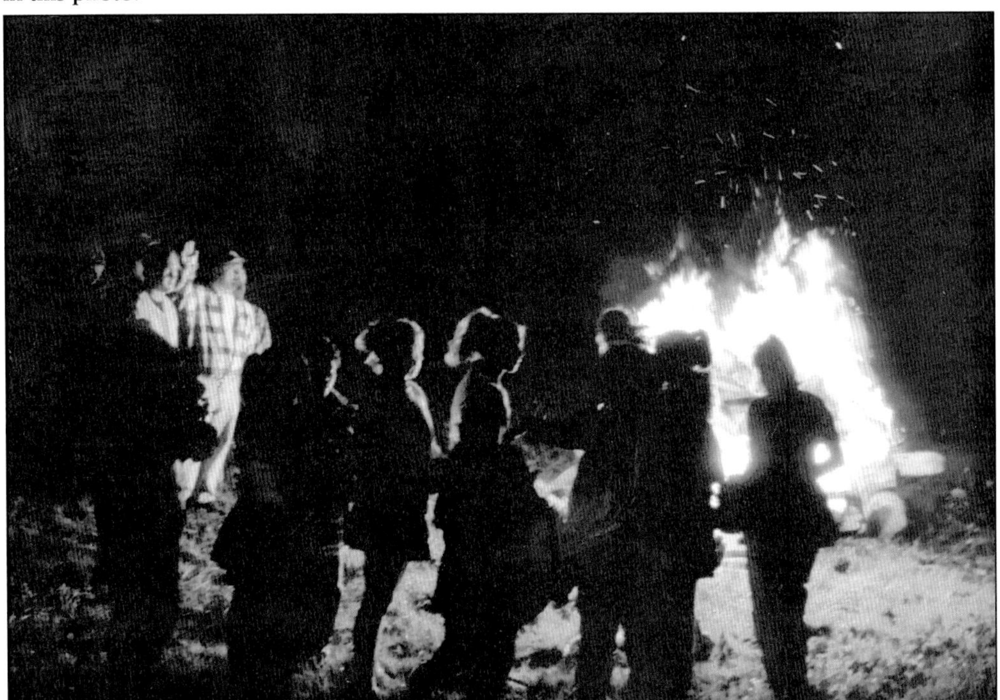

The Bonfire. No doubt there were pep rallies and bonfires sometime in the past history of the college. The current tradition of a homecoming bonfire began in 1999.

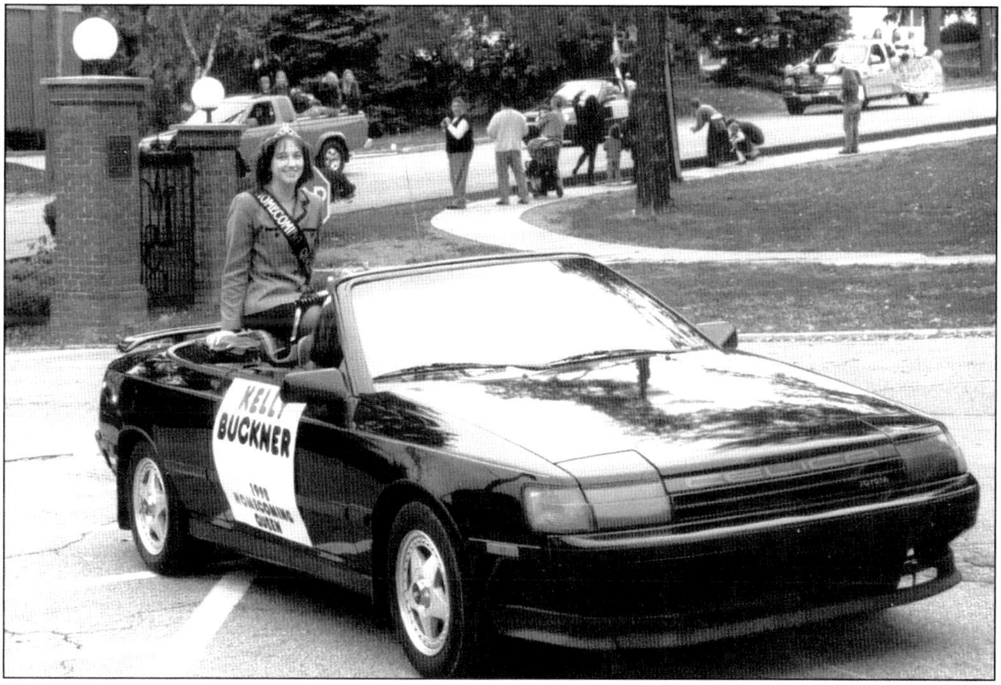

The Homecoming Parade. It is traditional for homecoming queen candidates and last year's queen to ride in convertibles. The parade consists of the marching band followed by the college president, the student government president, the homecoming queen candidates, and floats constructed by various student organizations. The West Liberty Volunteer Fire Department trucks bring up the rear.

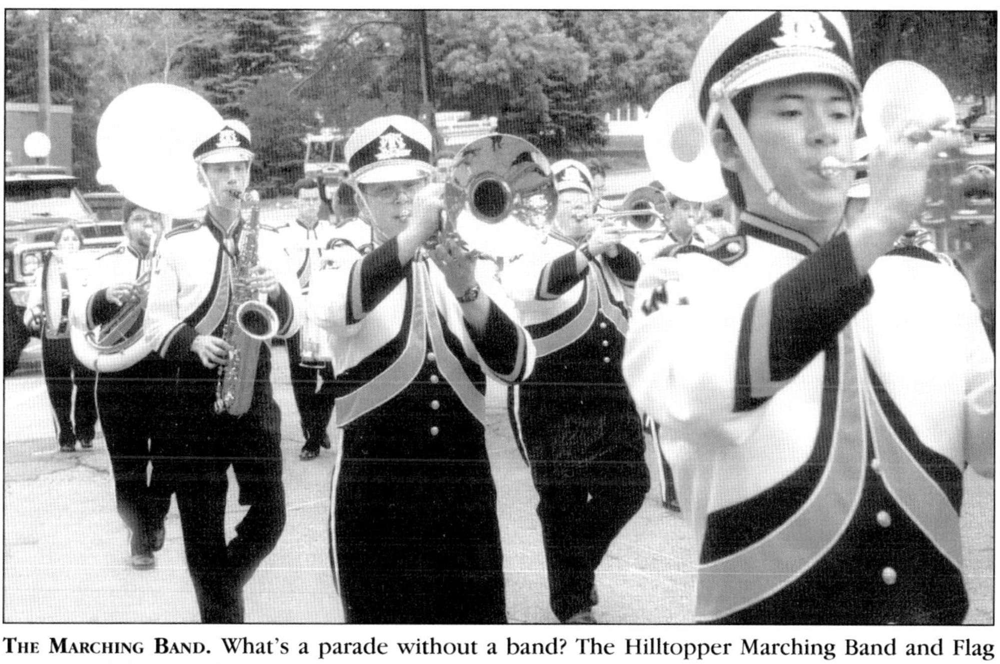

The Marching Band. What's a parade without a band? The Hilltopper Marching Band and Flag Corps lead the parade through the town and across the campus to Russek Field and the tailgate area where the alumni tent is located.

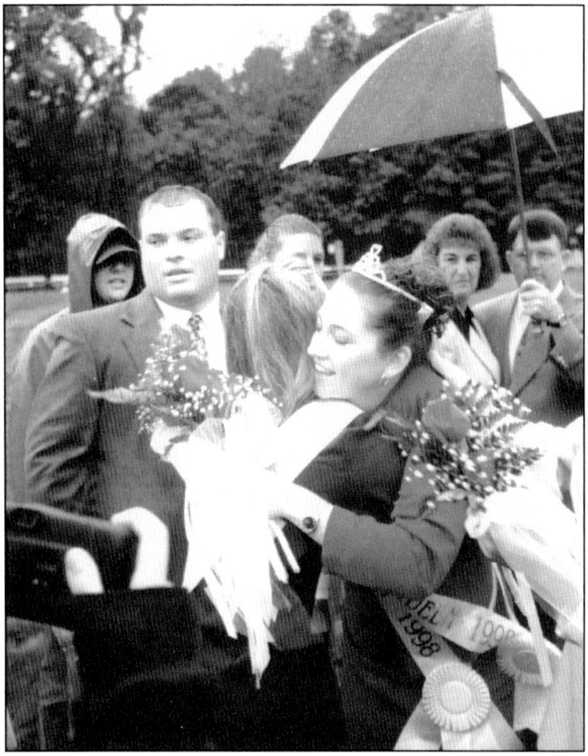

The 1998 Homecoming Queen. The new homecoming queen is crowned on the field at halftime by the previous year's queen in a ceremony in which all the candidates breathlessly await the announcement of the winner.

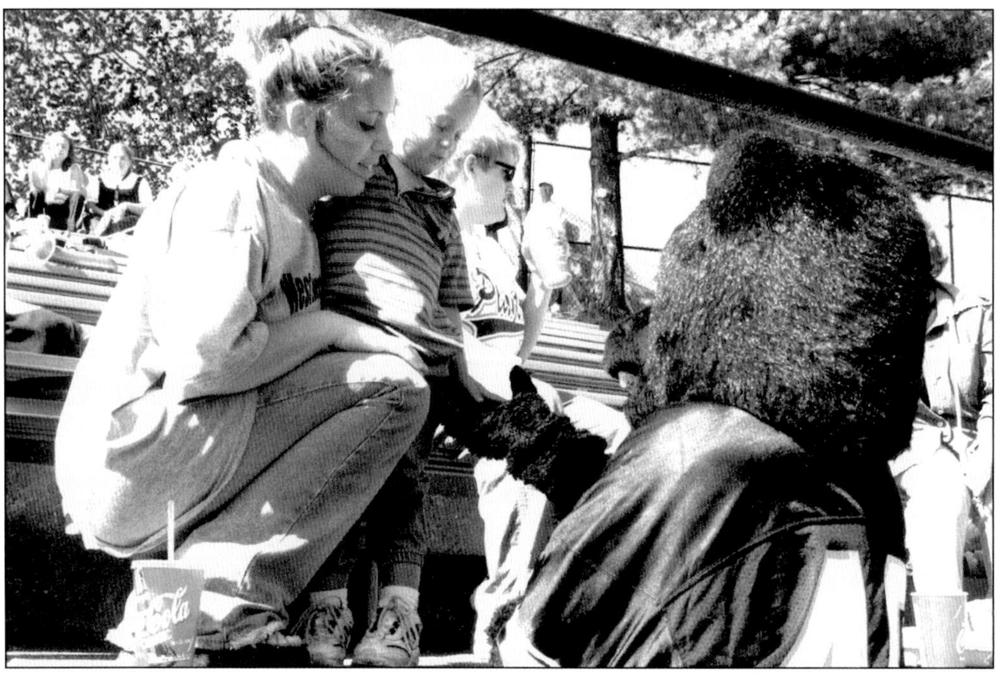

Topper and Friend. The homecoming dance and parties follow the game. Homecoming has grown increasingly important in the years since the alumni association was expanded as a result of the work done by President Campbell. Homecoming has grown from a one-day event to a series of events throughout the week.

Seven

ALUMNI WALL OF HONOR

In 1990, the West Liberty State College Alumni Association Board of Directors, at the suggestion of Professor Robert W. Schramm, who was a member of the board at that time, initiated a project that was designed to demonstrate to current students, visitors, and friends that the college has had some very distinguished graduates. The project, known as the "Alumni Wall of Honor," became a dramatic way for the college to honor and display pride in its accomplished alumni. The Wall of Honor is located in the Student Center in an area known as the Alumni Lounge. Photographs of the honorees are displayed on the wall of this room. A computerized kiosk featuring the photographs of each of the inductees and their biographies is also part of the display. New members of the Alumni Wall of Honor are added each year during homecoming weekend.

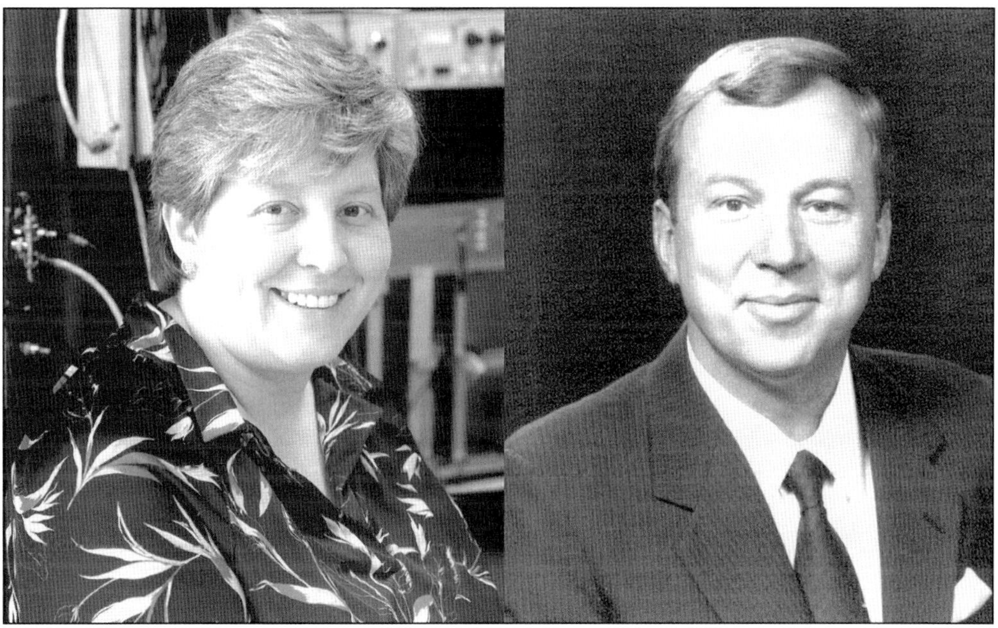

1990 INDUCTEES DR. THERESA A. NAGY ('68) AND PETER M. SONTAG ('69). As a visiting senior scientist at NASA, Dr. Nagy was manager for the Explorer class of satellites, the Astrophysics Theory Program, the Space Infrared Telescope Facility, the Advanced Technology Astrophysics Detector Program, and the NASA-wide super and scientific computing program. Mr. Sontag is chairman and CEO of USTravel Systems, Inc. This organization, which he created, is one of the largest travel companies in the world.

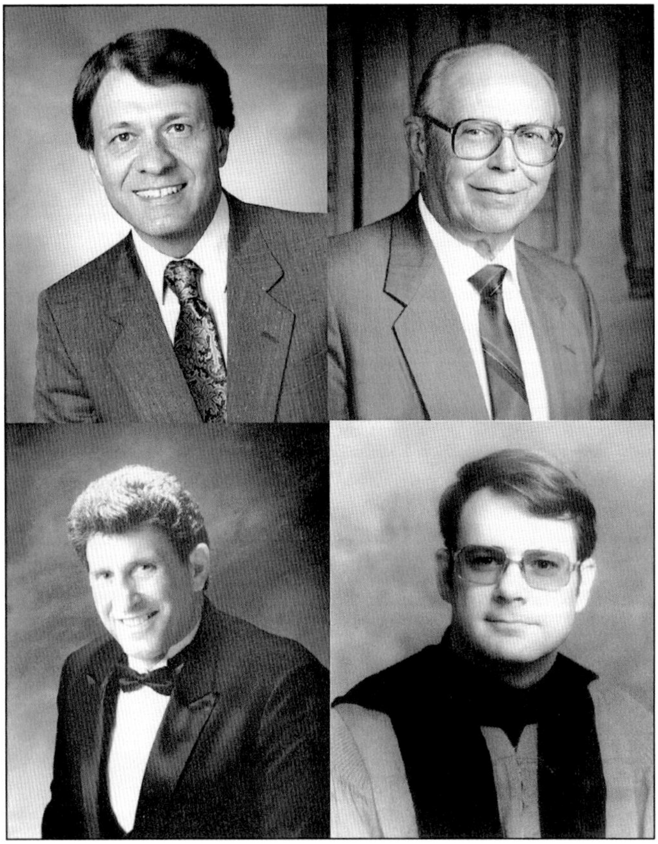

1991 Inductees. Pictured here, clockwise from the upper left, are Dr. Robert L. Joseph ('64), R. Clark Morton ('53), Dr. Richard F. Terry ('68), and Augusto Paglialunga ('61). Dr. Joseph is chief of the Ophthalmology Department at Wheeling Hospital. Mr. Morton served as an attorney for the U.S. Treasury Department, practices law in the Wheeling area, and serves on several local boards of directors. Dr. Terry is a practicing cardiologist in Wheeling and the key figure in the development of the Cardiac Catheterization Laboratory at Wheeling Medical Park. Mr. Paglialunga has performed leading tenor roles in opera houses and concert theaters in Europe, Canada, South East Asia, and the United States.

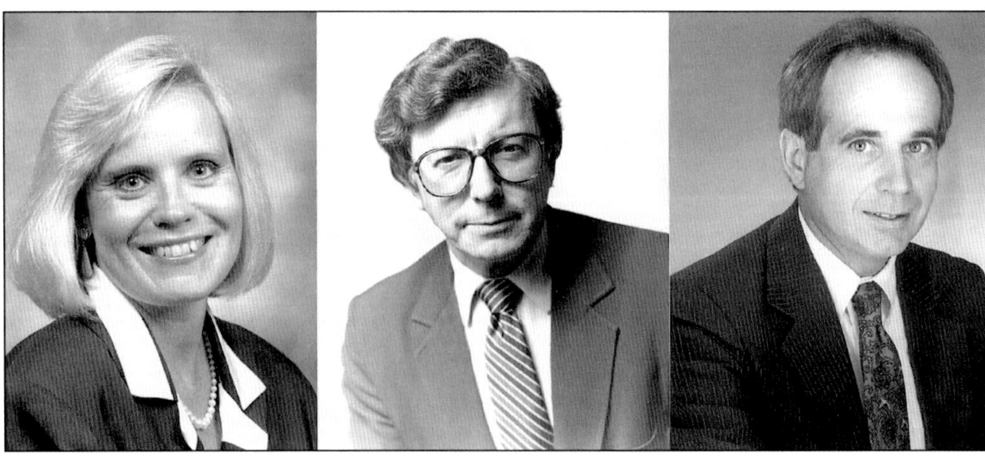

1992 Inductees. From left to right are Dr. Paula Myers-Keith ('74), Dr. Norman B. Moyes ('53), and Robert N. Susko ('70). Dr. Paula Myers-Keith, who has authored more than 25 papers, is the director of Biotechnology and Bioprocess Research at Pitman-Moore, Inc. Dr. Moyes is a professor of photography at Syracuse University and Boston University, and he has written five books. Mr. Susko practices law in Atlanta, Georgia. He is known for offering free counseling and representation to the indigent of the Atlanta area.

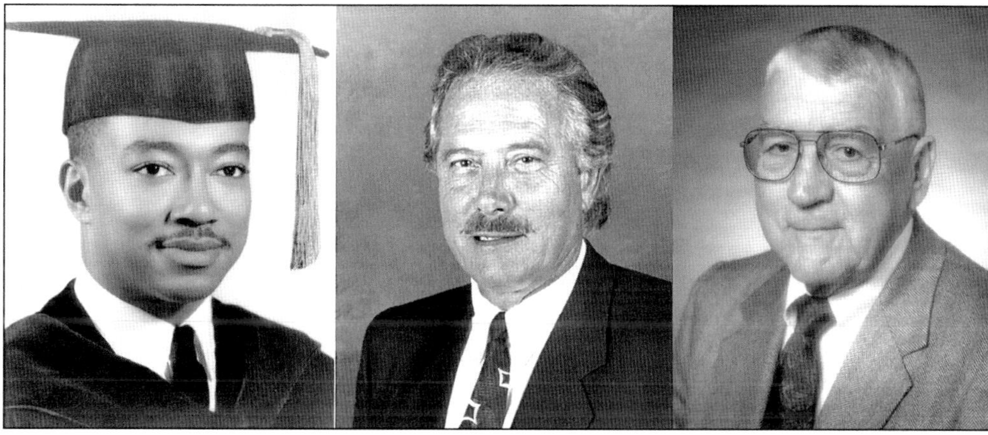

1993 Inductees. Pictured here are, from left to right, Dr. Robert W. Singletary ('59), Gary E. West ('58), and William F. McCreary ('50). Dr. Singletary practiced medicine in Ashtabula, Ohio and Pittsburgh, Pennsylvania before being appointed chief medical officer of U.S. Steel Company. Mr. West is president and CEO of Valley Welding, a 34-branch company located in seven states. Mr. McCreary is chairman of the board of CRM, a real estate tax service company that he founded. He was instrumental in founding several companies that have dramatically impacted the way the real estate business is done in California.

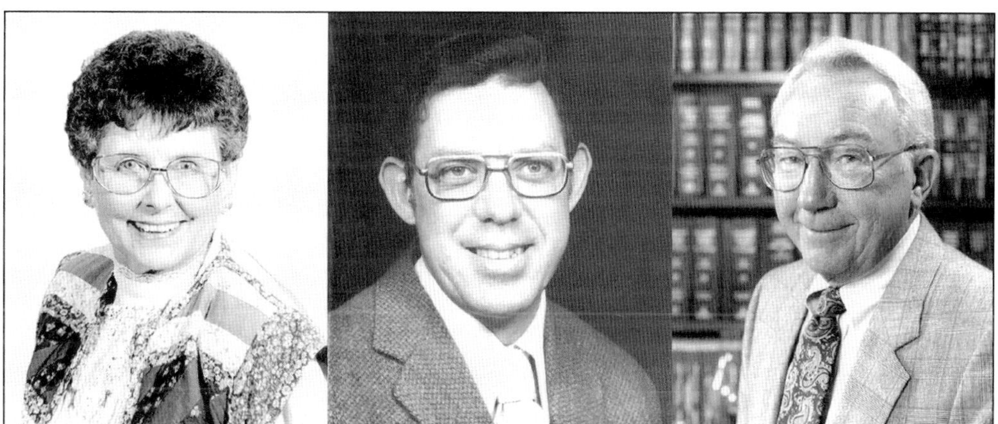

1994 Inductees. The following are pictured from left to right: Rhea R. Haxton ('54), James G. Marsh ('60), and Dr. William R. Grubler ('48). Ms. Haxton has been recognized as one of the outstanding art educators during her 27-year teaching career. Mr. Marsh established the major underpinnings for the discipline of satellite geodesy while employed by the Goddard Space Flight Center. He has received awards from NASA and the Space Agency of France. Dr. Grubler has served the community by providing free dental care and establishing a free dental clinic for those unable to afford such care.

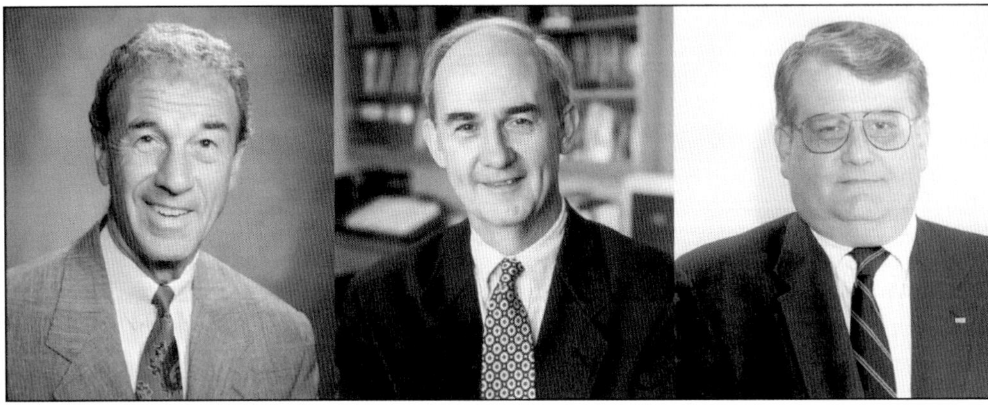

1995 Inductees. Seen here are, from left to right, Dr. Clyde D. Campbell ('53), Dr. Philip D. Stahl ('64), and Dr. Thomas A. Hatfield ('63). Dr. Campbell served as president of West Liberty State College for eleven years. As a result of his research in biochemistry and plastics, he holds numerous patents and is widely published in scientific journals. Dr. Stahl is the Edward Mallinckroft Jr. Professor of cell biology and physiology at Washington University Medical School. He has published more than 100 papers in scientific journals. Dr. Hatfield currently serves as the executive director of the National Art Education Association. He is recipient of the NAEA's art educator of the year award.

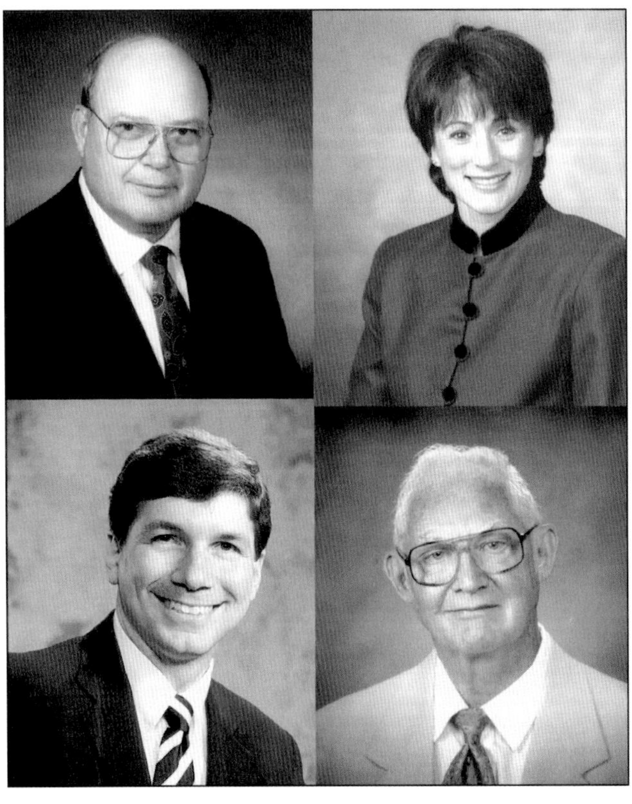

1996 Inductees. Clockwise from the upper left are James R. Hupp ('65), Cathy A. Priest ('72), Dr. Robert H. Sykes ('55), and Brian E. Joseph ('78). Mr. Hupp is president of American Office Systems, Inc., which he founded in 1983. Ms. Priest was selected by the Ohio Education Association as the 1996 Teacher of the Year. She has been a consultant for the Discovery Networks, is the author of nationally distributed academic contests, and a workshop facilitator for the Learning Channel. Dr. Sykes is professor emeritus of West Liberty State College. He has authored three books and countless journal and newspaper articles. Mr. Joseph is the founder of the Touchstone Research Laboratory, one of the most successful and innovative private companies in America.

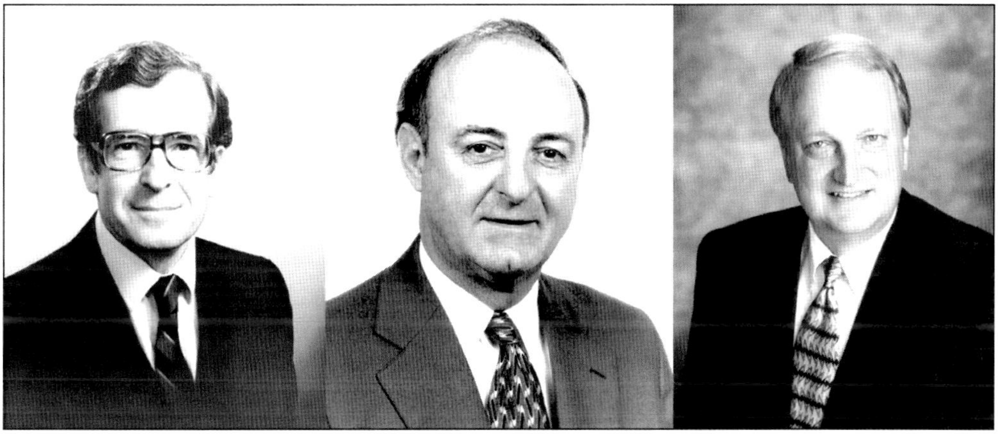

1997 Inductees. From left to right are as follows: Kenneth K. Kadar ('65), Dr. Henry R. Marockie ('61), and Arthur R. Mezerski ('69). Mr. Kadar, a member of the broadcasting industry, served his community through leadership positions in the Upper Ohio Valley United Way and the Special Wish Foundation. Dr. Marockie was appointed West Virginia state superintendent of schools in 1989. He also served as president of the National Council of Chief State School Officers. Mr. Mezerski is a three-time recipient of the Governor's Honors Academy Outstanding Educator Award and was recognized by the White House Commission on Presidential Scholars as a distinguished teacher.

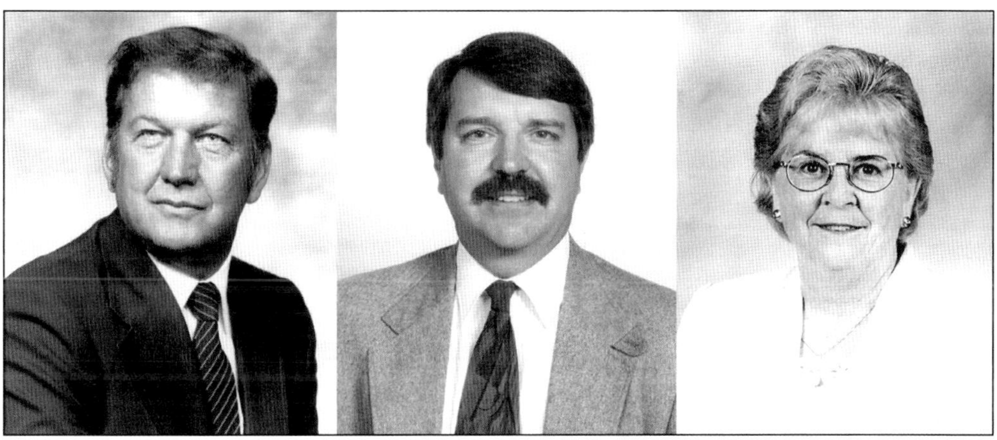

1998 Inductees. Pictured here are, from left to right, Donald A. Haskins ('59), Dr. William C. Mercer ('75), and Emmajo R. Shearer ('56). Mr. Haskins was the superintendent of Marshall County schools for 17 years and served two terms in the West Virginia House of Delegates. Dr. Mercer was selected as one of the "Top Physicians in America" by *Pittsburgh Magazine* in 1997. Ms. Shearer was clinic supervisor at WLSC for 20 years and clinic director at Ohio State University for 17 years where she was voted outstanding instructor in 1995 and 1998.

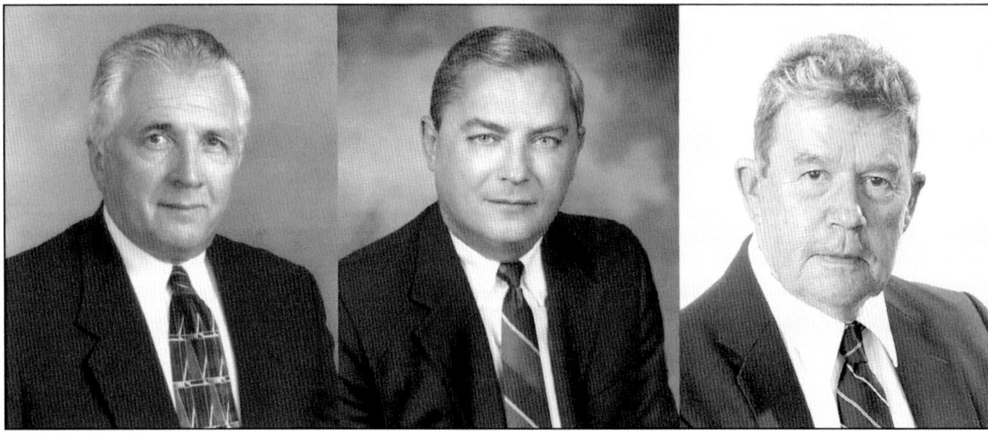

1999 INDUCTEES. From left to right are Dr. Dennis K. Flaherty ('67), Richard W. Glover ('63), and Dr. Edward F.J. Tucker ('65). Dr. Flaherty is recognized internationally as an expert in immunotoxicology, and he holds numerous patents. Mr. Glover is president and CEO of Theis Precision Steel Corporation, a company that has attained world leadership for specialty steels. Dr. Tucker has published six books, authored over 40 articles in scholarly journals, and landed over a million dollars in research and institutional grants.

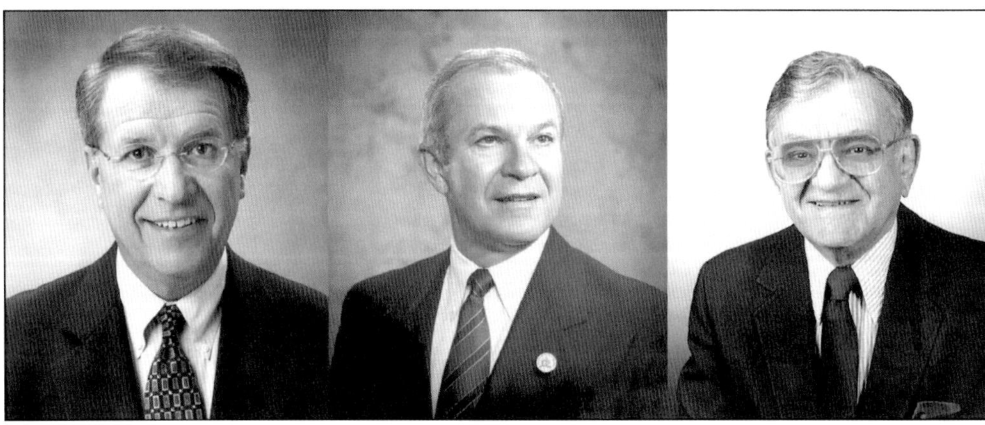

2000 INDUCTEES. Seen here are, from left to right, John R. Bonassi ('69), James P. Frum ('61), and Rudy Mumley ('50). Mr. Bonassi's varied career has led him from councilman and mayor of Greentree Borough, Pennsylvania to executive assistant to U.S. Senator John Heinz to director of marketing for the Dick Corporation. Mr. Frum is a past president and founding member of the West Virginia Speech, Language, and Hearing Association. Frum developed the Department of Audiology at Wheeling Clinic and Wheeling Medical Park. Mr. Mumley served twice as president of the Ohio Valley Athletic Conference and was the first director of the OVAC All-Star Football Game. He was charter member of the Upper Ohio Valler Dapper Dan Club and named "Man of the Year" in 1992.

AFTERWORD

As I examined the various documents that make up the 164-year history of West Liberty State College, it became clear that, except for the actions of certain key individuals, the history of the college would have been quite different; in fact, the college may not have lasted as long as it has. Some of these key people played major roles and some of them minor, but all of them exhibited similar traits of courage, intelligence, determination, and love for the institution. I have purposely featured these people in this publication and outlined their remarkable accomplishments.

There are four past principals and presidents in this group, namely, Shotwell, Shaw, Bonar and Elbin, whose presence at critical times in the history of the college can only be thought of as vital. These were all men of vision who saw what the institution could become and who provided the leadership necessary to make the dream come true.

West Liberty State College has also been blessed with a highly dedicated and talented faculty. While, over the years, the faculty has done its share of research and publication, it has always directed its primary efforts towards improving instruction and understanding the needs of students.

Now, as the college moves into the 21st century, one cannot help but wonder what it will be like in the future. But this is history, not physics, so there is no way to predict future events with any degree of accuracy. However, the current president, Dr. Ronald M. Zaccari, has already demonstrated those traits found in the key people who played such an important role in the past. It is, therefore, my belief that his strong leadership and keen perception of how the institution must adapt to the changing times will enable West Liberty State College to thrive and expand as the new millennium begins. I also believe that, no matter how the college changes in the future, it will always retain its small-college atmosphere and remain an institution where the education of its students is valued above all else.

Robert W. Schramm
April 2001

BIBLIOGRAPHY

Javersak, David T. *West Liberty State College 1837–1987.* Upper Ohio Valley Historical Review, Vol. XVI, No. 2, 1987.

Nodyne, Kenneth R. *Great Educator of the Upper Ohio Valley—Paul N. Elbin.* Upper Ohio Valley Historical Review, Vol. VIII, No. 1, 1978.

Regier, C.C., ed. *West Liberty Yesterday and Today.* Privately published, 1939.

Reuter, Frank T. *West Liberty State College: The First 125 Years.* Privately published, 1963.

West Liberty State College. *Archives*. Photographic files.

West Liberty State College. *Elbin Archive.* Photographic albums and scrapbooks.

West Liberty State College. *The Normal Trumpet.* 1921–1931.

West Liberty State College. *The Trumpet.* 1931–2000.

Index